T0361243

INTERNATIONAL INVESTMENT STRATEGIES IN THE PEOPLE'S REPUBLIC OF CHINA

International Investment Strategies in the People's Republic of China

YADONG LUO
University of Hawaii

Routledge
Taylor & Francis Group

LONDON AND NEW YORK

First published 1998 by Ashgate Publishing

Reissued 2018 by Routledge
2 Park Square, Milton Park, Abingdon, Oxon, OX14 4RN
52 Vanderbilt Avenue, New York, NY 10017

Routledge is an imprint of the Taylor & Francis Group, an informa business

Notice:
Product or corporate names may be trademarks or registered trademarks, and are used only for identification and explanation without intent to infringe.

Publisher's Note
The publisher has gone to great lengths to ensure the quality of this reprint but points out that some imperfections in the original copies may be apparent.

Disclaimer
The publisher has made every effort to trace copyright holders and welcomes correspondence from those they have been unable to contact.

A Library of Congress record exists under LC control number:

ISBN 13: 978-1-138-36307-6 (hbk)
ISBN 13: 978-0-429-43177-7 (ebk)

Contents

Appendices

List of Figures

ix

List of Tables

x

Preface

Recent years have seen an increased international investment by multinational corporations pursuing diverse strategic objectives. As a transnational economic flow and a dynamic and ongoing process, international investment often involves very complex choices. International investment strategies are mainly antecedent decisions focusing what, when, where, and how a foreign investor should invest in pursuit of its sustained competitive advantage in the global marketplace. Since antecedent decisions are made prior to the formation of foreign ventures, MNCs' choices regarding investment strategy attributes such as industry selection, timing of investment, project and location selection, entry mode selection, sharing arrangement, and partner selection need utmost managerial attention.

As transitional economies, most notably China, make political and economic transitions towards more market-based systems, MNCs have shown a greater interest in these markets. Reforms in this type of economy have continued unabated and their pace has even accelerated in recent years, contributing to a surge in international expansion activity. This activity has in turn profoundly transformed these economies to the point that they are today major players in the global integration of international business. As the world's largest emerging market economy and fastest-growing market, China is currently the second largest foreign direct investment recipient in the world, surpassed only by the Unites States. Since 1979 through the end of 1996, over 140,000 foreign invested enterprises representing $175.74 billion investment have commenced operation. The value of FDI in China in 1994 was close to $34 billion, accounting for 42.50 percent of the developing countries figure and 16.67 percent of the worldwide total in the same year. The share of industrial output by foreign-invested enterprises in total industrial output of the nation reached to 13 percent in 1995 and 17 million Chinese people are currently employed in these enterprises.

Having been isolated from the rest of the world for several decades, Chinese economy is characterized by a great deal of potential opportunity and needs on the one hand, and a tremendous amount of uncertainty and difficulty on the other. Those foreign companies best prepared to circumvent the former and exploit the latter are opt to survive and prosper. The success of international expansion in China depends largely on the formulation and implementation of appropriate investment strategies.

This book is written for international executives and business school students who have an interest in doing business in China. It is intended to provide important managerial lessons and insightful practical guidance for international executives active in the Chinese market. All the investment strategies addressed are essential in influencing the financial and market performance of international expansion in the country. It is my hope that this book, characterized by a strong combination of succinct analysis, conceptual foundations, empirical evidence, practical guidelines, and managerial recommendations, will be considered as one of the best books on international business in China.

This book is divided into three parts. The first part (chapters one and two) introduces various emerging characteristics of foreign direct investment in China and presents various current facets of investment environment facing foreign companies. The second part deals with operation-related investment strategies including industry selection (chapter three), timing of investment (chapter four), and project and location selection (chapter five). The third part focuses on cooperative-related investment strategies such as partner selection (chapter six), managerial networking (chapter seven), and entry mode selection and sharing arrangement (chapter eight). Overall, these strategies offer the insights into such critical issues as where, when, what, and how foreign companies should undertake investments and whom they should collaborate with.

In the course of writing this book, I have relied on the encouragement and support of numerous people. I would like to express my gratitude to the University Research Council, RFDC in the College of Business Administration, and the Center for International Business Education and Research, all at the University of Hawaii, for their financial support. I am very grateful to my colleague, Professor Oded Shenkar, for his constructive comments on several chapters in the book. I am also indebted to a number of friends and former colleagues at the Ministry of Foreign Trade and Economic Cooperation, P.R.C., and Jiangsu Provincial Commission of Foreign Trade and Economic Relations, for their great help in obtaining the most recent information, data, and policies. Finally, this book is dedicated to my family in recognition of their patience and support throughout this project.

Yadong Luo, Ph.D
College of Business Administration
University of Hawaii

1 Foreign Direct Investment in China: Patterns and Features

Chapter Purpose

This chapter describes background on foreign direct investment in China. The discussion is divided into five sections. The first section provides an overview of foreign direct investment in the world. This is followed by an introduction to some of the characteristics of foreign direct investment in China. The third section is a historical review of such investment over the past seventeen years (1979-1996). The next section illuminates what is occurring now, especially with respect to recently emerging policy changes. The last section speculates on the future of foreign investment in China.

1.1 Foreign Direct Investment: Worldwide Overview

Foreign direct investment (FDI) has been growing rapidly in recent years. It is increasing even faster than international trade, which has been the primary mechanism linking national economies. In 1995, FDI inflows increased by 40 percent worldwide, to an unprecedented $315 billion. Developed countries were the key generators of these record FDI inflows, investing $270 billion and receiving $203 billion (Table 1.1). FDI by developed countries in developing countries reached $100 billion in 1995, setting another record. Developed countries increased their share of world FDI inflows from 59 percent in 1994 to 65 percent in 1995, while outflows rose from 83 percent to 85 percent (Table 1.1).

FDI inflows are concentrated in a few countries. The largest host countries received two thirds of total inflow in 1995, while the smallest 100 recipient countries received only 1 percent (World Investment Report 1996). Similarly, the United States, Germany, the United Kingdom, Japan, and France represent the five largest home countries, which collectively accounted for about two thirds of all outflows in 1995 (World Investment Report 1996).

Table 1.1 FDI Inflows and Outflows: 1983-1995

Year	Developed Countries		Developing Countries		All Countries[#]	
	Inflows	Outflows	Inflows	Outflows	Inflows	Outflows
			Value ($ billion)			
1983-1987	58.7	72.6	18.3	4.2	77.1	76.8
1988-1989	139.1	193.3	36.8	15.2	177.3	108.5
1990	169.8	222.5	33.7	17.8	203.8	204.3
1991	114.0	201.9	41.3	8.9	157.8	210.8
1992	114.0	181.4	50.4	21.0	168.1	203.1
1993	129.3	192.4	73.1	33.0	207.9	225.5
1994	132.8	190.9	87.0	38.6	225.7	230.0
1995	203.2	270.5	99.7	47.0	314.9	317.8
			Share in total (%)			
1983-1987	76	95	24	5	100	100
1988-1992	78	93	217	7	100	100
1993	62	85	35	15	100	100
1994	59	83	39	17	100	100
1995	65	85	32	15	100	100
			Growth rate (%)			
1983-1987	37	35	9	24	29	35
1988-1992	-4	3	15	16	1	4
1993	13	6	45	52	24	11
1994	3	-1	19	17	9	2
1995	53	42	15	22	40	38

[#] The difference between 'All Countries' and combined 'Developed' and 'Developing Countries' is 'Central and Eastern Europe'.

Source: Adapted from World Investment Report 1996.

The United States remains both the world's largest host and home country. Receiving $60 billion in 1995, the United States inflows were twice that of the United Kingdom, which is the second largest recipient of FDI among developed countries. Reflecting high levels of merger and acquisition related investments by Western European multinational enterprises (MNEs), equity flow to the United States rose by 50 percent in 1995.

Most Japanese FDI has recently gone to East and South-East Asian countries and developed countries, aiming at establishing regional or global networks or supplying local markets. To increase international competitiveness, Japanese MNEs are establishing 'second generation' affiliates abroad. For example, 47 percent of Japanese affiliates in Hong Kong have already established their own foreign affiliates (World Investment Report 1996).

FDI flow has doubled between 1980 and 1994 relative to both global gross fixed capital formation and world GDP. The value added of all foreign affiliates accounted for 6 percent of world GDP in 1991, compared with 2 percent in 1982 (Table 1.2). As Table 1.2 shows, the outward FDI stock which the 39,000 or so parent firms invested in their approximately 270,000 foreign affiliates reached $2.7 trillion in 1995. Table 1.3 demonstrates that some MNEs have invested half of their total assets overseas and sent half of their total employees abroad. As a result, more than half of total sales are created by foreign affiliates. This evidence indicates that FDI plays a critical part in shaping economic globalization.

Table 1.2 Major Indicators of World FDI: 1986-1995

Indicators	Value at Current Prices 1995 ($bil)	Annual Growth Rate (%) 1986-1990	Annual Growth Rate (%) 1991-1994
FDI inflows	315	24.7	12.7
FDI outward stock	2730	19.8	8.8
Sales of foreign affiliates	6022	17.4	5.4
Royalties and fees receipts	41	21.8	10.1
GDP at factor cost	24948	10.8	4.3
Gross output of foreign affiliates	1410	11.0	11.4
Gross fixed capital formation	5681	10.6	4.0
Exports of goods and non-factor services	4707	14.3	3.8

Source: Adapted from World Investment Report 1996.

Table 1.3 Top Ten MNEs in 1994

Rank by foreign assets	Name	Country	Industry	Assets ($bil)		Sales ($bil)		Employment		Transnationality*
				Foreign	Total	Foreign	Total	Foreign	Total	
1	Royal Shell	Holland	Petroleum	63.7	102.0	51.1	94.8	79.00	106.00	63.6
2	Ford	USA	Motor & parts	60.6	219.4	38.1	128.4	96.73	337.79	28.6
3	Exxon	USA	Petroleum	56.2	87.9	72.3	113.9	55.00	86.00	63.8
4	GM	USA	Motor & parts	na	198.6	44.0	152.2	177.7	692.80	25.7
5	IBM	USA	Computer	43.9	81.1	39.9	64.1	115.6	219.84	56.4
6	Volkswagen	Germany	Motor & parts	na	52.4	29.0	49.3	96.55	242.32	60.4
7	GE	USA	Electronics	33.9	251.5	11.9	59.3	36.17	216.00	16.7
8	Toyota	Japan	Motor & parts	na	116.8	37.2	91.3	27.57	172.68	28.1
9	Daimler-Benz	Germany	Transport	27.9	66.5	46.3	74.0	79.30	330.55	42.8
10	Elf Aquitaine	France	Petroleum	na	48.9	26.2	38.9	43.95	89.50	56.7

* Transnationality index is calculated as the average of foreign assets to total assets, foreign sales to total sales and foreign employment to total employment; Employment unit: 1,000.

Source: Adapted from World Investment Report 1996.

Investment from developing countries to other developing countries is also increasing. For example, more than half of the FDI flows from Asian developing countries were invested in the same region in 1994. Total FDI coming from developing countries rose to $47 billion in 1995. The 50 largest multinational enterprises in developing countries, ranked by foreign assets, accounted for about 10 percent of the combined outward FDI stock of firms in their countries of origin. These firms's ratio of foreign to total sales is high (about 30 percent), but their ratio of foreign to total assets is low (about 9 percent). According to the World Investment Report (1996), their overall index of transnationality is about 21 percent, only about half of 42 percent for the world's top 100 MNEs.

Driven by privatization and economic recovery in Central and Eastern Europe, FDI inflows to these regions nearly doubled to $12 billion in 1995, after stagnating in 1994. The region accounted for 5 percent of world inflows in 1995, compared with only 1 percent in 1991. Investment inflow in Hungary, the Czech Republics, and the Russian Federation were all doubled in the last two years. This reflects the recognition by MNEs that Central and Eastern European countries, particularly those in Central Europe, are well on the way to becoming market economies.

South, East, and South-East Asia continue to be the largest developing host region, accounting for two thirds of all FDI in developing countries. The size and dynamism of emerging economies in Asia have made it increasingly important for MNEs from all countries to rapidly serve expanding markets, or to tap the tangible and intangible resources of that region for global production networks (Chen, 1990). Since 1992, China has been the largest developing country recipient of FDI. Although inflows are soaring in other countries as well, China is driving Asia's current investment boom.

1.2 FDI in China: Patterns, Situations, and Features

Overview

China officially opened its doors to foreign investment in 1979 with the promulgation of a joint venture law. Since then, through the end of 1996, Chinese authorities had approved the establishment of over 283,793 foreign invested enterprises (FIEs) involving $466.80 billion in foreign capital

(Table 1.4). Of these, over 140,000 FIEs representing $175.74 billion investment have commenced operations (Table 1.5).

According to *People's Daily* (May 22, 1995, p2), in 1994 a total of $80 billion in foreign capital had been invested in all developing countries. Worldwide, foreign direct investment amounted to $204 billion during the same year. The value of FDI in China alone was close to $34 billion, accounting for 42.5 percent of the developing countries figure and 16.67 percent of the worldwide total.

Table 1.4   Foreign Investment in China: 1979-1996
(Approved Investment in US $ million)

Year	Total Foreign Investment	Foreign Direct Investment	Other Foreign Investment*
1979-1982	6,999	6,010	989
1983	1,917	1,732	185
1984	2,875	2,651	224
1985	6,333	5,932	401
1986	3,330	2,834	496
1987	4,319	3,709	610
1988	6,191	5,297	894
1989	6,294	5,600	694
1990	6,987	6,595	391
1991	12,422	11,977	445
1992	58,736	58,124	612
1993	111,966	111,435	531
1994	81,971	81,406	565
1995	90,967	90,288	679
1996	73,547	73,213	334
1979-1996	474,854	466,804	8,050

* Other foreign investments include 1) international leasing; 2) compensation trade; and 3) processing and assembling.

Sources: (1) Data of 1979-1992: *China Statistical Yearbook* (1993), English Edition, China State Statistical Bureau, 1993, pp. 587; (2) Data of 1993: *The Bulletin of the MOFTEC, PRC*, Issue No. 2, 1994, pp. 10; (3) Data of 1994: the *Bulletin*, Issue No. 1, 1995, pp. 13; (4) Data of 1995: the *Bulletin*, Issue No. 1, 1996, pp. 1-5; and (5) Data of 1996: the *Bulletin*, Issue No. 1, 1997, pp. 19-20.

Table 1.5 Foreign Investment in China: 1979-1996
(Realized Investment in US $ million)

Year	Total Foreign Investment	Foreign Direct Investment	Other Foreign Investment*
1979-1982	1,767	1,166	601
1983	916	636	280
1984	1,419	1,258	161
1985	1,959	1,661	298
1986	2,244	1,874	370
1987	2,647	2,314	333
1988	3,739	3,194	545
1989	3,773	3,392	381
1990	3,755	3,487	268
1991	4,666	4,366	300
1992	11,291	11,007	284
1993	27,769	27,514	255
1994	34,122	33,787	335
1995	38,082	37,736	346
1996	42,600	42,350	250
1979-1996	180,749	175,742	5,007

* Other foreign investments include 1) international leasing; 2) compensation trade; and 3) processing and assembling.

Sources: (1) Data of 1979-1992: *China Statistical Yearbook* (1993), English Edition, China State Statistical Bureau, 1993, pp. 587; (2) Data of 1993: *The Bulletin of the MOFTEC, PRC*, Issue No. 2, 1994, pp. 10; (3) Data of 1994: the *Bulletin*, Issue No. 1, 1995, pp. 13; (4) Data of 1995: the *Bulletin*, Issue No. 1, 1996, pp. 1-5; and (5) Data of 1996: the *Bulletin*, Issue No. 1, 1997, pp. 19-20.

China is currently the second largest FDI recipient in the world, surpassed only by the United States (Table 1.6). Of the top countries listed in Table 1.6, China has the fastest FDI inflow growth. Among emerging economies and developing countries, China plays the leading role in absorbing foreign direct investment.

Table 1.6   Direct Investment Inflows in Selected Countries
(> US$2000 million in 1993)

Countries	1990	1991	1992	1993
United States	48,422	25,446	3,388	31,519
P.R. China	3,755	4,666	11,291	27,769
United Kingdom	32,897	15,934	18,165	14,449
France	9,040	11,073	15,894	12,141
Belgium-				
Luxembourg	8,162	8,919	10,791	8,616
Spain	13,681	10,423	8,115	7,184
Netherlands	8,765	4,934	5,883	6,803
Mexico	2,633	4,762	4,393	4,901
Italy	6,344	2,481	3,161	3,447
New Zealand	1,686	1,695	1,089	2,564
Australia	6,870	4,773	5,286	2,557
Canada	6,597	6,544	4,963	2,468
Sweden	2,029	6,315	241	2,438
Norway	1,004	-291	720	2,058

Source: (1) *Financial Market Trends*, OECD, 04/1994;
　　　　 (2) *China Statistical Yearbook*, Various Years.

Contributions

FIEs have played a major role in the modernization of the Chinese economy. As shown in Table 1.7, the share of total industrial output in China made by FIEs reached 13 percent in 1995. The share of total national export volume made by FIEs climbed to 31.3 percent in the same year. The tax contribution as a share of the nation's total was 10 percent. FDI already accounted for 18.3 percent of total gross domestic investment in 1994. Seventeen million Chinese people are currently employed in FIEs (*Bulletin of MOFTEC*, 1997), one million more than a year ago (Table 1.7). Table 1.7 thus reveals drastic growth in every major indicator of FDI contribution to the Chinese economy.

Table 1.7 Contribution of FDI to China's Economy: 1991-1995

Item	1991	1992	1993	1994	1995
Average amount per project ($mil)	0.9	1.2	1.3	1.8	2.5
FDI to gross domestic investment (%)	4.5	8.0	13.6	18.3	na
Volume of exports by FIEs ($bil)	12.1	17.4	25.2	34.7	na
Share of exports in total (%)	17.0	20.4	27.5	28.7	31.3
Share of industrial output (%)	5.0	6.0	9.0	11.0	13.0
Number of employees (mil)	4.8	6.0	10.0	14.0	16.0
Tax contribution as share of total (%)	na	4.1	na	na	10.0

Source: Adapted from World Investment Report 1996.

Foreign Sources

FIEs have diverse foreign sources. Tables 1.8 and 1.9 list the top 20 countries or regions of origin for FDI in China in 1995 and as of 1995, respectively. By the end of 1995, Hong Kong and Macau took the lead in direct investment in the mainland, contributing $80,548 million, or 60.38 percent of China's total FDI inflow. They were followed by Taiwan (8.68 percent), the United States (8.14 percent), and Japan (7.88 percent), respectively.

Interestingly, of the top 20 foreign sources, 10 each come from developed and developing countries or regions. In 1995, investors from the top ten developing countries or regions collectively undertook 73.49 percent of the total actual FDI in China, whereas their counterparts from the developed world accounted for only 23.08 percent (Table 1.8). Investors coming from top ten developing countries or regions also accounted for 72.94 percent of total accumulated FDI in China as of 1995 whereas investors from top ten developed countries only represented 21.55 percent. This suggests that FDI in China launched by developing country businesses has been more than three times as much as that made by developed country firms over the last sixteen years.

In addition to Hong Kong, Macau, and Taiwan, Singapore, South Korea, Thailand, and Malaysia are important sources of FDI in their neighboring country, China. Although the investment from the United States was surpassed by Japanese investments in 1995, the former still constituted

Table 1.8 Foreign Direct Investment in China from Top 20 Countries and Regions in 1995 (in US$ million)

Rank	Country(Region)	Number of Projects	Contractual FDI	Actual FDI
1	Hong Kong/Macao	17,713	42,111	20,500
2	Taiwan	4,847	5,849	3,162
3	Japan	2,946	7,592	3,108
4	United States	3,474	7,471	3,083
5	Singapore	1,279	8,666	1,851
6	Republic of Korea	1,975	2,998	1,043
7	United Kingdom	457	3,577	914
8	Germany	355	1,660	386
9	Virgin Islands	168	1,321	304
10	Thailand	304	638	288
11	France	183	642	287
12	Italy	213	507	263
13	Malaysia	243	1,061	259
14	Canada	560	982	257
15	Australia	471	1,257	233
16	Netherlands	105	602	114
17	Indonesia	80	344	112
18	Bermuda	19	285	109
19	Philippines	125	213	106
20	Switzerland	59	309	64

Source: *The Bulletin of MOFTEC*, Issue No. 2, 1996, pp. 15.

the largest source from developed countries by the end of 1995. Among top ten foreign sources as of 1995, three were from Europe: the United Kingdom, Germany and France. However, collectively they provided less than 4 percent of total FDI in China.

Although Hong Kong and Taiwan are the top two investment sources, in a broad sense, they are simply moving relatively labor-intensive activities into China in an attempt to escape rising labor costs and space constraints at home. Moreover, the average size of investment from these two sources is relatively small. For instance, the average equity pledged by US investors is nearly twice as high as that put forth by FDI from Hong Kong and about

Table 1.9 Foreign Direct Investment in China from Top 20 Countries and Regions by the End of 1995 (in US$ million)

Rank	Country/Region	Number of projects	Contractual FDI	Actual FDI
1	Hong Kong/Macao	157,664	241,559	80,548
2	Taiwan	31,849	29,462	11,585
3	United States	19,731	28,258	10,852
4	Japan	13,260	21,262	10,506
5	Singapore	5,846	17,306	3,923
6	Republic of Korea	6,222	6,778	2,259
7	United Kingdom	1,474	9,386	2,206
8	Germany	1,247	4,411	1,190
9	France	1,247	1,837	1,085
10	Thailand	2,132	3,519	918
11	Italy	863	1,332	779
12	Australia	2,321	3,372	761
13	Canada	2,738	3,690	736
14	Malaysia	1,238	2,708	582
15	Virgin Islands	293	2,504	450
16	Philippines	872	1,527	411
17	Netherlands	392	1,375	401
18	Indonesia	471	1,023	319
19	Switzerland	236	829	236
20	Kuwait	11	67	225

Source: *The Bulletin of MOFTEC*, Issue No. 2, 1996, pp. 16.

50% higher than the average FDI project from Taiwan and Southeast Asian countries (National Council, 1991).

While Hong Kong and Taiwan investors emphasize labor-intensive and simple industrial processing for light industrial and textile goods aimed at the international market, the U.S. and European firms tend to place their emphasis on capital- or technology-intensive manufacturing sectors in an effort to gain access to the growing Chinese domestic market. Japanese investors, while also interested in China's domestic market, have placed less emphasis than their U.S. counterparts on manufacturing and have instead become more involved in various forms of property development (Luo, 1997).

Sector Structure

FDI in China has been active in a variety of industries. Table 1.10 presents industrial patterns of foreign direct investment in China in 1993 and 1995. In 1995, the industrial sector accounted for 67.54   percent of total FDI,

Table 1.10 Foreign Direct Investment in China by Sectors
            (Approved Investment in US$ million)

Sector	1993 # of Projects	1993 Value	1995 # of Projects	1995 Value
Agriculture	1,704	1,191	903	1,736
Industry	56,549	51,174	27,687	61,648
Construction	3,167	3,878	944	1,918
Transportation & Tele-communication Service	915	1,490	268	1,697
Commerce/Food Service	4,842	4,606	1,851	3,427
Real Estate & Utility	11,322	43,771	3,279	17,835
(Tourism & Hotel)	(806)	(1,482)	(171)	(954)
Health Care, Sports & Social Welfare	206	477	174	837
Education, Culture & Arts	458	452	162	345
Scientific Research	881	588	275	278
Others	3,393	3,808	1,468	1,560
Total	83,437	111,435	37,011	91,281*

* There are some differences in statistical methods between MOFTEC and State Statistical Bureau, PRC.

Source: *China Statistical Yearbook*, 1995, pp. 560; 1996, pp. 603.

leading all other sectors in influencing the economy. The real estate and utility sector follows, involving $17,835 million in investments or 19.54 percent of the total in 1995. Commercial and food services, construction, agriculture, and transportation and telecommunication services are also important sectors, ranking from third to sixth, respectively.

Different sectors have idiosyncratic patterns of FDI growth. FDI in agriculture, industry, transportation and telecommunication services, and health care and social welfare services has boomed over the past years, growing from 12 percent to 75 percent between 1993 and 1995. FDI in other sectors, especially real estate and construction have slowed down. For instance, foreign investment in hotel and construction sectors were decreased by 55.35 percent and 102 percent, respectively, during the same period. This reflects structural changes in Chinese FDI policies over the past few years.

Location Patterns

FDI in China is located throughout the country. Table 1.11 shows that FDI was made in every province in 1994 and 1995. This is also demonstrated in Table 1.12, which indicates that FIEs have been registered and operated throughout China. However, the obviously uneven geographical distribution of FDI within various regions in China is a critical issue.

For example, in 1995, the total value of FDI in 18 Central and Western provinces or autonomous regions was $4,867 million, only 15.05 percent of the FDI in 12 Eastern provinces (Table 1.13). The number of registered FIEs in all Central and Western provinces or autonomous regions as of 1995 was 44,875, or just 23.78 percent of their counterparts in Eastern regions. Meanwhile, the portion of registered foreign capital in Central and Western regions by the end of 1995 was $40,249 million, constituting only 15.67 percent of the nation's total (Table 1.13). The distribution of FDI in China has not shown a marked change in recent years. By the end of 1994, the number of FIEs in Central and Western provinces or autonomous regions represented about 18 percent of the total number of FIEs (*People's Daily*, July 9, 1995, p2). This pattern has remained unchanged since 1994. Although over the last few years the Chinese government has called for an increase of FDI in the Central and Western region of the country, the flow of foreign investment to these areas still lags far behind that directed toward the Eastern region.

Table 1.11   Foreign Direct Investment in China by Locations (Realized Investment in US$ million)

Rank	Region	1994	1995
1	Guandong	9,463	10,260
2	Jiangsu	3,763	5,191
3	Fujian	3,713	4,044
4	Shanghai	2,473	2,893
5	Shandong	2,552	2,689
6	Tianjin	1,015	1,521
7	Liaoning	1,440	1,425
8	Zhejiang	1,150	1,258
9	Beijing	1,372	1,080
10	Hainan	918	1,062
11	Guangxi	838	673
12	Hubei	602	625
13	Hebei	523	547
14	Sichuan	922	542
15	Heilongjiang	348	517
16	Hunan	331	508
17	Anhui	370	483
18	Henan	387	479
19	Jilin	242	408
20	Shaanxi	239	324
21	Jiangxi	262	289
22	Yunnan	65	98
23	Gansu	88	64
24	Shanxi	32	64
25	Inner Mongolia	40	58
26	Guizhou	64	57
27	Xinjiang	48	55
28	Ningxia	7	4
29	Qinghai	2	2
30	Tibet		
	Regional Total	33,268	37,215

Source: *China Statistical Yearbook*, 1996, pp. 600.

Table 1.12 Some Indicators of Registered Foreign-Invested Enterprises (FIEs) as of the end of 1995 (US$ million)

Region	# of FIEs	Total investment	Registered Capital Total	Registered Capital Foreign
Guandong	59,582	204,627	129,131	92,949
Jiangsu	22,950	53,231	32,404	18,439
Fujian	16,527	36,715	22,882	18,541
Shanghai	14,487	67,729	36,029	23,309
Shandong	17,988	37,425	25,771	13,281
Tianjin	8,959	16,944	10,882	7,673
Liaoning	11,284	28,079	17,430	9,675
Zhejiang	11,237	24,371	14,806	8,165
Beijing	9,691	28,820	15,115	9,269
Hainan	8,606	21,135	12,378	10,054
Guangxi	4,876	13,453	8,463	4,970
Hubei	5,758	13,649	9,278	5,441
Hebei	5,368	12,278	8,197	4,270
Sichuan	5,897	12,680	9,303	4,976
Heilongjiang	4,388	8,554	6,348	3,284
Hunan	3,263	7,002	4,460	2,597
Anhui	2,949	6,103	4,229	2,320
Henan	4,382	8,954	6,753	3,352
Jilin	2,990	4,790	3,711	1,996
Shaanxi	1,894	4,593	2,998	1,772
Jiangxi	3,016	4,979	3,647	2,088
Yunnan	1,286	2,870	1,938	1,086
Gansu	1,037	1,636	1,114	601
Shanxi	1,364	2,404	1,903	908
In. Mongolia	1,074	1,987	1,426	654
Guizhou	997	1,969	1,572	954
Xinjiang	656	1,421	980	490
Ningxia	361	430	368	197
Qinghai	97	143	111	53
Tibet	51	203	72	34
National Total	233,564	639,009	399,123	256,884

Source: *China Statistical Yearbook*, 1996, pp. 601.

Table 1.13 Regional Pattern of FDI in China

Eastern Provinces	Central & Western Provinces
Beijing	Hebei
Tianjin	Shanxi
Liaoning	Inner Mongolia
Jilin	Guangxi
Heilongjiang	Jiangxi
Shanghai	Henan
Jiangsu	Hubei
Zhejiang	Hunan
Fujian	Anhui
Shandong	Sichuan
Guangdong	Guizhou
Hainan	Yunnan
	Tibet
	Shaanxi
	Gansu
	Qinghai
	Ningxia
	Xingjiang

Total provinces: 12	18	
FDI in 1995: $32,348m	$4,867m	
# of FIEs as of 1995: 188,689	44,875	
Registered capital by foreign investors as of 1995: $216,635m	$40,249m	

Source: The author's own calculation.

FDI Entry Mode

Foreign investors are generally free to choose their mode of entry into the Chinese market. Tables 1.14 and 1.15 depict the trends and patterns of FDI entry into China over four years (1993 through 1996). According to the Chinese government's classifications, these entry modes include:

(1) Equity joint venture (EJV): It accounted for 52.02 percent of the total amount of actual FDI in 1994 (Table 1.14) and 49.97 percent in 1996 (Table 1.15). An EJV involves the creation of limited liability companies with equity and management shared in negotiated proportions by the foreign and Chinese partners.

(2) Wholly foreign-owned enterprise (WFOE): It represented 25.46% of the total value of FDI in 1994 and 29.85 percent in 1996. According to China's Law on Wholly Foreign-owned Enterprises which was promulgated in April 1986, the WFOE is a company organized by a foreign company using entirely its capital, technology and management. The enterprise manages its operations independently and is responsible for all risks, gains, and losses.

(3) Contractual (or cooperative) joint venture (CJV): It constitutes about 19.71% of the actual value of FDI in 1994 and 18.99 percent in 1996. The CJV refers to a variety of arrangements and is a looser association of partners (although they may still involve establishment of a limited liability company) that agree to pursue a joint undertaking. The Chinese and foreign partner cooperate in joint projects or other business activities according to the terms and conditions stipulated in the venture agreement. Technology transfer and long-term licensing agreements are also included in this type.

(4) Joint exploration project (e.g., offshore oil exploration consortia): This represented 1.82% of the total amount of FDI in 1994 and less than 1 percent in 1996. Under these arrangements, the exploration costs are borne by the foreign partner, with development costs later shared by a Chinese entity. Although such explorations allow the foreign firm to manage specific projects, this type of FDI does not result in the establishment of new limited liability enterprises.

(5) Other FDI: This type constituted 0.99 percent and 0.59 percent of the total FDI in 1994 and 1996 respectively. It includes: a) processing and assembling agreements in which foreign firms provide Chinese manufacturers with raw materials or semi-products to produce final goods to be directly distributed in international markets; b) compensation trade agreements, under which foreign firms provide Chinese partners with inputs to manufacture products to be sold either in the domestic or in the international market, and c) international leasing agreements, whereby the foreign party retains ownership (and therefore equity and risk) of equipment used by China throughout the period of the lease.

Table 1.14 Foreign Direct Investment in China by Entry Modes in 1993 and 1994 (in US $ million)

Entry Mode	1993 Approved FDI	1993 Realized FDI	1994 Approved FDI	1994 Realized FDI
Equity JVs	55,175	15,347	39,355	17,750
Contractual JVs	25,499	5,237	20,347	6,726
Wholly Foreign Owned	30,456	6,505	21,472	8,689
Joint Exploration	304	424	232	622
Other FDI	531	255	565	335
1 International Leasing	65	46	17	20
2 Compensation Trade	271	89	203	113
3 Processing and Assembling	195	120	345	202
Total	111,966	27,769	81,971	34,122

Sources: *The Bulletin of MOFTEC*, Issue No. 2, 1994, pp. 10 and Issue No. 1, 1995, pp. 13.

Although the ratio of wholly foreign-owned ventures has been growing in recent years (about 7 percent prior to 1990 versus 29.85 percent in 1996), the equity joint venture is still the dominant mode, accounting for 50.84 percent in 1995 and 49.97 percent in 1996, respectively. For most industries, Chinese policy on foreign investment does not impose a ceiling on the proportion of foreign capital in the joint venture. In addition, although the joint venture law of 1979 stipulated that the equity share of a foreign partner could be no less than 25 percent, exceptions abound in practice.

Table 1.15 Foreign Direct Investment in China by Entry Modes in 1995 and 1996 (in US $ million)

Entry Mode	1993 Approved FDI	1993 Realized FDI	1994 Approved FDI	1994 Realized FDI
Equity JVs	38,839	19,364	31,884	21,287
Contractural JVs	17,791	7,502	14,337	8,090
Wholly Foreign Owned	33,601	10,298	26,699	12,718
Joint Exploration	57	590	293	255
Other FDI	679	346	334	250
1 International Leasing	42	29	42	24
2 Compensation Trade	531	277	142	172
3 Processing & Assembling	106	40	150	54
Total	90,967	38,082	73,547	42,600

Sources: The Bulletin of MOFTEC, Issue No. 1, 1997, pp. 19.

FDI Performance

With regard to the performance of FIEs operating in China, prior studies have drawn a controversial picture. While some studies show a satisfactory performance (Davidson, 1987; Kearney, 1987; National Council, 1987; Stelzer, Ma and Banthin, 1992; Osland and Cavusgil, 1996), others noted contrasting or uncertain results (Teagarden and Von Glinow, 1990; Shenkar, 1990; Beamish, 1993).

Davidson (1987) found in his field research conducted in 1984-85 with a sample of 47 Sino-U.S. joint ventures in China that, "Many of the firms in this sample went to China with high expectations. Almost half of the firms expected to recoup their initial investment within five years." In spite of these high expectations, over two-thirds of the firms reported that they had achieved or exceeded their performance expectations to date.

In a study by A. T. Kearney Inc. on the performance of 70 U.S., Hong Kong, Japanese and European joint ventures in ten major industry sectors, more than 50 percent of the foreign firms reported that they were accomplishing their objectives. In addition, 90 percent of the sample stated that had they had the knowledge acquired after entry, prior to the investment, their decision would have remained unchanged. The Kearney report concluded that most foreign investors report that their manufacturing FIEs were succeeding (*South China Morning Post*, August 19, 1987).

According to a survey conducted by the National Council for U.S.-China Trade (1987), among 120 U.S.-Chinese joint ventures, only "a handful" appeared to have failed. Recently, Stelzer *et al* (1992) conducted a survey of 306 senior executives overseeing U.S. investment projects in China. The study found most joint ventures were indeed profitable; 60 percent reported a five-year average ROI of 10 percent or higher. Nearly one third reported a ROI equal to, or exceeding, 18 percent. Only 12 percent of the sampling firms appeared to be losing money. When asked whether their China venture have met corporate expectations, about two-thirds of the surveyed companies claimed their ventures in China are meeting or exceeding anticipated performance. Based on interviews with 43 managers representing eight US-China joint ventures, Osland and Cavusgil (1996) find evidence in very joint venture in the sample that both sides are satisfied with the performance of the venture.

Other research paints a less positive picture. Beamish (1993), Shenkar (1990), and Teagarden and Von Glinow (1990) observed unsatisfactory performance. In the Beamish (1993) study, over half (14 out of 22) of the MNE partners indicated dissatisfaction with performance and felt that this situation was unlikely to change. Other researchers concluded that a high level of performance difficulties can be expected with Sino-foreign joint ventures in China, due to both their structural complexity and environmental diversity (Shenkar, 1990; Von Glinow and Teagarden, 1988).

Such contradictory evidence can be explained with consideration of a number of factors. First, different sampling sizes and time frames can translate into great variance in results. Such variance may be even larger within a highly dynamic investment environment such as the one prevailing in China. Second, prior studies have included samples of FIEs operating in different locations. Fundamental differences in policy treatment toward FDI across different regions or areas make firm performance dependent on location. This variability could explain the results. Third, earlier studies on the issue have not controlled for the industry effect which is likely to be very significant during the current transformation of the Chinese economy. As a result, samples taken from different industries have a great variance in performance.

We assessed the FDI performance in China based on the date obtained through a recent survey in 1996 of high level managers in FIEs in China. About five hundred questionnaires were distributed to general or deputy general managers of randomly selected FIEs in several Southern China provinces. These FIEs operate in various manufacturing sectors and are either wholly foreign owned or foreign dominant equity joint ventures. Sixty-five developed country funded FIEs and fifty-two developing country-funded FIEs returned the questionnaires in usable forms. This comes to a total of 116 sample FIEs.

FDI performance is measured in multiple dimensions comprising after-tax returns on assets, sales growth, competitive position in the market, and overall performance. These measures are widely used by firms in China and have captured the diverse objectives of FDI. The response format was a five-point scale comparison with the firm's major competitors, whether foreign or local, in the local industry (from bottom 20% to top 20%). The latest research suggests that the use of subjective measures of firm performance relative to competitors is particularly desirable in studying emerging businesses and is validated and shown to correlate with objective measures with a high degree of reliablity (Tan and Litschert, 1994).

As shown in Table 10, both developed country FIEs and developing country FIEs reveal an above-industry average, or moderately satisfactory performance along four dimensions including return on assets, sales growth, competitive position, and overall performance. More specifically, developed country FIEs demonstrate a better performance in market performance such as sales growth and competitive position in the market whereas developing country FIEs are more satisfactory with accounting performance (i.e., return on assets). For overall performance, all the FIEs reveal a moderately satisfactory performance comparative to their major rivals in the industry.

In Chapter eight, we will present an analysis of FDI performance by comparing equity joint ventures with wholly foreign owned subsidiaries and with local Chinese firms. Performance measures to be examined include not only profitability indicators, but also liquidity, leverage, and asset efficiency ratios.

Table 1.16 FDI Performance in China

Performance Measures	Developed Country FIEs (N=66)		Developing Country FIEs (N=52)	
	Mean	St.D.	Mean	St.D
Return on Assets	3.03	1.06	3.75	1.19
Sales Growth	3.30	0.96	2.57	1.24
Competitive Position	3.71	1.13	2.80	1.22
Overall Performance	3.18	1.08	3.08	1.09

1.3 Review of FDI in China Over the Past Seventeen Years (1979-1996)

Since economic liberalization was initiated in 1979, China has taken great strides in attracting FDI. The rapid growth of FDI flow has given a tremendous boost to the development of the national economy.

In the early years of the previous decade, the Chinese government adopted a series of preferential policies for Guangdong and Fujian province. Later on, the authorities set up the Shengzhen Special Economic Zone along with four other zones, and opened 14 coastal cities to FDI activity, all at the initiative of paramount leader Deng Xiaoping. In the 1990s, especially after a historical speech delivered by Deng affirming and extending the leadership's commitment to the liberalization policy, China's reform process has accelerated. Other measures were adopted including the establishment of Pudong's new development zone in Shanghai, and the opening up of additional cities along the Yangtze River as well as provincial capitals. A number of development zones have now been instituted throughout the territory. Overall, the role of FDI in nurturing and promoting China's economic development can be summarized as follows:

First, FDI has contributed to ease the shortage of capital needed for China's economic construction. The proportion of FDI in the total social fixed assets investment has been rising steadily, from an average of 2.5 percent in the 1980s to 18.3 percent in 1994.

Second, FDI has promoted the development of China's indigenous industries. The absorbed foreign capital has been mainly invested in advanced technologies, thus contributing to the modernization of Chinese industry. Products like stereo equipment, color TV sets and other consumer electronics which were imported in the past are now being exported in large quantities. Foreign invested enterprises have not only broadened the range of products available on the domestic market, they have also upgraded technology used in sectors of Chinese manufacturing.

Third, foreign invested enterprises now constitute a powerful engine fueling China's foreign trade. In 1993, the import and export volume of all foreign invested enterprises was valued at $67.07 billion or 34.4 percent of the country's total. In 1995, exports contributed by FIEs accounted for 31.3 percent of the nation's total export.

Fourth, foreign capital involvement has influenced the Chinese people's mentalities and modified their frames of reference. The establishment of foreign invested enterprises has introduced and popularized the concepts of market economy, new organizational and operational styles in the enterprises, market competition mechanisms and effective administration systems.

Despite the many positive developments that were discussed above, there still remain a few problems which have to be solved if the gains of foreign investment for both investors and host country are to be realized to their fullest extent. These problems are as follows:

First, the resource structure of FDI has relied too heavily on Hong Kong and Taiwan. By the end of 1995, 69.07 percent of the total amount of FDI were funded by Hong Kong and Macau and Taiwan investors. Since investors from these areas tend to focus more on labor-intensive products or real-estate projects, this structure is not beneficial in the long run. It can indeed slow the process of industrial structure rationalization and delay the process of transformation to a market economy.

Second, the motives animating foreign investors are often at odds with those held by the Chinese government. A sizable number of foreign investors seem to consider FDI as a vehicle to gain access to the Chinese market, either in the short or in the long run. Given the promising potential of this market, existing difficulties do not appear to constitute a deterrent. There are obviously other motivations for creating a venture, such as extracting resources, establishing a manufacturing base to supply other markets, or simply serving other ventures in China. However, the attraction of the domestic market constitute, by far, the most important factor in foreign investment decisions. In contrast, the Chinese government's interest in attracting FDI stems from very different considerations. Foreign investment is seen as a means to obtain advanced technologies and managerial skills needed to modernize the economy and to earn foreign exchange through the establishment of export industries. Some of the operation problems encountered by foreign ventures can be traced to the tension generated by the pursuit of different, and at times divergent, objectives by the foreign investor and various levels of governmental authorities in China.

Third, some governmental regulations and policies governing FDI are opaque. There is often a "margin" for either central or local authorities to "explain" the relevant laws, rules, regulations and policies. Under these circumstances, different officials have different explanations about policies and rules. This situation certainly has increased the instability of policy enforcement. Indeed, China has enacted hundreds of foreign investment laws, rules, and regulations which, however, lack in transparency. Foreign investors frequently complained about governmental "red tape" which remains a major impediment for business operations.

1.4 What is Happening Now?

China's FDI inflows rose by 147 percent between 1992 and 1993, but only by 23 percent in 1994 and 11 percent in 1995. Inflows increased from $28 billion in 1993 to $38 billion in 1995, almost equivalent to the average annual inflows of all developed countries in the first half of the 1980s. This raises the question of whether China's FDI growth is sustainable.

The Chinese central government has introduced measures very recently to prevent speculative investment (e.g., in real estate), and has forced some 'phantom' foreign affiliates to terminate operations. It has also strengthened monitoring by setting up 'administrative procedures for appraising foreign invested property' in early 1994. The appraisals aim at preventing speculative investments, or using inferior capital equipment. China has also become more selective in screening FDI projects to ensure compliance with economic development objectives. This is reflected in the government's newly adopted FDI guidelines that are in line with the national development plan and the country's industrial policies. Moreover, the nation is targeting large MNE investments. This is reflected in the incentives aimed at attracting large MNEs to technologically-advanced or capital-intensive projects (Luo, 1996).

China is moving towards national treatment - an effort to level the playing field for domestic and foreign firms and facilitate its entry into the World Trade Organization (WTO). Policy measures since 1994 are meant to eliminate those preferences for foreign investors that have distorted markets and have led to a bias against domestic firms. Such measures include the unification of the tax system and the elimination of exemption of import duties granted to FIEs.

To be more specific, in the tax reform undertaken in 1994, the turn-over tax regime and individual income tax regime were unified. As a result, both domestic and foreign firms are now governed by a unified set of rules on value-added, consumption, business operations and individual income taxation. A notable exception, however, is the corporate income tax regime, under which foreign investors still enjoy preferential treatment.

In April 1996, China substantially reduced the average general tariff level from 35.9 percent to 23 percent, covering nearly 5000 tariff lines with an average reduction margin of 36 percent. At the 1996 APEC meeting, China again announced that it would reduce the average general tariff level to 15 percent by the year 2000. China is phasing out the non-tariff measures and has submitted a timetable for the gradual elimination of the remaining non-tariff measures applied to around 400 tariff lines. FIEs face the same duties and import-related taxes as domestic firms on all imported equipment, materials, and all other items since April 1996. Although overall tariff rates had already been lowered considerably at the beginning of 1996, the abolition of the preferential import duties awarded to FIEs is important, given that nearly 70 percent of China's FDI is in the form of imported capital equipment or raw materials (National Council, 1991).

In 1996, China incorporated FIEs into the system of buying and selling foreign exchange through banks and realized the convertibility of the Renminbi (RMB) under current account on December 1 of the same year. At the same time, China keeps the foreign exchange swap center as a source of procurement and settlement of foreign exchanges. Nevertheless, more and more FIEs are likely to choose designated banks to buy or sell foreign exchanges because the new scheme offers much greater benefits. RMB convertibility under current account will help improve the investment and operating environment for foreigners. It provides a more adequate institutional guarantee of the legitimate revenues of foreign investors, minimizes the risks involved in the remittance of profits and gives a stronger sense of security to foreign investors. Meanwhile, the removal of restrictions on payment and transfer of foreign exchanges helps streamline the procedures for examination and approval, which will in turn increase the turnover rate of capital, thus improving business performance.

China is now experimenting with the Sino-foreign joint venture trading companies in Pudong, Shanghai. Pilot registration system for granting trading rights to production enterprises in the five Special Economic Zones (SEZs) has been introduced. Foreign banks have begun to do local currency business in Pudong on a trial basis.

1.5 Strategic Outlook

Recent policy changes are expected to have certain impacts on FDI over the next few years. The movement towards national treatment discourages 'round-tripping' (that is, capital outflows that are repatriated back to China disguised as FDI, taking advantage of tax and regulatory incentives to FIEs) and 'phantom' foreign ventures. Tighter screening and monitoring of FDI projects may significantly reduce the overvaluation of FDI that takes place through incorrect invoicing of imported equipment. In addition, tight monetary policies (likely to continue to be pursued by the government in the near future to curb inflation and cool the overheated economy) will have a bearing on FDI. This is because FDI projects usually have to be coupled with domestic capital (an entry requirement for FDI in some industries). More expensive domestic capital discourages domestic investment and hence diminishes the ability of foreign investors to find joint venture partners.

Further, FDI from Hong Kong, Macau and Taiwan, the top FDI sources for China, is losing momentum as the transfer of labor-intensive production to China slows down. Partly due to the fact that most labor-intensive production has already moved out from these economies and partially due to increases in labor and land costs in the coastal regions, export-processing production has become less attractive in China than in several other Asian countries such as Vietnam. The share of these three economies in China has, indeed, declined from 72 percent in 1993 to 63 percent in 1995. Moreover, the return of Hong Kong to China in 1997 also has some implications for FDI flows, depending on the smoothness of the transition and China's ability to maintain Hong Kong as a competitive international business center.

China's attractiveness to foreign investors, however, remains bright. First, China's growth performance is outstanding. With an average annual GDP growth of 12 percent in 1991-1996, China is one of the fastest growing economies in the world. This trend is expected to continue. Second, the liberalization of FDI policies is still under way. Some industries that had been off limits to foreign investors, including air transport, general aviation, retail trade, foreign trade, banking, insurance, accounting, auditing, legal services, the mining and smelting of precious metals, and the prospecting, extracting and processing of diamonds and other precious non-metal minerals, are gradually being opened.

Third, there is also a significant potential for FDI participation in infrastructure. Several build-operate-transfer (BOT) schemes have already been concluded. Foreign investors are now allowed to acquire state-owned firms. Fourth, to the extent that the Chinese currency becomes convertible, profit repatriation will be easier, making it more attractive to invest in China.

Lastly, according to the Ministry of Foreign Trade and Economic Cooperation (MOFTEC), China, the following tax policies will guide FDI in the future: (1) General preferential rate: For manufacturing businesses, a preferential income tax rate of 33 percent will apply; (2) Reduced tax rate extended to special areas: For FIEs located in the SEZs or manufacturing businesses in the economic and technological development zones (ETDZs), a 15 percent income tax will apply. The income tax rate of 24 percent will apply for foreign-invested manufacturing enterprises located in the old town of a city located at the coastal economic open areas, SEZs, or ETDZs; (3) Reduced tax rate extended to special sectors: For Sino-foreign joint ventures which meet certain qualifications and engage in energy, transportation, port or pier construction, a 15 percent income tax rate will apply; (4) Preferential rate extended to special businesses: The flow of FDI to high-tech businesses or export-oriented businesses will continuously be encouraged. Once confirmed as these two types of businesses, they will be granted special tax incentives; (5) Manufacturing FIEs with a term of operation over 10 years will be continuously granted tax exemption for two years starting from the profit-making year and given a half rate for three years afterwards; (6) If foreign investors make additional investments by profits made from the FIEs, they shall get a refund of 40 percent of the income tax they have already paid.

As a result of the above, the already great importance of FDI to China's economy is likely to grow. Thus, while FDI inflows to China might fall below $30 billion in the next few years, there is reason to believe that this will be a temporary adjustment rather than a response to a change in general economic factors. One strong piece of evidence supporting this speculation is that the top 12 MNEs from the United States that already have the biggest stakes in China are maintaining their commitment through ongoing construction and investment (see Table 1.17). All in all, China will remain one of the top FDI destinations in the world marketplace.

1.17 Top-12 US Companies with the Biggest Stakes in China by the End of 1996

1   Motorola: $1.2 billion. The company's most recent commitments include several joint ventures and a $560 million semiconductor wafer fabrication plant in Tianjing.
2   Atlantic Richfield: $625 million. Arco has completed China's largest offshore natural gas project, a $1.13 billion pipeline half owned by the Chinese government.
3   Coca-Cola: $500 million. Coke, Fanta, Sprite, and Hi C are bottled at 16 locations. Seven more facilities are being constructed.
4   Amoco: #350 million. Amoca started producing oil in March from a development project in the South China Sea.
5   Ford Motor: $250 million. Ford has three factories making auto components, light trucks, and vans; two other plants are under construction.
6   United Tech: $250 million. UT's Otis subsidiary makes elevators and escalators; Carrier manufactures air-conditioning equipment.
7   Pepsico: $200 million. Pepsi has 12 bottling plants, two joint ventures producing Cheetos, 62 KFC franchises, and 19 Pizza Huts.
8   Lucent Technologies: $150 million. The AT&T spinoff is involved in seven joint ventures, including a $70 million project to provide digital private-line service to Beijing.
9   General Electric: $150 million. GE is part of 14 joint ventures, including those that make X-ray and other medical systems. It owns 80% of the largest lighting manufacturer in China.
10 General Motors: $130 million. Delphi, a subsidiary, is a partner in three auto-parts facilities. Not counted, because the money is not yet committed, is GM's 50% partnership in a $1 billion project to build cars in Shanghai.
11 Hewlett-Packard: $100 million. HP has been investing in China for 12 years and is now manufacturing computers, medical systems products, and analytical chemical equipment.
12 IBM: $100 million. IBM has six joint ventures, producing computers, electronic cards, advanced workstations for the banking industry, and software.

Source: *Fortune*, May 27, 1996, pp. 118.

Bibliography and Further Readings

Beamish, P.W. (1993), 'The Characteristics of Joint Ventures in the People's Republic of China', *Journal of International Marketing*, vol. 1, pp. 29-48.
Bulletin of MOFTEC (1997), Bulletin of Ministry of Foreign Trade and Economic Cooperation, P. R. China, issue 1, pp. 1-8.
Casson, M. and Zheng, R. (1991), 'Western Joint Ventures in China', *Journal of International Development*, vol. 3, pp. 293-323.
Chen, E.K.Y. (1990), *Foreign Direct Investment in Asia*, Asian Productivity Organization, Tokyo.
Davidson, W.H. (1987), 'Creating and Managing Joint Ventures in China', *California Management Review*, vol. 29, pp. 77-94.
Luo, Y. (1997), 'Great China MNEs in the PRC: A Comparative Analysis of Their Investment Behavior and Performance Relative to Western MNEs', *International Business Review*, Special Issue (in press).
Luo, Y. (1996), 'Evaluating Strategic Alliance Performance in China'. *Long Range Planning*, vol. 29, pp. 532-540.
Luo, Y. and Sadrieh, F. (1995), 'The Relationships between Business Strategy Variables and Joint Venture Performance: Lessons from China', *Journal of Business and Management*, Fall, pp. 17-36.
Luo, Y. (1997), 'The Chinese Economy in Transition: From Plan to Market', *Asia Pacific Journal of Management*, book review (in press).
National Council (1991), National Council for US-China Trade, *Special Report on US Investment in China*, Department of Commerce, Washington, D.C..
National Council (1987), National Council for US-China Trade, *US Joint Venture in China: A Progress Report*, Department of Commerce, Washington, D.C.
Osland, G.E. and Cavusgil, S.T. (1996), 'Performance Issues in US-China Joint Ventures', *California Management Review*, vol. 38, pp. 106-130.
Pan, Y. (1996), 'Influences on Foreign Equity Ownership Level in Joint Ventures in China', *Journal of International Business Studies*, vol. 27, pp. 1-26.
Shan, W. (1991), 'Environmental Risks and Joint Venture Sharing Arrangements', *Journal of International Business Studies*, vol. 22, pp. 555-578.
Shenkar, O. (1990), 'International Joint Ventures' Problems in China: Risks and Remedies', *Long Range Planning*, vol. 23, pp. 82-90.
Stelzer, L., Ma, C. and Banthin, J. (1992), 'Gauging Investor Satisfaction'. *China Business Review*, November-December.
Teagarden, M.B. and Von Glinow, M.A. (1990), 'Sino-Foreign Strategic Alliances Types and Related Operating Characteristics', *International Studies of Management and Organization*, Spring, pp. 19-33.
World Investment Report 1996 (1997), UNCTAD.
Yan, A. and Gray, B. (1994), 'Bargaining Power, Management Control, and Performance in United States-China Joint Ventures: A Comparative Case Study', *Academy of Management Journal*, vol. 37, pp. 1478-1517.

2 International Investment Environment in China

Chapter Purpose

This chapter illustrates the general environment for foreign direct investment in China. The discussion is divided into six sections. The first section outlines the current economic environment. The next section focuses on current and emerging market demands. This is followed by an introduction to cost and revenue-related issues. The fourth section highlights recent tax policies. Environmental factors affecting international investment strategies are discussed next. The final section presents the most recent legal environment pertaining to foreign direct investment in China.

2.1 Emerging Market Economy

China's open market reform and rapid economic growth have enticed a tremendous surge in activity and market investment by multinational companies. China is second only to Japan as Asia's largest and fastest growing market for most products. Real growth in GDP has averaged 9% per year since 1981 and hit over 10% in the last five years. By the year 2000, China's consumer market will be larger than the United States or Western Europe.

In many ways, China is taking steps toward a market economy. Massive migration from the countryside to urban areas, though widely misinterpreted in the Western press as a threat to social stability in the PRC, represents the inevitable workings of a market economy. The gap between urban and rural wages in China is higher than in any other country. It is true that the tens of millions of people moving around China looking for employment are a worry to the leadership in Beijing. But this phenomenon indicates that jobs are no longer being allocated as strictly as they were in the past, and should be viewed as a sign that marketization is occurring.

Another sign of increasing marketization is the reduced relevance of 'the plan' to actual economic performance. China's economy is actually much more marketized than is recognized by the bureaucrats who continue to churn out plans in Beijing. Looking at the Eighth Five-Year Plan in hindsight makes it clear that there was very little connection between the plan set forth in 1990 and what actually happened. For example, many of the economic targets were fulfilled more rapidly than expected. Within just three years, enormous growth in GDP, trade, and FDI had already been achieved. Though the central government retains approval power over large-scale projects in critical industries, the grip over all sectors and levels of the economy as laid out in the Five-Year plan model has loosened. Table 2.1 presents some key indicators of China's economy in 1995.

China's effort to engineer industrial growth has included measures designed to gradually introduce market competition, encourage mergers and acquisitions, and foster the expansion of collective enterprises. As a result of industrial reform, firms have had increasing autonomy over determining how and with whom they will conduct business. From methods of production to decisions about hiring and firing workers, Chinese business organizations are becoming less and less dependent on central authority. Managers have more responsibility for finding productive inputs, determining appropriate production and inventory levels, and locating markets for their products. Bankruptcy and unemployment, unheard of in the past, have also increased in recent years, demonstrating that poor firm performance may result in failure for the firm and unemployment for the firm's managers.

As a result of these changes, Chinese industrial performance has improved considerably, leading to dramatic levels of macro-economic growth. As Table 2.2 indicates, the annual increase in industrial value added averaged 11.7 percent between 1981-1990. While the growth rate of this key indicator reached a two-decade low of 3.2 percent in 1990, it managed to climb to 21.7 percent just two years later. The estimates included in Table 2.2 also indicate that between 1981 and 1990, Chinese GDP grew at an average annual rate of 10.4 percent (8.7 percent per capita). GDP growth has been above 10 percent since 1992. The Asian Development Bank estimates that this rapid growth will continue to the end of this decade. The countries of Eastern Europe and the former Soviet Union that are also undergoing economic reform have not grown nearly as rapidly. Growth in Hungary was only 1.8 percent between 1981 and 1985; and in Poland, GDP growth averaged less than 2 percent between 1981 and 1989. As Table 2.3

Table 2.1 China's Economy in 1995

Nominal GDP	$692.6 billion
Real GDP growth	10.2%
Retail price inflation	14.8%
Cost of living index	17.0%
Population	1.198 billion
Per capita GDP	$578
Per capita urban income	$468
Per capita rural income	$190
Official unemployment rate	2.9%
M1 supply growth	16.7%
M2 supply growth	29.5%
Reserve money growth	20.6%
Foreign exchange reserves	
(excluding gold)	$73.5 billion
Exchange rate (4/15/96)	8.532/$1

Sources: International Monetary Fund, China Statistical Yearbook, and US Bureau of the Census.

indicates, average GDP growth in all developing economies was only 4 percent during these years, and average GDP growth in all post-socialist economies was negative.

The influence of the governmental planning system has been substantially reduced as the role of planners changes. Bureaucrats are no longer responsible for allocating machinery and equipment. Reports indicate that roughly 25 percent of manufacturing output now comes from foreign joint ventures and private firms. At the same time, township and village enterprises (TVEs), the most dynamic and entrepreneurial sector, is now playing a big part in shaping the Chinese economy. TVEs have rapidly emerged as a growing industrial force in China. As Table 2.4 shows, gross output produced by TVEs reached 4,258.85 billion yuan in 1994, which represented 30.46 percent of the nation's total in the industry sector. Similarly, the number of TVEs in industry is almost ten times greater than state-owned enterprises (*China Statistical Yearbook* 1995: 375). In 1994, 120.18 million people were employed by TVEs, nearly triple the number of

Table 2.2 Growth Rate of Chinese Economic Indicators (% per annum)

Year	Growth Rate of added value in industry	Growth Rate of GDP	Growth Rate of Per Capita GDP
1981-1990	11.7	10.4	8.7
1990	3.2	3.9	1.6
1991	13.3	9.3	8.1
1992	21.7	14.2	12.7
1993	20.7	13.5	12.0
1994	17.4	11.8	10.3
1995	13.6	10.2	8.9
1996*	8.5	8.0	6.8
1997*	8.9	9.0	9.0

Source: Asian Development Bank (1996); Chinese State Statistical Bureau (1995).
* Asian Development Bank estimates.

Table 2.3 International Comparison of GDP Growth

	Growth Rate of GDP (1995)
World	2.6
Industrialized countries	2.0
United States	2.1
Canada	2.4
United Kingdom	2.7
Japan	0.5
Developing Countries	4.0
Latin American	-0.3
Asia	7.9
China	10.2
Countries in Transition	-1.8

Source: Asian Development Bank (1996), China State Statistical Bureau (1995).

workers in state firms. While about 70 percent of state firms have undergone losses in past years, TVE net profits and contributed taxes have progressively increased (see Table 2.4). According to the *China Statistical Yearbook* (1995, pp. 366, 391), almost half of China's total pre-tax profits are now generated by TVEs. The success and growth of TVEs are also reflected in high levels of key financial ratios such as return on fixed assets, return on equity (funds), and return on sales (operating revenue) (Table 2.4). In no other transitional economy have TVEs played such a dynamic role. The central government has a limited ability to control the growth of these decentralized parts of the economy. Though central leaders can influence the variables that affect economic growth, they do not control the economy to the extent that they did in the past.

China is in a very strong position to increase the degree of currency convertibility. Though China officials give conflicting stories about the exact time frame for full convertibility, China already has current account convertibility. Most importers have ready access to foreign exchange, unless they seek to purchase a restricted item. There is also fairly wide access to foreign exchange which supports tourism and foreign-invested enterprises seeking to repatriate profits.

There are a few critical challenges that may impact the development of China's economy. First, state-owned enterprises (SOEs) are still losing money at a very rapid clip. About 44 percent of SOEs were operating in the red in 1995, almost double the percentage in 1992. Financing SOE losses puts enormous strains on the economy. Second, there is no evidence that the stage has yet been set for stabilizing macroeconomic fluctuations in the Chinese economy. Though China was successful in restricting the amount of credit that is funded through the banking system, there were two other major sources of unplanned credit: an increase in loans made by non-bank financial institutions and the People's Bank of China's injection of Chinese yuan (RMB) into the economy to keep the yuan from appreciating. Third, inter-firm debt (triangular debt) has continued to mount in recent years. By the end of 1995, state-owned firms accumulated account receivables amounting to about ¥150 billion. If China fails to make enterprises deal with each other on sounder economic terms, the prospects for reforming the state-owned sector will remain bleak. Lastly, management of state-owned assets remains to be resolved. The leadership is committed to the dominance of the state sector in certain industries. The way to implement more efficient management of state assets is to establish intermediary institutions to represent the State Asset Management Commission   (ASMC) by holding

Table 2.4 Township and Village Enterprises in China: 1990-1994

Item	1990	1991	1992	1993	1994
General Information					
Number of TVEs (million)	18.50	19.09	20.79	24.53	24.95
Number of Employees (million)	92.65	96.09	105.81	123.45	120.18
Gross Output (billion yuan)	846.16	1162.17	1797.54	3154.07	4258.85
Net Value of Fixed Assets (billion yuan)	166.87	195.93	258.59	376.80	519.62
Net Value of Circulating Funds (bil. yuan)	224.47	292.50	406.38	561.87	845.89
Performance					
Total Operating Revenue (billion yuan)	521.86	655.60	1004.09	1742.21	2508.90
Total Net Profits (billion yuan)	23.27	28.47	47.76	109.31	135.24
Taxes Paid (billion yuan)	27.55	33.38	47.02	64.85	107.90
Total Pre-tax Profits (billion yuan)	28.98	35.28	57.22	178.40	222.57
Total Wage Bill (billion yuan)	60.68	70.65	95.71	132.39	165.05
Financial Ratios					
After-tax Return on Fixed Assets (%)	10.60	10.80	13.80	21.20	20.50
Pre-tax Return on Equity (Funds) (%)	13.00	12.70	14.30	19.00	14.80
After-tax Return on Equity (Funds) (%)	5.90	5.80	7.20	11.60	9.00
After-tax Return on Operating Revenue (%)	4.50	4.30	4.80	6.30	5.40
Operating Revenue on Fixed Assets (%)	237.00	249.60	289.90	337.60	379.40

Source: Luo, Tan and Shenkar (in press).

shares in SOEs. Nevertheless, these state institutions may still have a vested interest in the maintenance of SOEs, even those operating at a loss. It may be difficult to close down a financially troubled SOE in which state financial institutions hold majority shares.

2.2 Market Demand

Chinese purchasing power is on the rise. Chinese people are demanding more products which are better and cheaper, and they want them faster. They want it all and some of them can pay. More than 200 million Chinese are expected to have purchasing power in excess of an annual $1,000 by the year 2000. This translates into big opportunities for western products. Over the next 25 years, China's economy should expand to almost $6 trillion, about 10 times its size in 1994, and the birth rate will be low. Although common sense needs to be applied to what is appropriate for the Chinese market, many western products are finding a warm reception due to their eye appeal and reputation for high quality and reliability.

China's urban population of 125 million in major coastal cities is crossing the $1,000 per capita income line and entering a phase of very high growth in demand (15% to 20% per year) for everything from blue jeans to electronic products, from motorcycles to processed foods, as well as for all of the industrial products (e.g., chemicals, pharmaceutical, and machinery) that feed consumption-based industries. Every year more than 50,000 international companies set up operations in China in search of market share before the market entry barriers get too high. Despite many daunting challenges, China is proving irresistibly attractive to most international companies.

Until now, growth has come mostly from manufacturers that took advantage of the country's immense pool of cheap labor, where wages averaged around $100 a month. Increasingly, though, these firms are moving to more advanced products. Within four years, China expects to ship out $100 billion worth of electronics and machinery. It may soon become one of the world's biggest exporters of color TVs, auto parts, and cellular phones, and will also start offering engines, power generators, and computer tomography scanners. There are some infrastructure inadequacies. Insufficient transportation, telecommunications, housing, water technology and energy may pose major obstacles to growth. Despite some challenges, however, China has created a lucrative sales and market potential. This has made it an attractive target for global revenue opportunities.

Potential market growth projections in China, for the years 1995 to 2000, suggest that demand for products such as telephones, VCRs, air conditioners, consumer electronics, washing machines, and detergents will grow rapidly. This is attributed to a greater number of households that have crossed the consumption threshold for these products, increased their income per household, and now have greater access due to advances in logistics and distribution. Although the national average household income was $685 in 1994, per-capita income has risen about 20 percent over the past years, and average income should reach $4,000 by 2020, compared with $35,000 in the United States (both measured in 1995 dollars). Buruma, Faison, and Zakaria report (1996) that, in 1995, (i) the average income of a Chinese businessperson is $581 a year; (ii) a factory worker: $420; and (iii) an agricultural worker: $213. A worker in a FIE earns at least 200 percent the salary of a comparable worker at a government-run company. But the latter receives insurance and subsidized housing.

How does a Chinese household spend its money? According to a recent survey (in 1996) by the *New York Times Magazine*, the average monthly expenses for a Chinese family are: (i) food: $22; (ii) savings: $11; (iii) clothing: $8; (iv) child education: $5; (v) rent and utilities: $4; (vi) medical care: $2; (vii) entertainment: $1; (viii) others: $4.

According to the same survey, the percentage of families who own certain consumer goods, from a survey of 3,500 households is as follows: (1) color television: 40 percent; (2) refrigerator: 25 percent; (3) VCR: 12 percent; (4) Telephone: 9 percent; and (5) computer: 2 percent.

Some of the top items on Chinese wish lists (in percentages): (1) washing machine: 22 percent; (2) refrigerator: 21 percent; (3) electric fan: 15 percent; (4) telephone: 11 percent; (5) automobile: 4 percent; and (6) computer: 4 percent. Table 2.5 illustrates Chinese household purchasing power in the last few years.

China's consumer market has experienced spectacular growth and is still growing. Foreign investors can now decide on pricing, location, distribution, and marketing strategy with much less, if any, government interference in unrestricted sectors. Many foreign companies that once struggled to make ends meet are reaping the rewards of investing in China. Below, the five American companies whose joint ventures yielded the highest gross sales in 1994 (in millions of dollars, and with rank among all joint ventures): 1. Chrysler: $497 (4th); 2. Motorola: $310 (6th); 3. Procter & Gamble: $234 (14th); 4. United Technologies: $184 (33rd); and 5. Coca-Cola: $119 (59th).

Some economists predict that China could become the second largest economy in the world, in absolute size, by 2010 (Tureq, 1995). China's current growing population of 1.198 billion people represents the bulk of tomorrow's world growth. China's pharmaceutical market at $8.1 billion is expected to grow to $19 billion by the year 2000, the sixth largest in the world. Five major vendors in the personal computer industry in China (Compaq, AST, IBM, Legend, and Hewlett-Packard) are competing heavily for shares of China's huge market potential. In 1993, only 0.1 percent of Chinese owned automobiles, a total of 1.2 million. About 70 percent were imports (bicycles, meanwhile, number upward of 450 million). China is thus a potentially huge market. If 1 percent of Chinese people could afford cars, that would be 12 million, roughly the market of the whole of Europe.

In the leading cities such as Shanghai, Beijing, and Guangzhou, which have the highest income levels in the country, the demand for brand name products is growing fast. Importantly, price controls by the government on 90 percent of consumer products have been lifted. Centralized, volume-based (or quota-based) state planning for manufactured products now applies to less than 20 percent of industrial output, down from 95 percent in 1979 (Pollock, 1994).

For example, Volkswagen established its Shanghai joint venture, VWS, in 1985 with an investment of ¥1 billion (about ($116 million) and a registered share capital of ¥350 million. The joint venture has been profitable since its second year, with production rising steadily from less than 10,000 cars a year to 100,000 in 1993. The company helped build its position by making concessions and agreeing to transfer technology and R&D management skills to its local partners. The Santana saloon, which has an ex-works value of ¥100,000, now uses 82 percent local content, up from 4 percent in the prototype. The company is now putting in another ¥2.5 billion to raise production by the end of 1997 to 150,000 units per year. A new model, the Santana 2000, is shortly expected. The company now controls over half of the Chinese car market. Table 2.5 illustrates the purchasing power of households owning durable consumer goods in Shanghai and Guangzhou.

Table 2.5 Purchasing Power: Households Owning Consumer Durables (% of Total Households)

	Shanghai		Guangzhou	
	1992	1993	1992	1993
Washing Machines	71%	85%	61%	72%
Cameras	42%	60%	24%	45%
Air Conditioners	1%	4%	7%	9%
Motorcycles	6%	12%	0.3%	1.7%
Colour TVs	83%	94%	85%	87%
Refrigerators	92%	96%	67%	70%

Source: Asiamoney, September 1994, pp. 51.

2.3 Cost and Revenue-Related Environment

One of China's attractions for FDI is undoubtedly its position as a low-labor cost manufacturing site. Indeed, many manufacturing projects, particularly in light industry (e.g., textiles, toys, consumer goods) seek to take advantage of the enormous Chinese labor pool.

Imported materials, parts, and components highly affect production costs. Most ventures must import some percentage of the input used in production because they are either unavailable in China or cannot be found at required quality levels and specifications. In general, the more advanced the product or technologies, the higher the venture's import content will be. High import content not only drives up production costs, but also, and perhaps more importantly, creates foreign exchange difficulties for the venture. The foreign exchange needs must be met with foreign exchange sales, which cannot be secured unless a certain level of competitiveness on the international market is achieved. This, in turn, depends to a large extent on costs of production.

According to the Regulations for the Implementation of the Joint Venture Law (1983), foreign ventures are required to sell at least 30% of their output on the international market. In practice, however, this rule has not been strictly enforced. On the international market, FIEs can either export directly to end users or export to other divisions of the foreign partner for use in other production facilities or for resale. On the domestic market, FIEs engaging in convertible-currency sales can target other FIEs and Chinese organizations with access to foreign exchange. Recently, an increasing number of foreign businesses are trying to sell domestically for a mixed Chinese yuan/foreign exchange price, with the foreign exchange portion covering as much of the costs of the product's imported inputs as possible.

A sizable number of FIEs have experienced liquidity and financing problems, not only in foreign exchange but also in Chinese yuan (Luo, 1995). One of the major factors is that many investors, both foreign and local, are reluctant to make cash contributions to the full extent of their contractual commitments either out of opportunism or in an attempt to reduce risk. Another major reason can be traced to the conditions created by the tight monetary policy instituted to control inflationary pressures. The credit squeeze has resulted in many FIEs experiencing delays in receiving both foreign exchange and Chinese yuan under existing loan agreements. In these situations, priority in new loans is given to those ventures that produce exports or bring in advanced technology.

The financial reforms undertaken by the Chinese authorities entered a new phase on January 1, 1994, with the unification of the official and swap exchange rates. This unified rate has greatly simplified financial dealings for foreign ventures, allowing them, in particular, to base their investment decisions and profit repatriation on a single benchmark.

2.4 Taxation Issues

Corporate Income Tax

A corporate income tax is assessed on the net profits of foreign ventures. For joint ventures, the standard national rate is 30% (payable to the central authorities) to which a local surcharge of 3% must be added. Wholly foreign owned subsidiaries are liable for a tax of 20 to 40% of profits as well as an additional local levy fixed at 10% of the national income tax.

Foreign ventures with a contract extending for more than 10 years are not taxed for the first two profit-making years, and benefit from a 50 percent reduction in income tax for the following three years. Foreign ventures that reinvest their profits in China over five consecutive years can claim a refund of up to 40 percent of disbursed taxes.

The local governments tend to offer the same tax concessions as the national government. A two year tax holiday and a three year 50% reduction of the national enterprise income tax is given to enterprises which are engaged in production and have an operating term of at least ten years. Unlike corporations in the West, which are assumed to continue perpetually, foreign funded enterprises in China must declare an approved operating period. This is fundamentally a formality. The period can be extended. As a practical matter, a corporation which commits to ten years could dissolve after two or five years. In fact, this strategy is often employed, to the consternation of the tax authorities.

An enterprise which exports at least 70% of its production also qualifies for a 50% reduction of the national income tax. An enterprise which is certified to be a technologically advanced enterprise may qualify for an additional three-year 50% tax reduction.

Foreign investors are exempt from individual income tax on dividends from foreign investment enterprises. If a foreign investor reinvests a dividend for at least five years, 40% of the enterprise income tax paid on such dividend will be refunded. If the reinvestment is made in an export oriented or technologically advanced enterprise, 100% of the enterprise income tax paid will be refunded.

If a foreign enterprise purchases materials in China on which value added tax (VAT) has been levied and then exports such materials, this VAT (17 percent) is refundable.

Location Differences

FIEs operating in a designated Special Economic Zone (SEZ) which is engaged in production and business operations qualify for a 15% income tax rate. Service enterprises in a SEZ qualify for a one-year exemption and a two year 50% reduction of income tax. Income derived from a SEZ by a foreign company is subject to only a 10% withholding tax. Goods produced in a SEZ (20% or more value added) are exempt from export duties. Some products in some SEZs qualify for a VAT exemption.

FIEs engaged in production also qualify for 15% income tax in an Economic and Technological Development Zone (ETDZ). The reduced 10%

withholding tax on interest and dividends applies to ETDZ-based income for foreign investors.

A production FIE in an Open Coastal City (OCC) qualifies for a 24% national income tax rate. If the FIE is also export-oriented, the national income tax rate is reduced to 12%. Technologically advanced FIEs qualify for a 15% tax rate. Local governments may reduce or exempt the local income tax at their own discretion. The withholding tax for foreign investors is again reduced to 10%.

Production FIEs in an Open Coastal Economic Area (OCEA) qualify for a 24% national income tax rate. Technologically advanced FIEs qualify for a 15% rate. The provincial government may exempt local income taxes on a case by case basis. The withholding tax rate is reduced to 10% for foreign investors.

FIEs certified as technologically advanced firms located within a High and New Technology Industrial Development Zone (HNTIDZ) qualify for a 15% national income tax rate. To qualify as a technologically advanced firm, 30% of the employees must be technical personnel with university degrees and 3% of gross revenues must be spent on research activities.

Any FIE located in a Border Open City (BOC), upon approval of the local tax agency qualifies for a 24% income tax rate. Some BOCs may lower the rate to 14%, give a 5 year exemption, and provide a five year 50% reduction for production FIEs.

Bonded Zones are exempt from customs duties. Goods imported into a Bonded Zone pay no import duties. Goods exported from a Bonded Zone pay no export duties. Companies are therefore able to import parts and materials, assemble them, and re-export them without customs duties. However, goods passing in and out of a Bonded Zone to China are subject to import and export duties. In effect, a Bonded Zone pushes the customs duty border back to its internal territory within China.

Export Encouragement

Previously, foreign business units had to pay a turnover tax ranging from 1.5 to 66 percent depending on their products. The new turnover tax, effective since January 1, 1994, applies to both foreign and domestic firms and consists mainly of a VAT, with the standard VAT rate fixed at 17 percent. The VAT paid is refundable if the final goods are exported to foreign markets.

The VAT and the Consumption Tax are both exempt or refundable for exports. Although the system is designed to provide for a full refund of Value-Added Taxes for exports, China has modified the policy for FIEs allowing a refund of only 9 percent rather than 17 percent. Several notices have been issued where some tax policy has changed or been clarified such that an item of taxation is disavowed. Taxes already paid under the void tax generally are retained rather than refunded. If a taxpayer failed to pay the tax in the past, no tax will be sought. But if the taxpayer paid the tax, no refund will be given. This approach seems peculiar from a Western perspective. It is, however, an expedient approach often resorted to in the PRC. The 9% VAT refund for FIEs happened during a transitional period where no refunds, though allowed under the law, were forthcoming as a matter of practice. The best approach is to consider the entire policy to be very generous, and to be grateful for any relief or refund awarded under any circumstances.

Tax Treaties

China currently has income tax treaties with 42 countries. These treaties generally provide for relief from double taxation. Residents of a tax treaty nation may be present in China up to 183 days without being subject to income tax. The United States, the United Kingdom, Canada, Australia, New Zealand, Singapore, India, Germany, Japan and Russia have all signed tax treaties with China.

Foreign investors can take advantage of tax treaties with China to obtain the most favorable tax treatment. The decision whether to invest or operate in China directly as a representative office, a branch of a foreign enterprise, a joint venture, or as a wholly owned subsidiary, and the decision as to which subsidiary should make the China investment are two crucial planning choices for MNEs which are greatly influenced by tax policies.

Tax treaties may entitle foreign investors to a reduction in the taxes China imposes on income, dividends, interest, royalties, or other distribution. Foreign investors are also eligible for tax credits in their country of residence if they pay taxes in China either directly or indirectly through their Chinese entity. Moreover, tax-sparing clauses in treaties may grant credit for taxes which China would otherwise have imposed in the absence of tax incentives provided under Chinese law.

Most Sino-foreign tax treaties entitle foreign investors in China to apply for direct and/or indirect credits in their country of residence for income taxes paid in China. Direct tax credits are those that are granted by the country of residence to a foreign investor who is subject to taxation in China. Indirect tax credits are credits a foreign investor receives from the country of residence for dividends obtained from a company subject to taxation in China and in which the investor holds a specific minimum equity interest. Representative offices or branches that perform services in China and do not set up a permanent establishment in China generally will not be subject to Chinese income tax.

A foreign investor in a joint venture or wholly owned business may seek direct or indirect tax credits in its country of residence for the payment of Chinese taxes, depending on whether the investor's national tax law classifies the FIE as a 'pass-through' entity such as a general or limited partnership or 'corporate' entity. In the former case, a foreign investor may be entitled to claim direct tax credits. Most foreign investors in the latter case may claim indirect tax credits in their country of residence for Chinese taxes paid by their FIEs under either an applicable treaty or the internal law of their country of residence. Investors unable to claim indirect tax credits with respect to a corporate FIE may decide to pursue direct tax credits by establishing a branch office of the parent company.

More important than tax credits, which merely reduce the incidence of double taxation, are the provisions of certain Chinese tax treaties permitting 'tax sparing'. Intended to allow investors to retain the benefits attributable to Chinese tax incentives without reducing foreign tax credits in the investor's country of residence, tax-sparing clauses entitle foreign investors to claim foreign tax credits that exceed the amount of tax actually paid in China. The tax-sparing clause deems a foreign investor to have paid, for foreign tax-credit purposes, the full amount of tax due to China, even if its FIE in China in fact paid less or even no tax as a result of special exemptions. This clause also applies in the context of dividend, interest, and royalty payments. China's tax authorities generally impose a 20 percent withholding tax rate on such payments. While certain treaties contain more or less favorable rates, the typical treaty reduces the rate of withholding tax on these items to 10 percent.

The United States has refused to agree to tax-sparing arrangements with China, as well as with other countries. This lack in the US-China treaty has encouraged some US companies to invest in ways that take advantage of other countries' more favorable treaties. For instance, to benefit from tax sparing provisions in the Sino-Singapore tax treaty, a US investor may choose to invest in China through a Singaporean subsidiary, rather than invest directly.

2.5 Legal Environment

Legal Code

A market economy is not only built upon individual autonomy and decision-making in running enterprises, but also on socially instituted legal systems and property rights. Chinese law is modelled on the Roman Law system, widely employed in Continental Europe, rather than on the common law system, familiar in Britain, the British Commonwealth and the United States. The source of law is therefore based on general codes, qualified by subsequent legislation, rather than on a mixture of legislation and precedents in an evolving corpus of legal judgements.

Five types of law applicable to foreign direct investment can be distinguished in the Chinese legal code: (1) National legislation promulgated by the National People's Congress, the State Council, and other organs of the central government (Ministry of Foreign Trade and Economic Cooperation, or MOFTEC, in particular). Frequently some legislation is termed 'provisional' or 'interim', to suggest its experimental nature; (2) Legislation at the municipal and provincial level which supplements (but may or may not be consistent with) national provisions. Additional laws are often passed to guide and control FDI at this level; (3) Legislation applied by analogy. Where no specific implementing regulations apply, Chinese officials have applied other laws by analogy; (4) Regulations which are internal and unavailable to foreigners, but which are nevertheless applied. Sometimes these are 'trial balloons' for forthcoming laws, at other times they seem to be created and applied in an arbitrary manner to cover uncertain circumstances; and (5) Models, such as sample contracts for joint ventures, have also been created. These provide a common structure upon which negotiations can be based.

The fundamental law, which lays down the general principles for business transactions is the Civil Code, called the *General Principles of Civil Law of the People's Republic of China*, instituted by the National People's Congress in April 1986. Other general principles are enshrined in the *Foreign Economic Contract Law* promulgated by the National People's Congress in March 1985 and in the *Law on Chinese-Foreign Equity Joint*

Ventures, the *Law on Chinese-Foreign Cooperative Enterprises*, the *Law on Wholly Foreign Owned Enterprises*, the *Income Tax Law for Enterprises with Foreign Investment and Foreign Enterprises*, the *Patent Law*, among others. For details of these major laws, please refer to the appendices.

Table 2.6 describes seven tidal changes in the legal treatment of FDI in China since late 1978 through today.

Table 2.6 Seven Tidal Changes in the Legal Treatment of FDI

1. Equity joint ventures: From *controlling* to *regulating*;
2. Wholly foreign owned subsidiaries: From *regional experimentation* to *national promotion*;
3. Regional policies: From *coastlining* to *opening inland*;
4. Tax regime: From *initial favors* to *proliferating encouragement* and *rationalization*;
5. Foreign exchange management: From *relief qualification* to *greater accommodation*;
6. Technology transfer and intellectual property protection: From *rudimentary access* to *more sophisticated operations*;
7. Foreign bank and foreign trade operations: From *experiment* and *simple presence* to *operational expansions*.

Intellectual Property Rights

Intellectual property protection in China has undergone considerable development since the first joint ventures were established in the late 1970s. At that time there was virtually no intellectual property protection offered by law in China. In the intervening period laws on trademarks in 1982, patents in 1984, and copyrights in 1990 have been passed, along with implementation regulations, while legislation on specific areas such as computer software protection has also been adopted.

Despite these advances, there have been many complaints from MNEs about copyright and patent abuse in China. In 1993, Chinese authorities dealt with more than 2500 cases involving intellectual property rights. Patent offices mediated 1400 disputes while Chinese courts ruled on 1171 cases relating to patent violations (Tan and Guo, 1995). Some investors have discovered that fakes can generate bigger business in China than the genuine products. Microsoft estimated that 98 out of every 100 of its software programs being used in China are illegal copies (Tan and Guo, 1995). On Beijing's 'Electric Street', computer programs sell at a dollar per disk, and it costs less than $35 to buy a fake copy of the Microsoft Windows advanced networking program.

Chinese authorities stated in mid 1994 that copyright and trademark violators would face harsh penalties, including possible life imprisonment and execution. Customs officials were also given a bigger role in tracking and stopping the flow of pirated goods. China's judicial system, however, moves slowly at best. The US Business Software Alliance presented evidence of stores selling pirated goods in March 1994 which masqueraded as coming from Microsoft, Lotus, and other software companies. It took Chinese authorities four months to respond with sweeps of the target stores. Based on the evidence seized, Microsoft, Lotus and Autodesk filed suit. But software companies fear that such delays on the part of the government gives suspects time to destroy incriminating evidence.

Law Enforcement

Law enforcement in China has been weak for many decades as a result of the public's poor concept of law, conflicting traditions and working practices, and the low quality of legal professionals. Interpretation and enforcement of laws are often carried out according to the whims of in-power officials. Indeed, as many as 100 various laws have sometimes been announced in a single week, but very few of them have been fully enforced. The resultant heavy workload has forced central level legislators to delegate certain functions to lower-level courts. This leads to constant confusion over whether some of the regulations passed are policy statements or enforceable laws. The lack of central control also leads to inconsistencies in interpretation and enforcement between central and local levels and among different authorities in the same region or the same level. In Beijing, the legislative process is hampered by debates over whether an issue should be settled based on political tenets, which would mean stricter interpretation of the law, or interpreted broadly for economic reasons. Lastly, the arrogant attitude of some Chinese officials undermines law enforcement. Some bureaucrats prefer to set their own policies rather than submit to a legal system imposed by others.

In an effort to improve the legal environment, state administrative and financial controls over the legal profession are gradually being removed. Lawyers are now encouraged to set up their own cooperative law offices and work towards self-sufficiency. These offices will be fully autonomous, electing their own directors and being responsible for their own profits and losses. China also plans to train 100,000 more lawyers by the end of this decade. Moreover, some forty-one foreign law firms are being allowed to set up practice in China, with another hundred awaiting licenses (Steidlmeier, 1995).

Commercial Arbitration

The number of commercial disputes in China is rising. In 1995, 902 cases were filed before the China International Economic and Trade Arbitration Committee (CIETAC), more than double those in 1990. To facilitate the resolution of these disputes, the Standing Committee of the Eighth National People's Congress adopted the Arbitration Law of the People's Republic of China on August 31, 1994, which came into effect on September 1, 1995. The Arbitration Law applies to both Chinese domestic firms and FIEs, addresses arbitrability and arbitration agreements, and defines the limits of authority of Chinese courts and arbitration tribunals in arbitration-related matters. The law governs arbitration cases involving foreign parties as well as cases including Chinese parties that are currently conducted under the auspices of local economic contract arbitration tribunals of the State Administration of Industry and Commerce (SAIC). In the future, domestic disputes are likely to be adjudicated by independent arbitration institutions. CIETAC and the China Maritime Arbitration Commission (CMAC) already administer foreign-related commercial and maritime arbitration cases, respectively.

The new law makes many of the procedures specified in the previous CIETAC rules legally binding. The Arbitration Law codifies the existing practice of designating an arbitral tribunal, stipulating that such tribunals be composed of one or three arbitrators. It also codifies CIETAC's current practice of allowing parties to submit foreign related disputes to arbitration institutions outside of China, if the parties so choose. Under this law, an arbitration award made by a foreign arbitration institution is enforceable in China. FIEs are treated as Chinese legal persons under Chinese law.

The Arbitration Law spells out several new provisions related to the court's role in arbitral proceedings. For instance, Chinese courts are now authorized to rule on a party's application to preserve evidence that another party, who would be put at a disadvantage by such evidence, might destroy. The Law also provides that a claimant may apply for the preservation of the defendant's property if the claimant can show that the defendant will not otherwise have the necessary assets available to satisfy the arbitral awards.

The Arbitration Law excludes from arbitration those disputes involving Chinese governmental departments. Such disputes are instead to be adjudicated by the administrative tribunals of the Chinese courts or other administrative departments. For example, under the Arbitration Law, patent validity would not be subject to arbitration and only could be adjudicated by the patent administrative authority. If a Chinese manufacturer who was a defendant in a hypothetical patent infringement case made a counter-claim that the claimant's patent was invalid, the arbitration institution might have to stay the proceedings, pending the patent administration authority's decision on the patent's validity.

The overall environment for arbitration in China has been strengthened through the enactment of the Arbitration Law. Though the Chinese courts have not enforced arbitral awards consistently in the past, enforcement has improved somewhat since the Arbitration Law's promulgation. While it may be difficult to erase all vestiges of local protectionism, Chinese arbitration practices, which incorporate much of the same language that is found in the New York Convention, is now in line with international norms, at least on paper.

Name Protection

The Regulations on the Administration of the Registration of Enterprise Names, which were issued by the State Administration for Industry and Commerce (SAIC) on June 22, 1991, set forth registration procedures, delineate the rights of name holders, and stipulate remedies for redress if registrants' names are used illegally. To ensure exclusive use of ownership names, foreign companies interested in exploring business opportunities in China should register their names under these Regulations. An owner's rights are now spelled out more clearly than before.

Under the Regulations, the holder of a registered company name is granted the exclusive right to use that name in its registered line of business. The Regulations stipulate that unauthorized users of a registered company name may be subject to penalties ranging from ¥5,000-50,000. The SAIC may also order the infringer to compensate the legitimate user for losses caused by the infringement. While the Regulations allow the registered owner of a company name to bring suit directly against the infringer in a Chinese court, administrative remedies are expected to be the usual course of action.

Article 25 of the Regulations explicitly provides that a dispute between a Chinese registrant and a foreign enterprise will be resolved by the SAIC on the basis of international treaties and agreements to which China is a party. These include the Paris Convention, which sets forth international patent and trademark protection. Registering one's name in China before any conflict arises is the safest course of action.

The Regulations stipulate that a registrable name must be composed of three elements in the following order: the business or trade name of the registrant, the line of business or specialty of the registrant, and an indication of the form of organization (e.g., Inc.). In addition to names which are deemed unacceptable because they are found to be too close to previously registered names, the Regulations prohibit: (1) Names with contents or words which are deemed harmful to the interests of the State or the public; (2) Names with contents or words that may deceive or mislead the public; (3) Names incorporating references to foreign countries, regions, or international organizations; (4) Names of political parties; government, or military authorities; mass organizations; social organizations; or designations of military units; and (5) Names containing numerals or words in *pinyin* (except if used in foreign names).

According to the Regulations, foreign companies must register a Chinese name composed of at least two characters consistent with the foreign name. If the applicant does not provide a Chinese name, the SAIC will most likely coin one itself. As the resulting name may be less than desirable, each foreign enterprise should supply its own name in Chinese for registration with the SAIC.

Most foreign firms entering the Chinese market have already made a point of building goodwill and market recognition for their companies' names abroad. This constitutes critical intangible assets. Though the process can be slow, a clear and comprehensive legislative mandate for formally protecting a well-recognized and admired name in China now exists. It is still too early to tell whether these new regulations will be enforced fully and effectively, but the structural foundation for implementation is sound.

2.6 International Investment Strategies and Environment

International Investment Strategies

The foreign parent firm faces a large number of complex decisions in considering foreign direct investment. FDI can be conceptualized as a dynamic and ongoing process that generally calls for both investment and business strategy decisions. International investment strategies are mainly antecedent decisions focusing on what, when, where, and how a foreign investor should invest. International business strategies are primarily process decisions concerning the optimization of global operations. It must be noted, however, that both types of choices are sometimes made simultaneously, becoming inseparable. Since antecedent decisions are made prior to the formation of a FIE, foreign parent's choices regarding investment strategy elements such as timing of investment, sharing arrangement, industry and partner selection and other factors critical to the performance of the FIE need utmost managerial attention.

International investment strategies involve two types of decisions: *operation-related* and *cooperation-related*. As shown in Figure 2.1, operation-related strategies include investment timing, industry selection, and investment orientation. Cooperation-related strategies in China are composed of partner selection, guanxi networking, and entry mode and sharing arrangements. While the two categories both influence an investor's success in exploiting market opportunities and product potentials in the host environment, operation-related strategies are formulated and implemented by the investor alone whereas cooperation-related decisions must be made and implemented by multiple parties in the joint venture or operation network. Moreover, operation-related decisions are more associated with a firm's technological, organizational, operational, and financial competencies whereas cooperation-related choices are more related to a firm's ability to cope with environmental change, mitigate contextual uncertainty, and reduce contractual risks. These strategies will be discussed in detail in subsequent chapters.

Foreign parent's investment strategy variables interrelate with the investment environment. The consistent characteristic of the strategy paradigm, regardless of perspective, is the assumed link between a firm's strategic profile and its external context. The strategic choice perspective asserts that this linkage has significant implications for performance. It is evident that both complexity and heterogeneity in the global operation

Figure 2.1 International Investment Strategies: Two Categories

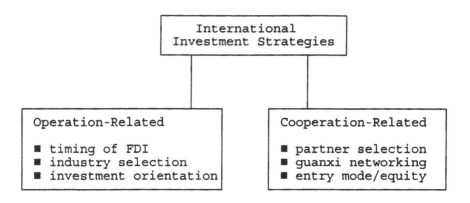

context are much greater than those within a domestic environment. As a result, investment strategies for FDI must be context-specific. Indeed, the adoption of a set of realistic investment strategies tailored to the investment environment represents a necessary condition for attaining a high level of performance.

In the Chinese investment environment, international investment strategies are particularly dependent on governmental policies, market conditions, and the industrial environment. The implementation of these context-oriented strategic elements is subject to frequent changes in the task and institutional environments. It is realized that MNEs investing in transitional economies encounter more sophisticated industry structures, more dynamic market conditions, stronger government intervention, more culture-specific business practices, and less protected intellectual property systems than in advanced market economies (Luo, 1995).

Environment for Investment Strategy

In recent years, the production and sales structures of FIEs in China have changed markedly. The percentage of capital- and technology-intensive projects has increased to about 35 percent of total number of ventures in 1994, and the growth rate is much higher than average for investments in telecommunications, transportation, and electric power. It seems that foreign investors in these industries rely on their specific competencies in an effort to achieve monopolistic competitive advantages from Chinese market structure imperfections. On the other hand, labor-intensive light industrial products continue to represent major export items, and the processing-exporting pattern remains unchanged. Apart from the obvious benefit of low labor costs, the preferential treatment accorded to export-oriented products by the authorities may also contribute to this pattern. These investment orientations are critical to firm performance because they involve the configuration between firm competence and host country environment.

Despite great improvements in recent years, China's industrial structure remains one of the bottlenecks hampering economic development. Some major structural problems include (1) inadequate power supply; (2) slower growth of the raw materials industry compared to the manufacturing industry; (3) obsolete manufacturing technologies; and (4) poor communications and transportation infrastructures.

In accordance with the Chinese industrial policy, foreign investors are encouraged to invest in high export projects and in new equipment or new material production that correspond to domestic needs, particularly in the energy, transportation, and telecommunications industries. In other areas, especially those that have already been developed domestically, those that involve the use of widely available technology, or industries assembling imported parts or producing for the domestic market, foreign investors face many restrictions and higher taxes. Tax treatment, as noted earlier, depends on the type of project. Joint ventures whose exports exceed 70 percent of total output (export-oriented) or bring in advanced technology (technologically-advanced) enjoy an income tax cut by half.

One prominent piece of foreign investment legislation in China is the Provisions to Encourage Foreign Investment, also known as the "22 articles", initiated by China's State Council in October 1986. In addition to a series of preferential policies, this law contained provisions that substantially decentralized ratification power, simplified approval procedures, and liberalized bureaucratic frameworks. It also provided foreign investors with freedom to choose entry mode and sharing arrangements.

Compared to other investment strategy elements, partner selection, investment timing, and guanxi networking are less restricted by the government. Nevertheless, foreign investors should keep a wary eye on the red tape and potential hindrance from various local authorities, whether administrative ('horizontal' authorities) or industry-based ('vertical' authorities). Horizontal authorities are found at at least three levels: provincial, regional, and county. Vertical authorities include foreign economic relations and trade commissions, foreign exchange administration bureaus, tax administration bureaus, customs houses, open affairs offices, local planning and economic commissions, and corresponding industrial administration bureaus.

Bibliography and Further Readings

Buruma, I., Faison, S. and Zakaria, F. (1996), 'The 21st Century Starts Here: China Booms; The World Holds Its Breath,' *New York Times Magazine*, February 18, section 6.

Curley, S.C. and Fortunato, D.R. (1996), 'Shoring Up the Bottom Line', *China Business Review*, January-Febrary, pp. 26-29.

Hickman, M.M. and Ho, H.K. (1992), 'Protecting Your Company's Name', *China Business Review*, July-August, pp. 10-12.

Hooijmaijers, M., van den Bergh, C. and Segers, J. (1995), *Dancing With the Dragon*, Amsterdam, Thesis Publishers.

Luo, Y. (1997), 'See You in Court: Lehman Brothers Sues Chinese Giants', in Phatak, A., *International Management: Concepts and Cases*, Cincinnati, Ohio, South-Western College Publishing, pp. 108-111.

Luo, Y. (1997), 'Business As Usual After Tiananmem Square?', in Phatak, A., *International Management: Concepts and Cases*, Cincinnati, Ohio, South-Western College Publishing, pp. 137-139.

Luo, Y. (1995), 'Business Strategy, Market Structure, and Performance of International Joint Ventures: The Case of China', *Management International Review*, vol. 35, pp. 241-264.

Luo, Y. (1990), 'A Review and Examination of Chinese Foreign Economic Legislation', *Intertrade* (English version), vol. 3, pp. 12-16.

Luo, Y. and Chen, M. (1995), 'A Financial Primer for Investors in China', *Business Horizons*, vol. 38(3), pp. 71-89.

Luo, Y., Tan, J. and Shenkar, O. (in press), 'Strategic Response to Competitive Pressure: The Case of Township and Village Enterprises in China', *Asia Pacific Journal of Management*.

Kelley, L. and Luo, Y. (in press), *Toward the Year 2000: Emerging Business Issues in China*, Sage Publishing Co.

Pollock, M. M. (1994), 'The Drawcard for the World's Multinationals', *AsiaMoney*, vol. 5, pp. 51-53.

Steidlmeier, P. (1995), *Strategic Management of the China Venture*, Westport, Connecticut, Quorum Books.

Sun, X. and Zeng, Y. (1996), 'Settling Out of Court', *China Business Review*, September-October, pp. 50-53.

Tan, C.L. and Guo, L.C. (1995), *China: Risks, Rewards, Regulations*, Singapore, Cassia Communications Pte Ltd.

Tureq, D. (1995), 'India & China: Asia's Non-Identical Twins', *The McKinsey Quarterly*, no. 2, pp. 24-37.

Wei, J. (1994), *Chinese Foreign Investment Laws and Policies*, Westport, Connecticut, Quorum Books.

3 Industry Selection Strategy in China

Chapter Purpose

This chapter describes the industry structure in China and its influence on foreign direct investment. An introduction of Chinese industry structure and its changes in recent years is followed by a presentation of current industrial policies toward foreign direct investment. The next section highlights the key industries and emerging investment opportunities. The following section discusses critical structural attributes of industry that have to be analyzed before making FDI decisions. Some important recent findings and results concerning Chinese industry are then presented. This chapter ends with implications for international investors active in China.

3.1 Introduction

In recent years, the intensity and propensity of FDI made by MNEs have greatly magnified. It has indeed been argued that MNEs can achieve higher performance than firms operating domestically because they benefit from the industry structural variance between the host and home countries. In industrial organization economics, a widely accepted conceptual framework holds that structural conditions determine the behavior and subsequent performance of a firm (Scherer and Ross, 1990). From an international perspective, when industrial structure of a host country is imperfect, FDI will flow in as a direct response if entry barriers are low (Hymer, 1976). Industrial structure imperfection in a foreign market constitutes a dominant factor which not only makes FDI preferable to trade or licensing (Contractor and Lorange, 1988) but also determines the relative attractiveness of one host country over other host countries and the home country (Dunning, 1979). Firms in oligopolistic industries enjoy the advantages of economies of scale and other characteristics that give them market power. This power allows them to overcome the disadvantages of being foreign and compete with local competitors in host countries where they have FDI facilities. Early researchers have reported the existence of a systematic linkage between MNE performance and industry structural variables in the advanced market economy context (Caves and Mehra, 1986; Kogut and Singh, 1988; Mitchell, *et al*, 1993).

However, the understanding of this issue in the context of the Chinese economy is incomplete. This is a gap, especially since this economy has recently become a major host for MNEs' direct investment. The industrial structure in China differs enormously from that in market economies. The differences are not merely limited to the degree of imperfection but extend to include structural uncertainty, information transparency, and governmental interference (Luo, 1997; Perkins, 1994). The current structural transformation in China, where some sectors are privatized and others are not, adds complexity and underlines the distinctive dynamism of these structures (Luo and Tan, 1997; Jefferson and Rawski, 1993).

3.2 Industrial Structure in China

China's transition from socialist central planning to a market-oriented economy is historically unprecedented. With neither a benchmark in past experience nor a well-formulated theoretical framework, China has proceeded in a trial-and-error manner. Since China's initial reform efforts began as experimental changes aimed at improving performance rather than, as in Eastern Europe, establishing a Western-style market system, it is not surprising that institutional change has been gradual and uneven, with many features of the pre-reform system surviving even today. Rather than attempting a 'big bang,' China's reform path is more akin to 'growing out of the plan'.

Industry, which by Chinese convention includes mining and utilities as well as manufacturing, is the largest sector of China's economy, accounting for 50 percent of total output, 80 percent of exports, and employing 102 million workers in 1992 (Luo and Tan, 1997). Its robust growth, amounting to well over 10 percent annually in the past years, undergirds China's standing as the world's fastest-growing economy. Industry also stands at the core of China's reform problem. Efforts to revitalize and restructure domestic industry are closely linked to reforms in pricing, banking, public finance, ownership, social welfare, and research and development. If China's recent accomplishments carry distinctive implications for policy design, it is industry, where reform has side-stepped privatization and other standard remedies, that is the most likely source of these lessons.

Reform has meant an expansion not only of markets, but also of industrial competition. Market forces tend to equalize financial returns to production factors employed in different lines of business. Naughton (1992) observes sharp reductions in the dispersion of profitability across all Chinese industrial sectors. There is also evidence of convergence in financial returns on capital, labor and materials across ownership types (Jefferson, *et al*, 1992). These tendencies are attributable to the decline and convergence of profit rates due to the continuing erosion of barriers that formerly protected state enterprises against competition from collective firms, imported products, and FIEs. As a result of past efforts to build 'complete sets' of industries in every province, market concentration by leading state enterprises tends to fall considerably below comparable figures for the United States and Japan. With military industries converting to civilian production, declining barriers to internal trade, FIEs' market expansion on the rise, and the prospect of sweeping reductions in import restrictions if China joins WTO, we see the competitive market a well-entrenched fixture in China's industrial economy. This emerging structural environment will influence not only the market and financial performance of FDI but also how investment strategy will be formulated.

The growing irrelevance of traditional planning mechanisms not only contributes to macroeconomic instability, but also unleashes opportunistic investment behavior that results in an undesirable industrial structure (Luo, 1997). The continuing fall in profit rates throughout industry, coupled with the expansion of enterprise claims on profit flows, has also caused the government to suffer a crushing revenue decline. Fear of inflation has left the state with little choice but to restrict the growth of subsidies and push an ever-growing list of industries into the hurly-burly of the marketplace. In addition, the central government has expanded the role of market transactions in coal, petroleum, steel, and other sectors formerly regarded as bastions of mandatory planning. By 1993, central planning controlled only 7 percent of industrial output (Luo and Tan, 1997). Even these mandatory commodity allocations often depend on market prices. These initiatives have contributed to the continued outward shift of industry's efficiency frontier.

A continuing inflow of foreign direct investment has played a pivotal role in this shift. Among economic sectors, the manufacturing sector leads with 54.94 percent of total FDI in 1994 (Luo and Tan, 1997). These investments have infused local enterprises with both technological and organizational skills. These skills, combined with China's readiness to assimilate them, have helped push the economy into a higher orbit. Indeed, the contribution of foreign direct investment to the transformation of China's industry structure is substantial. However, the impact of FDI on China's industrial structure is idiosyncratic according to the type of industry. This can be seen from the following details. First, structural influence of FDI on heavy industry, chemical industry, and raw materials industry is very limited. For instance, there have not yet been any FIEs established in the steel and aviation transportation industries. The output share of FDI in oil refining, petroleum chemicals, cement, and electric power generation industries is all less than 5 percent of an industry's total (see Table 3.1). Second, FDI tends to dominate 'import-substitution' industries (e.g., elevator and car manufacturing) where it has early-mover advantages in the country. As shown in Table 3.1, FIE shares in these industries exceed 50 percent. In addition, there are very few competitive local rivals due in large part to the shortage of technology or capital. Instead, the major competitors are other FIEs and foreign exporters. For instance, despite the dominance of FIEs in the elevator industry (60 percent), China imported more than 5,000 elevators in 1995. Third, structural influence of FDI in light industry, electronics products, machinery, and pharmaceutical industries is enormous. The vigor of competition between FIEs and Chinese domestic firms is intense. The market shares possessed by all FIEs range from 13 percent (pharmaceutical) to 72 percent (color TV display tube). The majority of FDI in China, in terms of both the number of projects and the contributed capital, was launched in these categories of industry.

As indicated in Table 3.2, 68.33 percent of total FIEs in China are investing and operating in various light industries, with the rest in heavy industries. Among light industries, 66 percent of FIEs use farm products as raw materials (Table 3.2). In heavy industries, most of the FIEs (78 percent) focus on manufacturing sectors. The number of FIEs in the excavation and raw materials sectors and their role in contributing to these sectors' GDP, sales, profits and taxes are extremely limited. The major reason lies in the vigorous controls and centralization maintained by the central government over those industries that are 'strategically vital' to the Chinese economy.

Although more FIEs have invested in light industries rather than in heavy sectors, these two types of industries each have an equal impact on shaping the Chinese economy. Table 3.2 suggests that these two categories are proportioned similarly in gross output, added industrial value, total sales revenue, total profit before tax, and total contributed value added tax (VAT). In addition, the differences in total assets, liabilities, and owners' equity between the two broad sectors are fairly minimal (Table 3.2).

Table 3.1 Structural Pattern of FDI in China in 1995

Industry	FDI's Output Share* (% of nation's total)	Investment'
Steel, Aviation	0.00%	none
Oil Refining	<1.00%	2 FIEs
Petroleum Chemicals	<5.00%	NA
Electric Power Generation	<1.00%	$1.9 bil. 18 FIEs
Cement	2.90%	18 FIEs
Elevator	60.00%	5 FIEs
Car	70.00%	296 FIEs
Wash and Cleanse Products		$0.2 billion
Detergent	32.00%	NA
Soap	27.20%	NA
Soft Drink	39.70%	$0.7 billion
Beer	20.00%	$0.5 billion
Electronic Products	33.33%	$8.0 billion
Glass	17.00%	NA
Pharmaceutical	13.00%	1,500 FIEs
Color TV Display Tube	72.00%	NA

* FDI projects in these industries are generally oriented on local markets, thus output share can be regarded as proxy of market share.
' All FIEs in the table refer to large and medium sized foreign-funded enterprises.

Source: Adopted from Luo and Tan (1997).

The financial and output performances of FIEs (total population) in every industry in 1995 are presented in Table 3.3. 12 percent of FIEs invested in garment and fiber products industries, 8.5 percent in textiles, 6.13 percent in plastic products, and 5.85 percent in electronics and telecommunications. These are followed by investments in raw chemical materials and chemical products (5.30%), nonmetal mineral products (5.14%), leather, furs, down and related products (5.07%), metal products (4.78%), food manufacturing (3.85%) and food processing (3.82%).

The following factors may contribute to the distribution of FIE investment described above. First, under the incremental reform approach, the central government still maintains control restricting or prohibiting FIEs from entering and operating within certain industries. FDI is therefore more actively involved in light industries or industries in their maturity stage of

Table 3.2 Major Economic Indicators of FIEs in 1995

	# of FIEs	Gross Output	Added Value	Total Assets	Total Liability	Total Equity	Total Sales	Total Profit*	Total VAT
National Total	49559	10714	2586	13348	7908	5441	10116	792	306
By Ownership									
FIEs from foreign countries	20190	5326	1354	6486	3588	2898	5051	470	169
Equity joint ventures	15078	4088	1017	5257	2901	2356	3897	410	151
Cooperative joint ventures	1848	414	131	489	253	236	354	29	9
Wholly foreign owned	3264	824	206	740	434	306	800	31	9
FIEs from HK, Macau & Taiwan	29369	5388	1233	6862	4320	2543	5066	322	138
Equity joint ventures	18927	3891	911	5168	3323	1845	3665	274	114
Cooperative joint ventures	3497	549	116	652	418	234	522	18	11
Wholly foreign owned	6945	948	206	1043	579	464	878	30	13
By Light/Heavy Industry									
Light industry	33863	6283	1374	6935	4166	2769	5902	374	153
Using farm products as materials	22365	3876	879	4241	2548	1692	3631	228	96
Using nonfarm products as materials	11498	2407	495	2694	1617	1077	2271	146	57
Heavy industry	15696	4431	1212	6414	3742	2672	4214	419	153
Excavation	340	75	52	101	13	88	40	10	1
Raw materials	3155	1131	317	2321	1394	927	1086	123	52
Manufacturing	12201	3225	843	3991	2335	1656	3088	285	100

* Profit before tax.

Source: China Statistical Yearbook (1996): 424-425.

Table 3.3 Performance of FIEs Across Different Industries in 1995

	# of FIEs	Gross Output	Added Value	Total Assets	Total Liability	Total Equity	Total Sales	Total Profit*	Total VAT
National Total	49559	10714	2586	13348	7908	5441	10116	792	306
Coal mining & processing	29	3	0.5	4	2	1	2	0.2	0.1
Petroleum & gas extraction	5	58	47	75	0.5	75	24	9	0
Ferrous metals mining & processing	12	0.2	0.1	0.6	0.2	0.4	0.2	0.1	0
Nonferrous metals mining & processing	40	2	0.6	3	2	1	2	0.1	0.1
Nonmetal mineral mining & processing	250	12	3	19	9	10	11	0.6	0.4
Other mineral mining & processing	2	0.1	0	0	0	0	0.1	0	0
Logging & transport of timber & bamboo	3	0	0	0.1	0	0.1	0	0	0
Food processing	1893	623	102	548	364	184	606	27	10
Food manufacturing	1909	301	68	395	215	180	283	27	13
Beverage manufacturing	1202	271	75	440	222	219	285	42	15
Tobacco processing	10	6	3	12	7	6	6	3	0.4
Textiles	4218	824	182	1035	651	384	761	27	16
Garments & other fiber products	5965	737	174	604	376	227	684	28	12
Leather, furs, down & related products	2513	523	103	403	278	125	483	11	6
Timber processing, bamboo, cane, palm fiber products	1270	115	23	156	97	60	100	3	3
Furniture manufacturing	741	68	16	92	62	31	62	4	2
Papermaking and paper products	1079	173	37	266	149	118	164	12	6
Printing and record pressing	860	74	20	137	65	72	71	6	3
Stationery, educational and sports goods	1188	186	37	160	94	66	178	5	2
Petroleum processing & coking products	133	29	4	31	23	8	29	1	0.4
Raw chemical materials and chemical products	2625	503	129	648	394	254	453	53	21
Medical and Pharmaceutical products	868	188	68	276	144	133	165	31	10
Chemical fibers	363	111	20	190	126	64	99	3	3

Continued from the previous page

	# of FIEs	Gross Output	Added Value	Total Assets	Total Liability	Total Equity	Total Sales	Total Profit*	Total VAT
Rubber products	470	155	32	192	117	75	147	12	5
Plastic products	3038	376	70	490	279	210	346	10	8
Nonmetal mineral products	2548	353	105	789	428	362	316	27	16
Smelting and pressing of ferrous metals	380	230	50	305	191	114	235	13	6
Smelting and pressing of nonferrous metals	459	173	30	194	125	70	161	9	3
Metal products	2371	439	91	575	344	231	404	21	9
Ordinary machinery manufacture	1450	336	96	486	261	225	319	42	14
Special purpose equipment manufacture	1303	156	45	213	114	99	147	13	5
Transportation equipment manufacture	1409	813	189	918	541	377	803	101	35
Electric equipment and machinery	2230	631	139	729	438	290	599	42	16
Electronics and telecommunications	2900	1518	374	1360	860	500	1474	112	30
Instruments, meters, cultural & office machinery	999	169	45	172	97	75	162	12	4
Other manufacturing	2559	218	55	233	127	106	200	9	4
Electric power, steam & hot water production	229	337	150	1185	699	486	329	74	27
Gas production and supply	17	3	1	7	4	4	5	0.2	0.2
Tap water production and supply	17	0.3	0.1	3	1	2	0.2	-0.1	0

* Average exchange rate in 1995: US$1 = ¥8.3507.

Source: China Statistical Yearbook (1996): 424-425.

life cycle. Second, Great China multinationals, especially those from Hong Kong, Macau and Taiwan, often seek cost minimization and export benefits by focusing on less technology-intensive or less capital-intensive industries. This strategy not only fits their organizational capabilities, orientations, and strengths, but also enables them to enjoy preferential treatment by the Chinese government, which aims at encouraging export.

As far as economic contributions are concerned, however, FDI has had a significant impact on industrial development. Table 3.3 shows the importance of such industries as electric power, electric equipment and machinery, machine building, and transportation equipment manufacturing in contributing added industrial value and value added taxes to the country. It has been reported that an increasing number of Western MNEs have commenced operations in these technology- and capital-intensive sectors. Their asset size and economy of scale are substantially greater than those of Great China MNEs. As a result, despite smaller numbers of FIEs in these sectors, the industrial value they add is greater. This pattern is likely to be reinforced in the future because Western MNEs in China are more long term oriented than their counterparts from Asian countries.

3.3 Industrial Policies Toward FDI in China

The Chinese government has determined the industrial sectors appropriate for FDI in order to comply with the State plan for national economic growth and social development, with gradual advances in step with world economic development. FDI guidance is usually maintained through laws and regulations relevant to specific sectors and through periodically compiling and updating the *Orientation Directory of Industries for FDI*, with specific implementation by various levels of related government departments in charge of FDI projects.

Industries Encouraging FDI

According to regulations stipulated by the Chinese government, FDI is sought for infrastructure facilities, basic industries and technological renovation of enterprises, as well as funding or technology-intensive industries. Following are the industries for which the Chinese government encourages FDI:

1. New agricultural technologies, comprehensive agricultural development, and energy or communications and key raw materials industries urgently needed for development;
2. New, high, or advanced technologies urgently needed by the State or new equipment or materials that can improve product performance, conserve energy and raw materials, upgrade enterprises' technological level, or result in manufacturing import-substitution products that meet market needs;
3. Projects generating more foreign exchange revenues in satisfying international market demands, which improve product quality, open new markets, or increase product export volume;
4. New technologies or equipment projects that comprehensively utilize resources, recycle resources, or reduce environmental pollution;
5. Other projects stipulated in state laws, decrees, or regulations.

FDI-Restricted Industries

Following are the areas restricted from foreign direct investment:

1. Sectors in which China has already developed or introduced advanced technologies and where the production capacity is already satisfying domestic needs;
2. Sectors in which China is implementing a trial introduction of foreign investment, or businesses monopolized by the state in selling, transacting, or operating;
3. Exploration or mining of rare natural resources;
4. Other projects stipulated in state laws, decrees, or regulations, such as those with quota or permit restrictions.

The projects restricted from obtaining FDI are classified into Restricted Category A (e.g., wristwatch chips or assembly, refrigeration boxes, cans, aluminum materials, photocopiers, one-time syringes, cassette recorders, ordinary antibiotics, luxury office buildings) and Category B (e.g., offshore or inland fishing, table salt, cigarettes, cotton or woolen textiles, chemical fibers, film, sedan cars, air-conditioners, color television sets, video recorders, arterial railways, aviation and water transportation, foreign trade, luxury hotels, banks, insurance, publishing, printing). A complete list is regularly compiled, modified, announced, and implemented, by government departments.

FDI-Prohibited Industries

FDI is prohibited in the following sectors:

1. Projects that do not contribute to China's national security, national economy, social development, or social or public interest;
2. Projects that pollute the environment, destroy natural resources, or endanger human health;
3. Projects that manufacture products using technologies uniquely owned by China;
4. Other projects stipulated in state laws, decrees, or regulations.

All industries, apart from those specifically encouraged, restricted or prohibited, allow foreign direct investment. Foreign investors thus have great flexibility in selecting industries for investment.

Sectors Newly Opened to FDI

The following sectors have been opened to FDI since 1992:

1. Energy: inland petroleum prospecting and mining, power generation, and energy recycling;
2. Communication and telecommunications: Highways, harbors, railways, civil aviation, and telecommunication facilities;
3. Natural resources: Exploration and mining of low-grade gold;
4. Forestry: Forest planting on barren hills or wasteland to develop forestry, in the form of either equity or cooperative joint ventures with Chinese partners;
5. Merchandising and foreign trade: Commodity retail business in some major central cities, in the form of either Sino-foreign joint ventures or wholly foreign-owned ventures, and foreign trade business in designated development zones;
6. Financing and banking: Banks in some open coastal cities, in the form of either joint ventures or wholly foreign-owned businesses;
7. Tertiary sector: Real estate development and management of urban renovation projects in large or medium-sized cities.

As China does not have much experience pertaining to FDI in these industries, the opening up of these areas is on a trial basis and will be only gradually expanded over time.

Measures Promoting FDI

The Chinese government has adopted a series of preferential steps to boost FDI in those industries they wish to encourage. Major steps include:

1. Regardless of where it is located, a project exceeding US$30 million, upon approval by the state tax authorities, is entitled to enjoy the same preferential taxation treatment applied in economic and technological development zones;
2. FIEs engaged in the building and operations of energy or communication infrastructure facilities (coal, electric power, local railway, highway, or harbor), with a large investment and a long projected time for return on investment, may expand their business scope in relation to their business, subject to approval;
3. FIEs introducing new, high, or advanced technologies urgently needed by China, or new equipment or materials to manufacture import-substitution products, with the capability of balancing their own foreign exchange, may be free from the requirement to export;
4. When the total investment amount exceeds US$100 million, the percentage of the registered capital against the total investment may be made lower than stipulated by the regulations, subject to approval;
5. Priority will be given to FIEs requesting export quotas when their products involve such quotas.

Measures Confining FDI in Restricted Industries

These restrictive measures include:

1. The length of operations of Sino-foreign joint ventures must be specified in the joint venture contract;
2. For projects falling within the Restricted Category A, 100 percent of the total investment is to be the registered capital if the total investment is below US$10 million; 70 percent of the total investment is to be registered capital if the investment is between US$10 and US$30 million; and 60 percent of the total investment is to be registered if the

investment is above US$30 million. Further, a Chinese partner in the project must use their own funds for investment in fixed assets. Projects approval is confined by quota limitations set by the State Council;

3. For projects within quota limitations and Restricted Category B, project proposals are to be reviewed and approved by the government department in charge directly under the State Council and filed with the State Planning Commission or the State Economic and Trade Commission.

4. Projects falling within Restricted Category A, upon approval, may be treated as though in allowed areas and thus free from restrictions, should either of the following specified conditions be satisfied: (i) the export value takes up over 70 percent of their total production; (ii) the existing manufacturing capabilities are used to improve the level of their products, so that the export value is increased by over 30 percent annually.

3.4 Industry Profiles and Opportunities

Civil Aviation

Recently, China's State Council has approved conditional investment in the civil aviation industry, on a trial basis, from foreign businesses. Major regulations include:

1. Foreign investors are allowed to invest in the civil aviation industry in the form of either equity or cooperative joint ventures;

2. Foreign investors are allowed to invest in the construction of airport flight areas (including runways, sliding ways, aircraft parking area, etc) or in the construction of airport facilities such as terminals, cargo warehouses, land services, aircraft maintenance, catering, airport hotels and restaurants, and aircraft fueling, or establish air transportation or aviation enterprises in service of agriculture or forestry;

3. Foreign investors engaging in the construction of airports may expand their scope of business, with approval, to include managing airport facilities, as listed above;

4. Foreign investors, especially foreign air cargo shipment enterprises, are allowed to purchase shares of Chinese air cargo shipment enterprises

or exchange shares with their Chinese counterparts, or set up air cargo shipment enterprises;
5. Stipulations have been made with regard to foreign businesses' share of investment in the civil aviation industry and nomination of the board chairman and the general manager.

Telecommunications

In China, a large part of the present passenger travel is for business and administration, much of which could be avoided with an efficient telecommunications system. Large projects are now being funded by FDI, because the government is not able to finance all the investment necessary to fully develop telecommunications. In 1993, officials of the State Planning Commission signed an agreement with the telecommunications giant AT&T to organize training and manufacturing of a variety of communications products in China.

Investments in telecommunications projects will be about US$50 billion, of which 50 percent comes out of local funds and 50 percent from foreign capital. This will be used to provide 75 million phone lines by the year 2000, adding to the current 25 million lines.

Energy

Though China is one of the world's largest producers of fuel, it is also one of its largest consumers. This is mainly because fuel is used very inefficiently. China's energy problems are compounded by the geographic imbalances between the location of fuel reserves and the areas of demand, combined with an inadequate transport system. There is also an over-dependence on coal as the major source of energy.

Because the industrial output is expected to have grown 400 percent between 1980 and 2000, while the energy output will only grow 200 percent in the same period (Hooijmaijers, van den Bergh and Segers, 1995), energy efficiency must be enhanced. Considering the fact that coal is less efficient than other sources of energy, major changes in energy use have to be organized.

China is in the midst of a major overhaul of its electric power generating network. According to Ministry of Power Industry, China will need to add 17 to 20 new power plants each year to reach its goal of 300 gigawatts of generating capacity by the year 2000. Central, provincial, and local authorities are actively seeking FDI in this sector. A second oil exchange has been opened in Shanghai in 1994 as one of the moves in the direction of increased electric power. The Three Gorges hydro-electric project on the Yangtze River exemplifies China's search for alternative energy sources.

China will have probably the world's largest nuclear energy network by 2050, with a heavy reliance on Western designed power plants. In its quest to feed its power hungry economy, China has taken some actions to attract FDI in this sector as well. A shortage of capital, combined with the projected long term energy deficit, has forced China to seek the cheapest power it can buy.

The BOT (build-operate-transfer) model is widely used in power plant investing. Foreign businesses may set up BOT project firms by means of either equity or cooperative joint ventures with Chinese partners or as wholly foreign owned ventures. Although no special laws or regulations pertain to BOT projects, procedures and approval are guided by the prevailing policies concerning FDI.

Automobile Industry

By world standards, China's auto industry is relatively small. The country is fast on its way to becoming a major auto market, however. Prior to 1979, China produced only about 160,000 vehicles each year, and trucks and buses accounted for over 90 percent of total vehicle output. In 1992, for the first time, China produced 1 million vehicles, including sedans and minivans. Industry officials have set a target of over 3 million vehicles to be produced annually by the year 2000. With the ultimate goal of producing passenger cars entirely designed and manufactured in the country, China named the automotive sector a 'pillar' industry in the Eighth Five-Year Plan (1991-1996) along with electronics, machine building, and petrochemicals. Over the next few years, China will attempt to consolidate the industry by bolstering passenger car production, improving the quality of vehicles and services, and increasing the percentage of local content.

China's automobile industry is highly fragmented. It currently has more than 200 assembly plants, with an annual production capacity ranging from 100 units in small garage factories to 150,000 units in modern facilities financed through joint ventures. The components sector is even more variable. It is estimated that of the thousands of auto parts makers in China, only a tiny percentage have the ability to produce quality products.

Protecting China's infant auto industry remains a priority for the central government. Domestic assemblers and parts suppliers enjoy considerable government support. The original six major passenger car producers in China - Shanghai Volkswagen, First Autoworks, Second Autoworks, Beijing Jeep, Tianjin Daihatsu, and Guangzhou Peugeot - together with Shenyang Jinbei Automotive Corp., Nanjing IRECO, and Jinan Heavy Truck Corp., are the largest vehicle producers in China. By 1992, these companies produced 75 percent of China's total vehicle output.

New foreign entrants will find themselves joining European, American, and Japanese companies producing a wide range of vehicles including minivans, sedans, pickups, vans, buses, and heavy trucks. The early foreign movers in the industry were grouped into a 'Big Three, Little Three' policy designed to consolidate auto manufacturing and develop economies of scale.

To succeed in China's auto industry, foreign companies need both to offer the right technologies and gain access to the right players. During upcoming years, the Chinese government will continue efforts to consolidate the industry though expansion of major production bases such as the First and Second Autoworks. Meanwhile, Chinese officials will seek to improve research and development capabilities. China is also counting on the development of the domestic auto industry to stimulate growth in supporting industries such as steel, plastics, and glass. Facing some restrictions in the assembly of passenger autos, foreign investors may start with technologically advanced auto part production, and then move to equity or cooperative joint ventures for producing complete units. In the non-passenger sector, a foreign investor faces no official restrictions on approval of new projects. Opportunities to produce buses, motorcycles, trucks, and the like are abundant. In the year 2000, industry analysts estimate that the market demand for total vehicles per year in China will be over 3,000,000 units.

Ports and Rail

China plans to spend over $6 billion developing ports and waterways between 1994-2000. Options for foreign participation have been dramatically expanded in recent years. Foreign companies can now invest and participate in the management of joint venture wharves and ports. They are also permitted to set up wholly foreign owned enterprises to build and operate special-purpose wharves and waterways. Foreign loans from Japan's Overseas Economic Cooperation Fund, the World Bank, and the Asian

Development Bank have been obtained by the Chinese government for port and berth construction at Qinghuandao, Dalian, Tianjing, Shijiazhung, Shanghai, Ningbo, Lianyungang, Xiamem, and Guanzhou. In recent years, 90 percent of foreign investment has gone toward container wharf projects. A number of foreign companies that have invested in real estate development, power plants, and manufacturing projects have also been permitted to build special-purpose wharves to cater to the shipping needs of their mainline projects.

Ports in China generally have locational advantages. They are usually nearby major centers of population, industry, and economic development. Clusters of ports are evolving in three of China's most developed regions: Southern China, the Bohai Sea Rim in the north, and the Yangtze Delta in the east. Dalian, in the Liaoning province, has the largest shipyard in China. Shanghai in cooperation with the Rotterdam harbor, Netherlands, has built some Rotterdam harbor systems in Shanghai and plans to implement more within the next few years. Container handling improvements for the future are concentrated in Lianyungang (Jiangsu province), Tianjing, Dalian, and Shanghai.

All major international shipping companies have agencies in the most important harbors of China: Shanghai, Tianjin, Guangzhou, Dalian, and Qindao (Shangdong province). The two largest Chinese shippers include *China Ocean Shipping Corporation* (COSCO), which is state-owned and represent one of the biggest shipping companies in the world, and *China National Foreign Transportation Corporation* (Sinotrans). Their businesses include transport by water, air, and land, handling of cargo from railway stations and harbors, storage, customs clearance, inspections, and the like. Although foreign companies are officially   permitted to   handle these operations, in practice, a lot of resistance comes from governmental bureaucrats.

China's transport system is mainly based on the railways. China's railways carry 70 percent of the nation's cargo and 60 percent of its passengers. The total length of railways is about 54,500 kilometers (which is still short given the size of China). Approximately US$48 billion in investments in railways has recently been approved by the government for the period between 1994 and 2000. Half of the funds provide for the construction of new lines and the other half is reserved to create double tracks and electrification on existing railways.

Electronics

The electronics industry is among the fastest growing sectors in China. It is largely concentrated in the coastal provinces of Guangdong, Shanghai, Jiangsu, Beijing, and Tianjin. The restructuring of state-owned companies in this industry is proceeded very rapidly. Over 260 firms under the Ministry of Machinery and Electronics Industries have been decentralized. China's electrical appliances industry produces a wide range of household appliances, from refrigerators, air conditioning, cleaning, ventilating and heating appliances to kitchen, cosmetic and health care utensils and a variety of accessories.

There are several reasons for the boom in China's electronics industry, which is also highly competitive internationally. First, export aspirations has made producers spend more on R&D and quality control to meet international standards. Second, localization of parts and components greatly drives down the cost of production, which enhances the cost leadership in the world. Third, Great China MNEs from Hong Kong, Taiwan, and Singapore have brought in many innovative ideas, technological skills, capital resources, international channels, and managerial expertise, further facilitating the competitive edge of the Chinese electronics industry in the global market. Today, IBM, Hewlett Packard, Hitachi, Siemens, Philips, Olivetti, Toshiba, among other firms, all have made dramatic investments in China.

Building Materials

The major products of the building materials industry in China are cement and cement products, sheet glass, sanitation products, bricks, tiles, hermetically sealed waterproof materials, furnishing materials, asbestos, gypsum, talcum, graphite, mica, diamonds, and other non-metallic minerals and mineral products. There are over 220,000 manufacturing firms employing over 400,000 workers in the industry. Although located everywhere, major plants are situated in Jiangsu, Shangdong, Zhejiang, Guangdong, and Hubei.

In recent years, many new building materials have been introduced, produced, and used extensively in China. Examples include frame structures and lightweight board used in the construction process. The labor productivity of workers using these new materials is significantly higher than those using brick and concrete construction. Demand for these materials is extremely high. FIEs manufacturing these materials have mushroomed in many regions.

The future demand for building materials is estimated to bypass the market supply. In many cities, a vast shortage of housing and office space outnumbers the running projects. The development of a large number of small new towns all over the country further drives the market demand. Many firms in the industry, both incumbents and new entrants further face the challenge of an increasing demand for high quality by sophisticated FIEs and local firms.

Pharmaceuticals

When China catches a cold, pharmaceutical companies have to pay attention. According to the survey by Swanson (1994), 90 percent of the more than 100 urban consumers interviewed stated they had used a cold medication in the previous six months, and 50 percent said they had taken painkillers. China's overall pharmaceutical market sized at US$7.5 billion in retail sales in 1992.

China is essentially self-sufficient in providing low-cost and well established drugs. In recent years, however, Beijing has welcomed high-tech foreign pharmaceutical companies to enter this industry. In some sub-sectors, foreign drugs have dominated the market. SmithKline Beecham's cold medicine Contac, which is manufactured at the company's Tianjin joint venture, is one of the market leaders in China.

One of China's main challenges is to revamp its medical reimbursement system, under which hospital charges traditionally have been controlled and subsidized by the government and the bulk of each patient's medical charges has been reimbursed or paid for by his work unit (*danwei*). The work unit sets aside some of its own money for employee health care and also receives funds from local and central government authorities.

Some reforms have been made in recent years. As hospitals become financially accountable, their charges to patients are growing. Though price controls are still in place on most hospital fees for basic operations and procedures, inflation and the proliferation of more advanced, expensive, treatments are straining government health care budgets.

One goal is to unify the variety of reimbursement methods currently used in China's cities. In most cases, a work unit sets a percentage of price limit on coverage depending upon an employee's age and rank and then establishes a standing care agreement with specific hospitals (usually three hospitals). Workers either pay the amount exceeding the coverage limit or pay the balance in full and later receive reimbursement directly from the work unit.

Since an increasing number of workers are no longer part of the 'iron rice bowl' work system that provides cradle-to-grave benefits, more and more urban residents are falling outside this system. Moreover, as China's work-unit health systems do not cover the self-employed or those in private enterprises, more patients are buying medicines at local drugstores. As a result of rising health-care fees and health care reform, both *danwei*-employed and self-employed workers in urban areas and the vast rural population now view purchasing over-the-counter (OTC) medicines on their own as a more appealing option than seeing a doctor and seeking reimbursement for prescribed medicines. Consequently, China's OTC sector offers great potential for strong consumer sales and brand awareness. Already, drugstores in Beijing, Guangzhou, and Shanghai sell about 25 percent of their OTC products without a doctor's prescription.

Petroleum

Despite the rapid development of China's petroleum sector - especially in the last decade - supply lags at least 25-30 percent behind demand (Tansey, 1994). Industry analysts estimate that each percentage increase in China's gross domestic product leads to a corresponding 0.7 percent increase in consumption of oil products. With production unable to keep pace, China will likely import increasing quantities of petroleum in the future. The State Planning Commission estimates that China may be importing more than 1 million barrels of oil per day by the year 2000.

Recently, the central government has appointed two State companies, the China National Chemicals Import & Export Corp. (Sinochem) and the China International United Petrochemical Corp. (Unipec) as the primary agents for all oil imports. The China National Petroleum Corp. (Sinopec) and China National Petroleum Corp. (CNPC) remain as the State refiner and State producer, respectively. CNPC may use the China National United Oil Corp. (Sinoil) as its main agent. Distribution is to be handled by Sinopec, unless special permission is obtained from the State Planning Commission. No entity may resell or barter petroleum to other units. If a foreign company wishes to sell oil extracted in China on the domestic market, it must sell the oil to CNPC, which maintains a monopoly over purchasing rights. Moreover, all crude and refined product prices are now set by the State.

China started cooperating with foreign investors in offshore exploration. The National Offshore Oil Corp. (CNOOC) was formed in 1982 to specialize in working with foreign companies and overseeing exploration efforts. To date, nearly two-thirds of all foreign offshore contracts (about 50) have been signed with US companies. Together, foreign firms spent over $3 billion dollars on offshore exploration and about $1 billion on offshore development from 1982-1993. Two oil fields operated by the ACT Group in South China Sea (Agip, Chevron, and Texaco) are producing 2.5 million tons of good quality crude annually. A number of foreign firms including Texaco, British Petroleum, and Japan's National Oil Co. are now involved in exploration and development in the Bohai Gulf, Pearl River Basin, and nearby areas. ACT's two fields in these regions produce 1.5 million tons of petroleum annually while Amoco explores about 2.5 million tons per year. Two other fields, operated by Phillips and Pecten, went into production recently, with a combined peak production of 3.1 million tons.

Currently, over 70 percent of China's total production is generated from Daqing, Shengli, and Liaohe. Given the age of these fields (around 30 years) and the high rate of drilling there in the past, all are likely to see production fall in the short or medium term. As a consequence, China recently decided to open 11 provinces and regions in South China plus 13 blocks in the East China Sea to foreign participation.

Machinery

China's machine building industry mainly concentrates on the production of farm machinery, metallurgical equipment, mining equipment, chemical industry equipment, lift and transport equipment, printing machines, power equipment, transportation and transmission lines and electrical appliances, instruments and meters, and food processing machinery.

In the machine building industry, there are approximately 300,000 workers employed in a large number of small firms and a small number of exceptionally large, state-owned firms. A vast number of TVEs have recently mushroomed in this sector. Non-state-owned enterprises now account for almost 50 percent of employment in the industry.

Through joint venture establishment, China's import of advanced machinery and high technology has made a marked rise. The emergence of more competition among local firms as well as with foreign producers has facilitated the advancement of the industry.

Because of the shortage of qualified technicians with advanced expertise in handling modern machinery, a large proportion of production is likely to continue along traditional lines of machinery and equipment production. It is also important for foreign investors to incorporate training in the joint venture contract when entering the Chinese machinery building industry.

3.5 Critical Structural Attributes in China

It should be noted that despite great improvements in recent years, the industrial structure of China remains one of the bottlenecks hampering economic development. Inter-industry variance in after-tax profitability still abounds during transition, due primarily to long-rooted industry structure imperfections, the gradual approach of economic reforms, and a cumbersome consolidation tax system. Similarly, there is also an immense difference in sales growth across industries, attributable mainly to the government industrial policy which does not allow all sectors to be decentralized and privatized at the same time. In addition, one major structural 'headache' lies in the central government's need to control the ownership of state firms' assets while allowing them to be acquired by or merged with domestic or foreign investors. The higher asset intensity industries thus are subject to greater government interference. In other words, inter-industry variations in asset intensity can lead to differential treatment for firms in different industries. Moreover, the growth in the number of firms in an industry is enormously idiosyncratic across industries. Controlling the number of new firms established in the industry is a predominant means for the government to monitor structural development. This entry barrier consequently leads to the heterogeneity of the degree of competition in different industries. Furthermore, industry structure is highly uncertain, arising mainly from the transitional nature of the national economy and the experimental nature of an array of new industrial policies. These structural characteristics lead to the following structural attributes that are important in China. These are: (i) industry profitability, (ii) industry sales growth, (iii) industry asset intensity, (iv) the growth in the number of firms in an industry, and (v) industry structural uncertainty. Table 3.4 shows the major structural characteristics of Chinese industries in recent years.

Table 3.4 The Calculation of Growth Rate (GR) for Chinese Industry Structure Attributes (Part I)

Industrial Sector	(1) GR(%) of # of Enterprises 88-91	90-93	(2) GR (%) of Net Output 88-91	90-93	(3) GR(%) of Sales 88-91	90-93	(4) GR (%) of Net Fixed Assets 88-91	90-93
Coal Mining & Dressing	0.78	1.76	20.35	34.65	12.39	24.25	16.26	10.21
Petroleum/Natural Gas Extraction	6.47	30.89	9.75	40.56	26.46	48.04	27.03	23.14
Ferrous Metal Mining & Dressing	4.49	21.23	22.08	42.63	30.81	36.57	13.39	9.28
Nonferrous Metal Mining & Dressing	7.48	5.07	21.87	28.44	12.33	24.89	14.99	17.91
Building Materials & Other Nonmetal Mineral Mining	-0.67	4.23	22.51	59.80	14.66	44.22	11.92	40.20
Salt Mining	3.35	-1.25	16.25	16.89	14.89	11.13	20.49	18.63
Other Minerals & Dressing	6.26	45.86	32.63	100.00	13.33	130.62	25.99	73.05
Logging & Transport of Timber & Bamboo	-7.59	1.58	5.07	17.56	19.80	21.21	7.74	5.50
Purification & Supply of Tap Water	7.13	6.44	35.42	56.46	44.49	36.50	22.35	18.93
Food Processing	-3.43	-12.41	23.71	35.18	13.50	11.49	17.21	7.73
Grain Processing	-4.07	-6.01	21.48	26.01	12.24	15.89	18.54	17.14
Beverage Processing	-3.39	-1.18	30.37	33.98	21.79	16.93	18.97	22.23
Tobacco Processing	2.67	7.24	22.81	12.35	8.86	14.75	34.77	30.53
Forage Industry	3.37	-1.31	43.52	29.49	26.42	29.31	32.30	24.45
Textile Industry	2.22	0.04	16.03	24.51	13.59	16.99	19.38	17.88
Cotton Textiles	6.34	-1.63	15.48	6.20	12.14	9.67	22.10	14.78
Woolen Textiles	4.66	-0.40	12.30	20.78	18.94	17.69	15.21	11.29
Silk Textiles	-1.76	-0.62	28.00	11.59	10.12	11.89	16.96	21.46
Sewing Industry	-2.70	1.30	25.93	47.74	27.28	33.43	24.17	35.70
Leather, Furs & Related Products	1.31	5.28	22.51	49.80	30.20	44.29	22.06	32.15
Timber, Bamboo, Cane, Palm & Straw Products	-0.63	5.26	8.17	58.31	25.10	41.78	17.58	24.12
Furniture Manufacture	-6.68	-6.20	9.60	30.48	17.37	26.42	12.93	17.26
Paper Making & Paper Products	3.66	3.97	16.29	17.45	16.49	24.07	16.39	22.71
Printing	2.25	6.21	19.58	35.70	20.96	26.54	13.05	26.43
Cultural, Educational & Sports Goods	3.39	5.41	19.40	36.58	30.99	32.88	21.79	30.89
Arts & Crafts	1.64	0.28	22.74	17.96	19.83	23.50	22.08	22.39

Continued from the previous page

Industrial Sector	(1) GR(%) of # of Enterprises		(2) GR (%) of Net Output		(3) GR(%) of Sales		(4) GR (%) of Net Fixed Assets	
	88-91	90-93	88-91	90-93	88-91	90-93	88-91	90-93
Power Generation, Stream & Hot Water Supply	-2.10	-67.61	21.70	37.25	20.94	32.13	18.17	28.62
Petroleum Processing	8.11	34.57	9.11	38.63	44.70	43.50	24.55	24.89
Coking, Gas & Coal Related Products	4.22	-2.69	26.10	0.05	23.86	23.31	28.42	27.65
Chemicals & Allied Products	7.09	6.83	21.78	20.02	12.18	19.62	20.89	20.24
Basic Raw Chemical Materials	7.40	0.93	23.95	5.46	12.91	15.51	27.28	20.24
Organic Chemical Products	8.51	5.78	16.13	10.36	6.17	12.68	24.78	7.37
Daily Use Chemical Products	7.96	2.83	37.13	16.61	15.18	13.60	23.76	15.62
Medical & Pharmaceutical Products	7.46	10.67	31.38	34.59	28.88	28.73	27.59	31.97
Chemical Fibers	12.29	24.78	33.10	23.88	19.46	16.82	14.36	30.99
Rubber Products	2.10	3.46	21.31	17.89	20.29	21.32	14.76	20.09
Plastic Products	3.22	4.56	23.84	33.86	30.39	27.96	20.37	24.90
Building Materials & Other Non-Metal Mineral Products	-2.23	0.88	16.76	48.37	24.60	39.83	13.25	21.01
Cement Manufacturing	0.49	-0.44	22.44	47.95	28.35	35.41	15.37	13.97
Smelting & Pressing Ferrous Metals	7.45	19.86	10.58	59.90	27.35	44.78	14.61	23.97
Smelting & Pressing Non-Ferrous Metals	8.38	12.76	20.46	39.00	22.16	29.71	14.87	24.31
Metal Products	-2.12	-0.48	16.74	41.41	21.94	34.82	15.39	25.93
Machine Building Industry	0.07	1.49	13.28	29.42	28.52	8.84	9.16	-7.62
Industry Equipment	2.14	0.29	12.65	23.56	25.15	29.49	8.37	11.28
Daily Use Machinery	3.74	-0.18	-1.32	10.52	31.20	26.46	10.97	13.19
Transportation Equipment	3.09	12.22	7.15	55.01	49.91	57.73	12.91	28.99
Electric Equipment & Machinery	1.76	5.81	21.10	36.22	22.80	37.17	17.23	27.23
Daily Use Electric Equipment	-0.03	-0.82	24.37	33.17	27.80	27.14	20.14	26.08
Electronic & Telecommunication Equipment	6.75	10.83	27.46	34.22	36.28	37.05	23.80	29.70
Daily Use Electronics Apparatus	4.19	-2.49	23.26	14.51	30.87	18.46	23.83	21.96
Instruments, Metals & Other Measuring Equipment	-0.19	12.35	16.00	44.72	29.50	52.64	10.42	30.54
Mean (%)	**2.48**	**5.64**	**20.63**	**36.44**	**23.73**	**32.80**	**18.81**	**24.16**
Standard Deviation	**4.31**	**16.28**	**8.20**	**17.14**	**9.19**	**19.69**	**6.15**	**11.87**

Table 3.4   The Calculation of Growth Rate (GR) for Chinese Industry Structure Attributes (Part II)

Industrial Sector	(5) GR(%) of After Tax Profit 88-91	90-93	(6) GR(%) of Pre-Tax Profit 88-91	90-93	Comprehensive Growth Index 88-91 Mean(%)	St.D	90-93 Mean(%)	St.D
Coal Mining & Dressing	62.17	29.90	167.97	63.40	46.65	57.52	27.36	19.65
Petroleum/Natural Gas Extraction	-17.34	-23.24	-17.53	126.71	5.81	18.14	41.03	44.62
Ferrous Metals Mining & Dressing	8.13	31.07	11.09	33.65	15.00	8.90	29.07	10.94
Nonferrous Metals Mining & Dressing	-2.24	-0.03	1.19	4.50	9.27	8.18	13.46	10.86
Building Materials & Other Nonmetal Minerals Mining & Dressing	2.31	29.80	7.98	35.23	9.78	7.73	35.58	16.83
Salt Mining	-2.66	-5.98	3.29	-0.96	9.27	8.36	6.41	9.56
Other Minerals & Dressing	26.00	25.99	44.22	51.83	24.74	12.36	71.23	35.18
Logging & Transport of Timber & Bamboo	72.28	71.25	-18.87	28.56	13.07	29.13	24.28	22.90
Purification & Supply of Tap Water	26.10	64.53	25.19	58.59	26.78	11.53	40.24	21.60
Food Processing	-13.45	-4.45	-2.75	-0.95	5.80	13.16	6.10	15.17
Grain Processing	1.04	3.60	1.96	6.66	8.53	9.48	10.55	10.40
Beverage Processing	-11.42	114.83	8.51	32.08	10.81	14.55	36.48	36.90
Tobacco Processing	-499.9	-3177.1	11.79	10.52	-69.83	192.61	-516.91	1189.70
Forage Industry	4.90	38.96	14.98	24.85	20.92	13.55	24.29	12.40
Textile Industry	-20.73	-546.19	-0.51	-8.64	5.00	13.55	-82.57	207.65
Cotton Textiles	-140.80	-16.73	-16.91	-14.71	-16.95	56.73	-0.40	11.89
Woolen Textiles	-29.57	511.12	-18.22	32.84	0.55	18.11	98.89	184.63
Silk Textiles	-14.60	-18.37	4.05	-5.84	7.13	13.55	3.35	13.17
Sewing Industry	-3.42	32.26	4.79	25.81	12.68	13.41	29.37	14.16
Leather, Furs & Related Products	-33.17	128.17	-9.12	50.41	5.63	21.99	51.68	37.52
Timber Processing, Bamboo, Cane, Palm Fiber & Straw Products	-56.35	158.18	-31.54	84.64	-6.28	28.69	62.05	194.43
Furniture Manufacturing	-35.17	106.55	-14.09	41.25	-2.67	18.25	35.96	34.78
Paper Making & Paper Products	-33.22	-8.47	-11.98	9.35	1.27	18.51	11.51	11.40
Printing	0.82	8.77	4.92	13.72	10.26	8.07	19.56	10.69
Cultural, Educational & Sports Goods	-2.27	26.60	1.84	22.76	12.52	12.18	25.85	10.15
Arts & Crafts Articles	-12.10	14.19	1.44	13.88	9.27	13.12	15.37	7.67
Power Generation, Stream & Hot Water Production & Supply	17.08	23.34	15.69	19.85	15.24	8.05	12.26	36.16

Continued from the previous page

Industrial Sector	(5) GR(%) of After Tax Profit		(6) GR(%) of Pre-Tax Profit		Comprehensive Growth Index			
					88-91		90-93	
	88-91	90-93	88-91	90-93	Mean(%)	St.D	Mean(%)	St.D
Petroleum Processing	-13.43	57.16	3.75	20.67	12.80	18.08	36.57	12.04
Coking, Gas & Coal Related Products	-52.02	-106.07	-25.29	-148.79	0.88	30.05	-34.42	67.82
Chemicals & Allied Products	-15.45	-19.83	-0.10	0.25	7.73	12.91	7.42	14.18
Basic Raw Chemical Materials	-21.99	-23.15	-3.91	-1.00	7.61	16.79	3.00	13.93
Organic Chemical Products	-14.77	3.26	-4.16	0.56	6.11	12.89	6.67	4.08
Daily Use Chemical Products	-2.56	-6.40	9.46	3.75	15.16	12.62	7.67	8.32
Medical & Pharmaceutical Products	-4.65	29.14	2.61	27.25	15.55	14.23	27.06	7.71
Chemical Fibers	6.45	5.58	14.08	7.20	16.62	11.33	18.21	9.32
Rubber Products	-8.73	14.02	2.60	15.94	8.72	10.91	15.59	5.89
Plastic Products	-18.94	13.72	-7.08	18.46	8.63	17.70	20.58	9.64
Building Materials & Other Non-Metal Mineral Products	-19.80	121.24	-1.72	61.39	5.14	14.74	48.79	37.76
Cement Manufacturing	-16.71	246.56	1.91	78.76	8.64	15.16	70.37	82.70
Smelting & Pressing Ferrous Metals	-14.12	66.05	2.20	51.12	8.01	12.57	44.28	17.19
Smelting & Pressing Non-Ferrous Metals	-16.38	10.18	-3.43	17.97	7.68	13.17	22.32	9.95
Metal Products	-15.38	32.62	-3.51	29.66	5.51	13.55	27.93	13.71
Machine Building Industry	-25.41	26.66	-11.99	13.56	2.27	17.47	12.06	13.08
Industry Equipment	-23.61	26.25	-10.97	23.68	2.29	15.88	19.09	10.12
Daily Use Machinery	-41.23	458.67	33.40	31.62	6.13	24.83	91.71	164.42
Transportation Equipment	1.50	58.79	6.90	57.14	13.58	16.64	44.98	17.94
Electric Equipment & Machinery	-22.49	39.14	-7.11	31.17	5.55	16.52	29.46	11.30
Daily Use Electric Equipment	6.36	100.86	7.05	35.38	14.28	10.32	36.97	30.94
Electronic & Telecommunication Equip.	-17.55	39.26	-9.15	34.24	11.27	19.63	30.92	9.45
Daily Use Electronics Apparatus	-34.54	17.45	-19.98	8.95	4.61	24.30	13.14	8.05
Instruments, Metals & Other Measuring Equip.	-13.92	34.17	-5.40	36.40	6.07	14.36	35.14	12.52
Mean (%)	**-19.85**	**-62.55**	**4.51**	**26.02**	**8.38**		**10.42**	
Standard Deviation	**81.58**	**515.60**	**29.67**	**38.15**	**15.38**		**89.05**	

<u>Source:</u> Adopted from Luo and Tan (1997).

Industry Profitability

Inter-industry variance in profitability has been an enduring characteristic of the Chinese economy. The breadth and depth of the removal of government-induced asymmetries in an industry during transition depend largely upon that industry's profit level. In high profitability industries, although more competitive entry from both domestic and foreign firms can gradually erode supra-normal profits on invested capital, continued government hinderance of the structural adjustment process results in appreciable barriers to entry and enables existing local firms and FIEs in these industries to keep their market power and advantageous competitive position vis-a-vis new rivals for some time. Additionally, when operating in high-profitability industries, FIEs are likely to confront more government hinderance in material supply and product distribution and face high latent competition pressure from new rivals and great market fluctuations, since the objective of the economic transition in formerly planned economies is to orient the industry structure toward less disequilibrium and greater market force determination.

Industry Sales Growth

Industry sales growth has been a key component of market attractiveness for both local firms and FIEs. Growth serves as an indicator of disequilibrium, a condition favorably associated with entry, and as an indicator of industry evolution. Porter (1980) argues that rapid industry growth ensures strong financial performance for incumbents even though new entrants take some market share. Moreover, when a sector of the Chinese economy is freed from government control over market supply, a rapid initial development will usually ensue. This take-off is reflected in a surge in industry sales growth, which is in turn likely to be mirrored in the sales growth of FIEs in the industry. Furthermore, when the local market for a particular industry appears to grow dramatically, it is reasonable to expect that FIEs will pursue local market expansion rather than export growth, because the predominant strategic objective of foreign investors entering China is to acquire market share in growing industries.

Industry Asset Intensity

This intensity represents a plausible indicator for capital requirements, a proxy for entry barriers, and a determinant of economies of scale. The imperfect capital market argument in industrial organization studies contends that firms in an industry which requires a large initial capital investment can obtain monopolistic profits in the long run because few truly qualified competitors can enter the industry, and exit barriers created by substantial resource commitments may not be fully recoverable (Scherer and Ross, 1990). Although inter-industry mobility turns out to be higher during transition than pre-transition in China, high asset intensity discourages entry of new firms into the industry. As a result, FIEs in a high asset intensity industry are likely to have high profitability. Additionally, a high-asset-intensity industry usually requires foreign investors to commit a great deal of investment capital or other distinctive resources. According to the resource-based theory, the strategic objectives of firms are determined by their core competencies or resources. By contributing their distinctive resources to local capital- or technology-intensive industries, FIEs manifest their long term commitment to indigenous production and host market expansion rather than export.

Growth in the Number of Firms in an Industry

In examining the degree of competition in an industry in market economies, the most widely used measure is the leading firm concentration ratio (e.g., CR4 for the U.S., CR5 for the U.K., and CR3 for Germany). However, this ratio is neither applicable nor available in China because the degree of inequality of firms' share in an industry does not necessarily reflect the vigor of competition, as a consequence of government intervention and the 'state-owned' identity of leading firms (Luo, 1997). Following the decentralization and privatization of most industry sectors that had been unable to meet market demand, the number of firms in these now more competitive industries has drastically grown; this growth constitutes a good proxy for the degree of competition in the transition phase (Jefferson and Rawski, 1993). The increase in the number of firms in the industry is likely to boost competition, decrease disparities in a firm's profitability between industries, and slow down the average growth rate of local sales for individual firms. Whenever a host industry appears to be highly competitive as a result of an increase in the number of firms in the industry, FIEs are likely to shift their focus from local market development to production factor exploitation (Ghoshal, 1987). This strategic choice, aimed at production cost-minimization and globally-integrated network utilization, is expected to result in high export sales for the FIEs.

Industry Structural Uncertainty

An important feature of the Chinese economy is the dynamic nature of industry structure. The degree of decentralization and privatization and the stage of structural transformation differ enormously across industries. Unlike those in market economies that often arise due to market force fluctuations, structural uncertainties in China are attributable mainly to the changes in government rules and policies. Fluctuations in price, sales, and material supply are all considerably high. Information imperfection in the country compounds the structural uncertainty which, *ceteris paribus*, increases the operational risks of FIEs. Under these circumstances, FIEs in high-uncertainty industries are expected to confront more operational risks. According to FDI theory, foreign ventures can reduce their vulnerability to local industry structural uncertainty by minimizing their reliance on local settings. In an effort to do so, foreign investors can decrease the portion of local marketing and increase the portion of export. Thus FIE's export performance is proposed to be negatively related to industry structural uncertainty.

3.6 Empirical Analysis

Recently, Luo and Tan (1997), Luo (1997), and Luo (in press) have examined the relationship between industry structural attributes and FIE performance. The key results of these studies can be summarized as follows:

First, industry profitability is found to have a significant impact on overall performance of a FIE and a strong positive effect on its efficiency and local market expansion, but a negative effect on its export and risk reduction. This evidence suggests that industry profitability in China vigorously affects all the major dimensions of FIE performance, but is heterogeneous according to the dimension considered. The trade-off between efficiency and risk reduction and between local market expansion and export performance supports the notion in FDI literature that FIE performance is multi-dimensional and its evaluation should correspond to the roles of the venture stipulated by the parent firms. Additionally, asset size is found to mediate the positive function of industry profitability on a firm's efficiency.

Second, industry sales growth is significantly related to FIE's overall performance and positively linked with firm profitability and domestic sales growth. However, FIE's export growth is an inverse function of industry's sales growth. This finding demonstrates that FIEs in China attain economic rents from local industry sales growth, participating in local expansion at the expense of exports. When domestic industry conditions are unfavorable, FIE's strategic aim necessitates cost-minimization and is reflected in the high performance of exports.

Third, industry asset intensity has no significant effect on FIE's overall performance, but has a modest positive influence on a firm's profitability and a negative influence on the firm's export and risk reduction. This finding, based on the Chinese context, is consistent with observations by Bettis (1981) of firms in developed market economies. Bettis found that capital requirement is positively associated with a firm's profit level at the expense of risk reduction. Also consistent with our earlier prediction, the results demonstrate that FIEs investing in high asset intensity industries appear to manifest a long-term commitment to local production rather than to export expansion. In addition, FIE's type of project is also found to moderate the form of the relationship between industry asset intensity and firm efficiency.

Fourth, the growth in the number of firms in an industry is positively associated with FIE's profitability and local market expansion in a significant way. Unlike advanced market economies, high growth in the number of firms in an industry in China does not simply represent increased competition. Rather, it mirrors industry growth when government-instituted control over market supply is lifted during the economic transition.

Finally, it is observed that industry structural uncertainty has a significant effect on FIE's overall performance. Specifically, FIE's operational risk is an increasing function of industry's uncertainty. Nevertheless, the form of this univariate relationship is moderated by FIE's operation length. A greater length of operations in China lessens the unfavorable impact of structural uncertainty on the operational stability of FIEs in this context.

Overall, these studies reveal some similarities in the structure-performance relationship for international production between China and a developed market economy on which early studies are often based. The similarities reside in performance implications of such structural variables as industry profitability, sales growth, and asset intensity. Nevertheless, in two areas the relationships diverge according to context. First, whereas market economy-based studies find that the growth in the number of firms in an industry is negatively related to a firm's accounting return and market growth, the studies based in China observe a positive relationship. Indeed, when government-instituted controls over industry supply are lifted during a transitional phase, high growth in the number of firms in an industry signals industry growth rather than simply increased competition. In other words, it seems that 'emerging economies' are aptly named, since the explosion in the number of participants in newly competitive industries does not exhaust its potential. Second, while market economy-based studies demonstrate that there is not necessarily a causality between industry structural uncertainty and operational risks facing firms, the studies based in China show a positive relationship between the two, implying that macro environmental factors outweigh micro firm characteristics in China. This may derive from the nature of industry structural uncertainty. If, as is very probable, uncertainty is attributable mostly to government policies, then no single firm can escape the risks of changing rules and their consequences.

3.7 Implications for International Executives

Some findings by previous studies have managerial implications for international investors interested in China. These include: (1) industry profitability and its sales growth are important for FIE's overall performance and both have a profoundly favorable influence on FIE's economic efficiency and market growth in the country. Nevertheless, they are negatively associated with either risk reduction or export growth; (2) industry asset intensity, a proxy for an industry's economy of scale and capital requirement, has a positive effect on FIE's profitability, although it is not significant for FIE's overall performance; (3) the growth in the number of firms in an industry is positively, rather than negatively, linked with FIE's market growth and accounting return. High growth in this number seems to be not a representation of increased competition, but rather a signal of more business potential once the various government-instituted interventions are gradually eliminated; (4) industry structural instability is significantly and positively related to FIE's operational risk. It is difficult for FIEs to avoid the risks derived from the uncertainty of Chinese industrial policies; and (5) the relationship between industry structural variables and firm performance is modified by such firm-level attributes as length of local operations, type of project, and FIE size.

These results suggest that industry structural attributes in the Chinese economy are not only important to the overall performance of international expansion of foreign businesses, but also crucial to several aspects of FIE performance taken separately. It is found that the relationship between an industry's profitability, sales growth, and asset intensity and FIE performance in the Chinese context is similar to that in developed market economies, but the effects of structural uncertainty and growth in the number of firms are different. Moreover, the results indicate enormous differences in the effect that different variables have on FIE's overall and unidimensional performance. In addition, each individual structural variable affects differently the various dimensions of FIE performance. Overall, evidence from China supports the notion by Buckley and Casson (1985), Teece (1985), and Porter (1986) that industry attractiveness in host countries constitutes a significant source for explaining variations of MNE performance. Nevertheless, given the contextual assumption implicitly made by most international operation studies, a serious need for testing the effects of industry structure variables in a different setting was apparent. From both practical and theoretical standpoints, contexts different from those of developed market economies should not be ignored.

Industry structural characteristics constitute an important driver of international investment performance in China. As a critical investment strategy element for foreign investors, industry selection in the host country influences not only economic efficiency and local market expansion but also operational risk and export growth. In the process of industry selection, foreign investors should assess all the important structural attributes of the industry they opt for, including sales growth, profitability, asset intensity, growth in the number of firms in the industry, and structural uncertainty. Foreign investors seeking profitability should enter those industries which reveal high profitability, high sales growth, or high asset intensity. For foreign investors seeking market growth in China, it is advisable to enter those industries which exhibit high growth in the number of firms or high sales growth. Alternatively, foreign investors pursuing risk diversification are warned not to enter high structural uncertainty or high profitability industries. Dynamically, length of operations in China can facilitate the positive influence, or mitigate the negative effect, of related structural attributes on foreign investment performance.

During the past seventeen years, China's industrial economy has achieved important progress toward building a market system. The accumulation of market experience and the confidence inspired by a large increase in living standards have created a consensus favoring a market-based economy with a limited role for state ownership, government planning, and bureaucratic regulation of economic activity. Today, competition is emerging as a powerful force for beneficial change in all segments of China's semi-market industrial system. As a result, this episode of partial reform raises the level of industrial output and enhances economic welfare while creating the foundation for a market system. The steady decline in entry and trade barriers in the new system opens up the Chinese market to MNEs. Indeed, the potential benefits for China from FDI are enormous, and it would be a rational choice for the government to maintain a policy of welcoming transnational investors. In late June 1994, the State Planning Commission (SPC) released its industrial development outline for the remainder of the decade. The SPC's blueprint gives special attention to FDI in 'pillar' industries such as petrochemicals, autos, construction, electronics, and machinery, and infrastructure industries such as transportation, telecommunications, oil drilling, and power generation. Indeed, given the country's population of 1.2 billion, the consumer and investment market will be practically impossible to saturate if the economy stays on a reasonably healthy and stable path. The government has planned that in the next ten years China will invest $500 billion in its infrastructure alone, and a sizable portion of that amount needs to come from the international capital markets. The energy industry, for example, will need to raise $20 billion in foreign capital before the year 2000.

Although extremely promising, the Chinese market can present daunting challenges to unwary investors. The Chinese government has taken a series of measures to make FDI in important industries consistent with its planned priorities. For example, the government requires all new projects in the auto industry to produce autos with 80-90 percent local content within a few years of operation, to hold no more than 50 percent share of equity in any new joint venture, to establish R&D facilities within ventures, and to balance foreign exchange through export of vehicles or components. In the aircraft manufacturing industry, Boeing was required to successively assist the main Chinese aircraft manufacturer in Xian in establishing the capacity to produce spare parts, to manufacture whole sections of aircraft, and to assist in establishing a capacity to produce complete aircraft within China.

In plunging into the Chinese market, MNEs should keep a wary eye on the dynamics of structural transformation and on government policies during this process. Today the globalization of markets and products has intensified competitive rivalry in industry after industry, where a large number of companies battle each other for market share in more and more countries. This rivalry has driven down profit rates and made it all the more critical for companies to maximize their efficiency, quality, customer responsiveness, and innovative ability. China and other formerly centrally-planned economies are now no longer totally new territory for most MNEs. In fact, many of them have established second generation ventures there. Only those who pioneer new industries, markets, products, ways of doing business, and government relations are able to gain a competitive edge over local or foreign rivals. It is the authors' hope that this study's assessment of the effect of Chinese industry structure on FDI performance will invite further studies of this important global business issue, particularly in the context of emerging or transitional economies.

Bibliography and Further Readings

Hooijmaijers, M., van den Bergh, C. and Segers, J. (1995), *Dancing With the Dragon*, Amsterdam, Thesis Publishers.

Bettis, R. A. (1981),'Performance Differences in Related and Unrelated Diversified Firms', *Strategic Management Journal*, vol. 2, pp. 379-393.

Buckley, P. J. and Casson, M. (1985), *The Economic Theory of the Multinational Enterprise*. London: The MacMillan Press.

Caves, R. E. and Mehra, K. (1986).'Entry of Foreign Multinationals Into US Manufacturing Industries'. In Porter, M. E. (eds.), *Competition in Global Industries*, Harvard Business School Press, Boston, MA, 1986.

Contractor, F. J. and Lorange, P. (1988),'The Strategy and Economic Basis for Cooperative Venture'. In Contractor, F. and Lorange, P. (eds.), *Cooperative Strategies in International Business*. Lexington, Mass.: Lexington Books, 1988.

Davidson, W. H. (1980), 'The Location of Foreign Direct Investment Activity: Country Characteristics and Experience Effects', *Journal of International Business Studies*, vol. 12, pp. 9-22.

Dunning, J. H. (1979),'Explaining Changing Patterns of International Production: In Defense of the Eclectic Theory', *Oxford Bulletin of Economics and Statistics*, vol. 41, pp. 269-296.

Ghoshal, S. (1987) Global Strategy: An Organizing Framework. *Strategic Management Journal*, vol. 8, pp. 425-440.

Hymer, S. H. (1976), *The International Operations of National Firms: A Study of Direct Foreign Investment*, Cambridge, MA: MIT Press.

Jefferson, G. H., Rawski, T. G. and Zheng, Y. (1992), 'Growth, Efficiency and Convergence in China's State and Collective Industry', *Economic Development & Cultural Change*, vol. 40, pp. 239-266.

Jefferson, G. H. and Rawski, T. G. (1993), *A Theory of Economic Reform*, University of Pittsburgh, Department of Economics, Working Paper No. 273.

Kogut, B. and Singh, H. (1988), 'Entering US by Joint Venture: Competitive Rivalry and Industry Structure', In Contractor, F. and Lorange, P. (eds.), *Cooperative Strategies in International Business*. Lexington, Mass.: Lexington Books.

Luo, Y. (1997), 'Industry Attractiveness, Firm Competence, and International Investment Performance in a Transitional Economy', *Bulletin of Economic Research*, vol. 49, pp. 1-10.

Luo, Y. (in press), 'Structure-Performance Relationships in the Transitional Economy Context: An Empirical Study of the Multinational Alliances in the P. R. China', *Journal of Business Research*, in press.

Luo, Y. and Tan, J. J. (1997), 'How Much Does Industry Structure Impact Foreign Direct Investment in China?', *International Business Review*, vol. 6, pp. 337-359.

Luo, Y. (1997), 'Performance Implications of International Strategy', *Group and Organization Management*, vol. 22, pp. 87-116.

Luo, Y. (1995), 'An Investigation of Strategic Marketing Factors Affecting Performance of International Joint Ventures in China', *Journal of Transnational Management Development*, vol. 1, pp. 71-89.

Luo, Y. (in press), 'International Joint Ventures in China: Industry Structure and Its Performance Implications', In Kelley, L. and Luo, Y. (eds), *Toward the Year 2000: Emerging Business Issues in China*, Sage.

Mitchell, W., Shaver, J. M. and Yeung, B. (1993), 'Performance Following Changes of International Presence in Domestic and Transition Industries', *Journal of International Business Studies*, vol. 24, pp. 647-669.

Naughton, B. (1994), *Growing Out of the Plan: Chinese Economic Reform, 1878-1993*. New York: Cambridge University Press.

Perkins, D. (1994), 'Completing China's Move to the Market', *Journal of Economic Perspective*, vol. 8, pp. 23-46.

Porter, M. E. (1980), *Competitive Advantage*. New York: Free Press.

Porter, M. E. (1986), *Competition in Global Industries*. Boston, Mass.: Harvard Business School Press.

Scherer, F. M. and Ross, D. (1990), *Industrial Market Structure and Economic Performance*, Third Edition, Houghton Mifflin Company, Boston.

Swanson, M. (1994), 'Unofficial and Untapped: China's Over-the Counter Drug Market', *China Business Review*, March-April, pp. 34-39.

Tansey, R. (1994), 'Black Gold Rush', *China Business Review*, July-August, pp. 8-16.

Teece, D. J. (1985), 'Multinational Enterprises, Internal Governance, and Industrial Organization', *American Economic Review, Papers and Proceedings*, vol. 75, pp. 233-238.

4 Timing of Investment in China

Chapter Purpose

This chapter aims to shed some lights on the timing of entry into the Chinese market. It begins with the introduction of the importance of FDI timing into emerging economies, followed by the discussion of conceptual foundations. The third section illustrates the economic effect of timing of entry into China. A framework of timing strategy is discussed next. The following section provides some survey results on the relationship between FDI timing and firm performance. Managerial implications and guidance for international executives are finally highlighted.

4.1 Introduction

As the year 2000 approaches, more markets are opening throughout the world. In Eastern and Western Europe, the post-Soviet republics, Greater China and Asia, and North America, trade and investment walls that have stood for decades are beginning to crumble in the face of political unrest and technological innovation. In anticipation of these changes, a do-or-die atmosphere is enforcing many European, Japanese, and U.S. companies to make critical decisions fast on whether, when, and how to expand into uncharted territories. Although Western companies have experience with deregulation over the past two decades, this deregulation is largely a domestic event and less traumatic. When expanding internationally, competitive dynamics, risk factors, and social-institutional environments that unfold when taking the plunge into a foreign market are markedly different from that revealed when artificial constraints are lifted and new entrants are allowed to rush in as a consequence of deregulation. The actions required to survive in the early years of a foreign market's opening are not the same as those that bring success in the second phase of open-market domestic competition.

Having been isolated from the rest of the world for many decades, transitional economies such as Eastern Europe, the post-Soviet republics, and China are characterized by a tremendous amount of uncertainties and difficulties on one hand, and a great deal of potential opportunities and markets on the other hand. While these countries have generally been characterized by a number of political, economic, and social uncertainties affecting both foreign and domestic firms, certain events create particular anxiety on the part of foreign businesses. These include, for example, the evacuation of most expatriate personnel to Hong Kong in the aftermath of the Tiananmen Square Incident in China in 1989, and the panic surrounding the violent coup in Russia in 1991 and 1993. These devastating but rare events aside, relatively small-scale environmental changes such as sudden changes in tax codes and regulations are numerous. The frustration caused by these changes for doing business in transitional economies has been well documented. MaCarthy, Puffer and Simmonds (1993), for example, suggest that foreign investors seem to be riding a "roller coaster" in Russia.

On the other hand, the rapidly expanding economies together with the existence of a pent-up demand, long stifled by ideologically-based government interventions, often lead to the inability of local producers to fully exploit market opportunities and exhaust business potentials, thus providing foreign investors with much more opportunities than in home markets. In China, for example, its GDP has grown tenfold in the past fifteen years, and will continue to expand to almost $6 trillion, almost 10 times its size in 1994, over the next twenty five years. The output and export created by foreign-funded enterprises have accounted for fifteen percent and thirty five percent of China's total GNP and export, respectively. The heterogeneity of industry and market structures between transitional economies and advanced market economies also increases the likelihood that foreign firms will achieve higher performance than operating domestically. Moreover, distinctive technological and organizational skills often enable foreign companies to create a new segmented product-market in which they can pioneer.

Under the above circumstances, foreign investors have to ask whether or not they will be better off to become an early entrant or to wait and see. This is a critical yet trade-off issue since each of these two strategies has economic advantages as well as disadvantages. Recently, reforms in transitional economies, most notably China, have been pursued and their pace has accelerated, contributing to a surge in FDI activity. This activity has in turn assisted transform these markets to the point that they are today major players in the integration of global economy.

4.2 Conceptual Issues

In the general literature on FDI and MNEs, a few systematic attempts to analyze the optimal timing of FDI include Aliber (1970), Buckley and Casson (1981), and Rivoli and Salorio (1996). Aliber (1970) and Buckley and Casson (1981) used the neo-classical model of minimizing the cost or maximizing the net present value incurred in switching from licensing or export to FDI as the criterion for optimal timing. FDI will occur when switching at time *t* from one mode (e.g., export) to another mode (FDI) generates lower recurrent variable costs and a non-recoverable set-up cost. Building upon extant theory, Rivoli and Salorio (1996) argue that when environmental uncertainty is high or information is exogenous (e.g., in emerging economies), FDI timing does not merely depend on cost minimization because the presence of uncertainty may increase the value of the "wait and see" option. Moreover, FDI decisions are not always based upon the costs of a shift from licensing or export to FDI; instead, they often involve a shift from a home production base to an overseas site to accomplish various strategic goals.

The population ecology model suggests that a firm can achieve its competitive edge through either the *r*-strategy or *k*-strategy (Hannan and Freeman, 1977). An investor using the *r*-strategy enters a new product-market at an early stage when the population contains few other members. In contrast, a firm using the *k*-strategy joins later when the population members are more numerous. Thus, the development of a new population of businesses may be viewed as a series of waves, with additional businesses appearing with each successive wave. When a new product-market emerges that is substantially different from existing ones, its early development is usually characterized by high uncertainty and radical change. Once initial market uncertainties are reduced by the first entrant, late entrants increasingly pursue strategies which are efficiency-oriented to cope with intensifying competition and reduced uncertainty. The population ecology model suggests that *r*-strategists have the best chance of success in market expansion at the expense of risk. In contrast, late entrants pursuing *k*-strategies are likely to enjoy a high level of efficiency in their concentrated segments but face more institutional barriers. Wherever environmental resources are unequally distributed between 'niches' in the environment, and conditions in the environment of a new population change over time, the population ecology model suggests that firms that enter with each successive wave need to have different resources, capabilities, and strategies if they are to carve out a sustainable competitive position. In essence, the ecological framework corroborates the microeconomic model of firm behavior in timing of investment. According to the microeconomic model, early entrants may gain advantages from early association with the product category and accumulated experience, but assume the risks associated with technological obsolescence, preventing proprietary technology from diffusing to competitors, and the burden of educating a changing market.

According to the above theories, early movers into emerging economies are expected to have considerable preemptive opportunities and benefit from market, product, and technological leadership. Teece (1987) contends that the level of technology appropriability, the existence of a dominant design, and the presence of complementary assets determine a firm's ability to preempt opportunities in a dynamic market. As a result, a non-dominant firm in the home market may be able to pioneer in emerging economies, especially in those industries that are in an embryonic or growing stage. It is misleading to assume that emerging economies can provide opportunities for every foreign entrant at any time. Under the 'garbage can' theory, investment opportunities are 'garbage cans' that have streams of choices, problems, and solutions, and have participants with limited time, resources, and energy flowing through them (Cohen, March and Olsen, 1972). In emerging economies, the windows of opportunity during a given period are often manipulated by central governments through controlling the number of firms, especially in abnormally profitable industries. Success often goes to those investors who reach first into the can and quickly grab a combination of streams of choices, resources and solutions to make a successful deal (Luo, 1997).

Early movers, however, assume substantial costs of the "liability of foreignness" in emerging economies. According to the MNE theory, such a liability not only stems from the general costs of doing business overseas that investors encounter in every foreign market, but also from the dramatic differences in institutional structures, organizational forms, and managerial psyches, which add to the scale and scope of uncertainties and risks of potential failure. It usually takes time for governments in emerging economies to learn how to deal with foreign investors and decide how to create and enforce legislation of FDI. Moreover, local partners are frequently state-owned, thus in a position to influence changes in the "rules of the game" in their favor, in effect, creating further transaction hazards for early investors from abroad. Further, in the early stages of market reform, a certain degree of managerial antipathy for FDI persists: local decision-makers resent dominant foreign control of indigenous enterprises. In contrast, late movers can wait until first movers have made their mistakes, taken pains to educate local governments, partners and consumers, and lobbied for a more accommodating legal and institutional framework for FDI. In other words, late entrants benefit from early investors' endeavors in two key areas: learning and environment-stabilization (Luo and Peng, 1998). Late movers are hence in a better position to "leapfrog" over initial market hurdles and obstacles.

The competitive market entry of a foreign investor in relation to its performance is influenced by the entry position of local firms. The niche width perspective of the ecological framework divides r- or k-strategies into generalists (MNEs) and specialists (local firms), both of which are able to exploit emerging market opportunities. An early mover of FDI can be a late entrant in the host market when domestic rivals are able to pioneer and benefit from first mover advantages in an industry. Researchers in international market entry, such as Mitchell, Shaver and Yeung (1993), have demonstrated that early foreign investors are more likely to enter new niches where there are few threats from local rivals to their core product. In new product-market niches, local firms are more likely to be early followers or late entrants because they are wedded to historical ways of doing business and unlikely to be proactive (Mascarenhas, 1992), given the risks of disruption of their existing organization or cannibalization of existing products.

In emerging economies such as China, local firms are often unable to fully exploit market possibilities and exhaust business potentials in existing and emerging product-markets due to the persistence of a pent-up demand long stifled by ideologically-based government interventions. As major rivals of MNEs in the indigenous setting, hierarchical state firms have little economic incentive to preempt business opportunities. Since the compensation of state firm managers is not often linked with firm performance, and a large proportion of purchasing, production, and marketing activity is controlled by the government, state firms tend to be risk averse, less innovative, and less proactive. The high degree of organizational inertia stemming from bureaucratic structure and government control compounds the indolence of state firms in reacting to market opportunities. As a result, when emerging economies open the door to FDI while lifting control over industry supply, early movers of FDI have the preemptive advantage in newly competitive industries. Moreover, distinctive competence in product differentiation often enables an MNE to create a new segmented product-market in which it can pioneer (Luo, Peng and Tan, 1997). Thus, early entrants of FDI in emerging economies may have first-mover advantages not only in locally existing industries but also in those markets they have developed. The achievement of these advantages, nevertheless, will be influenced by the degree of competition in the industry. In few highly regulated sectors, state firms remain dominant players because they are still institutionally protected by the government. They collude in, and control over, marketing and distribution, supplier relationship, and pricing strategy. In many deregulated industries, foreign businesses and local firms compete against each other building upon their own competitive advantages and organizational capabilities. Foreign entrants in competitive industries are less influenced and threatened by local incumbents than when trying to enter government-regulated sectors.

The microeconomic model maintains that the income effect of a foreign investor's timing may also be influenced by the timing of market entry of other foreign firms in the same industry. Mills (1988) shows that whether perfect-Nash-equilibrium timing strategies eliminate economic rents depends on whether it is costly for rivals to credibly threaten preemption. Where credible threats are costless, the investor's rents are eliminated. However, where credible threats are costly because the market is very large or the environment is highly uncertain and complex, rivals have less impact on the investor's timing and its outcome. In the early phase of FDI in an emerging economy, the impact from other foreign firms is less influential because MNEs operate in less competitive markets and face more uncertainty and complexity. In a later stage, however, this impact is greater as more foreign firms compete against each other in a more familiar and competitive market.

4.3 Economic Effects of Timing of Investment

Broadly, the decision on timing of investment is based upon the potential entrant's assessment of entry barriers erected by the host government and existing firms relative to the factors promoting entry. Potential entrants weigh the expected benefits and costs of entry, and entry occurs when the former outweigh the latter.

Comprehending Timing's Economic Return

When entering the market, a pioneering firm generally has more advantages over a late mover. During this period, the pioneering firm is able to invest strategically in facilities, distribution channels, product positioning, patentable technology, natural resources, and human and organizational know-how. The first-mover opportunity may arise from the situation where the firm develops unique product or process for a new market opportunity not perceived by other firms, or where the firm is the first to act upon an opportunity perceived by many others. Despite the importance of the firm's initiative, the availability of first-mover opportunity sometimes depends purely on luck. In addition, if imitation is expensive or takes place with a long time lag, preemptive investment during the initial period can be leveraged into significant long-run benefits for the first-mover firm. Furthermore, the cost of acquiring resources is lower due to the lack of competition in the early period when other firms have not yet entered the market. Moreover, market pioneers may benefit from the first-in advantages of holding technical leadership, seizing scarce resources, and creating buyer switching costs. Finally, early movers have the preemptive right to marketing and distribution channels and the robust sustained pioneering information and brand advantages. In brief, pioneering investors tend to outperform the follower firms in acquiring market power. Empirically, cumulating evidence based on advanced market economies demonstrates that successful market pioneers hold higher market shares than late entrants. In general, the order of entry has much to do with market share variance.

Transnational investors entering foreign markets are likely to have more preemptive investment opportunities in foreign markets than in their home markets. This is largely due to the different market and industry structures between home and host economies. By investing in an emerging market, a later mover in the home country could become an early entrant in the host country. It could enjoy more favorable business opportunities in sectors that are in an initial or growing stage of industry life cycle in the local environment, or in industries in which it has distinctive competitive advantages and is encouraged by the host governments to invest. It is wrong, however, to assume that any foreign entrants could obtain business opportunities from emerging economies at any time and in any place. As a general rule, business opportunities are like "garbage cans" with a variety of choices, problems, solutions, and participants flowing around them. Only those investors who reach the can first and grab important things quickly can be successful. In the emerging economy, "window of opportunity" during a specific time and in a specific region or industry is available for only a limited number of foreign investment projects to have long-term abnormal profit. For example, to pursue economic reform and political stability, the State Council's Planning Commission of China required local authorities and industrial ministries to set up a ceiling on the number of foreign-funded projects for modernizing the economy of the regions or sectors. Under this condition, early investors not only enjoy superior market expansion, but also have more privileges and options in selecting their industries, locations, and project's market orientations (e.g., import-substitution or local market-oriented). In addition, early movers are offered by the host government priorities of natural resources, scarce materials, existing distribution channel use, promotion arrangement, and infrastructure access. Moreover, early investors have superiority in selecting better local firms for equity/contractual joint ventures or for supply-purchase business relations. Furthermore, early movers are in a better position for formulating strategies to deal with competition from the local firms, particularly the state enterprises. They could place their strength in businesses, industries, and markets where competition from local firms is weak, or where they have better technological and organizational competencies.

Appraising Timing's Operational Risk

As pioneers, early movers are confronted with more operational risks and uncertainties. The causes for the operational risks can be either contextual or transactional, the former stemming from investment environment uncertainties in the host country, and the latter from the business activity variations in the indigenous setting. In other words, the former represents country or industry-specific risks, while the latter represents firm or business-specific ones. At the contextual level, some of the uncertainties can be overcome when the governments of newly emerging market economies have learned how to deal with foreign businesses. Take China for an example, laws addressing FDI have gradually been drawn up to accommodate and monitor the increased inflow of foreign direct investment. In addition to this learning process, political and social uncertainties resulting from the transitional stage often widen the variations of contextual conditions. Furthermore, dramatic changes of industry and market structures in the transformational emerging economies bring about significant variations to the investment environment. The contextual risks and uncertainties are expected to diminish with the time, the transition proceeding, and the emerging market being more integrated with the global economy. Consequently, early comers will face higher contextual risks and uncertainties.

Comparatively, earlier movers of foreign businesses are less familiar with the local environment, therefore, many of them select joint venture as the entry mode of FDI. In the joint venture business, however, the objectives of the local partners are usually very divergent, because they are frequently host government agencies or state-owned firms that can impose or affect the changes of rules and regulations. Under this circumstance, the pursuit of self-interests rather than common goals as well as the lack of autonomy of local partners usually result in significant uncertainties for the joint venture operations. These uncertainties and risks are often beyond the control of foreign investors, therefore, they cannot be "internalized" through the global integration of transnational business as they otherwise could in the advanced market economy. Obviously for early ventures, the risks are more substantial than late ones, because late investors can choose to establish partnership with non-state-owned local firms which have substantially more autonomy in strategic and operational decisions than state-owned enterprises. In sum, for foreign-funded enterprises investing in the emerging economy, the earlier the investors are, the more operational risks they are expected to take in the early period of FDI.

According to Aliber (1970), one of the most important issues in FDI decision making in the international context is the "cost of doing business abroad". However, this cost can be reduced by the learning curve effect, according to earlier FDI and MNE literature. Whenever there are elements of uncertainties, the learning effect is more obvious. The effect is even more emphasized in the transitional economies since the rules of the game in these economies are different from those in market economies. Therefore, a first mover in a foreign market will pay higher cost in learning how to deal with local environment than a later comer. Other scholars in the business field also recognized that later transnational investors can gain learning experience from the earlier investors. In addition to the costs of doing business, early movers also have to pay higher switching and start-up costs. Later movers, on the other hand, can "free ride" on innovators' investment if imitation is easy, and thereby gain the best profits without having to pay as much as innovators. As a result, late movers are likely to outperform the early investors in terms of profitability in the beginning stage of FDI. Figure

4.1 schematically presents an organizing framework that has incorporated both economic merits and costs of foreign direct investment timing.

Figure 4.1 Timing of FDI - Risk-Return Model

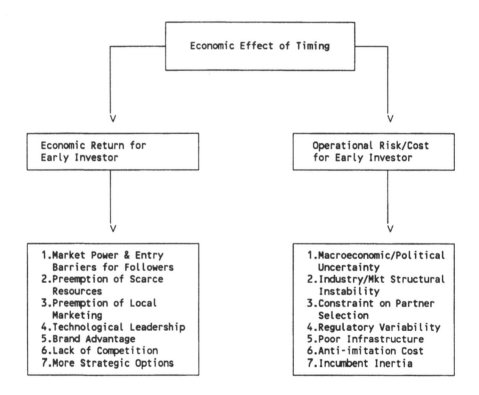

4.4 A Framework of Timing Strategy Formulation

Based on the above discussion, early timing of FDI has the following several advantages: i) market advantages such as new market, new segmentation, new distribution channel, buyer switching cost creation, and lack of strong competition, ii) product advantages such as new product, new product positioning, material supply, and brand loyalty, iii) technology advantages such as new patentable technology and seizing technology leadership over local firms and other foreign businesses, and iv) resource access advantages such as facilities, information, partner selection, scarce materials, human and natural resources, and other investment infrastructure. The disadvantages of early FDI timing can be summarized as the following: i) risk effect such as high contextual risks and operational uncertainties, ii) cost effect such as high searching costs, switching costs, start-up costs, and costs of doing business abroad, and iii) imitation effect, i.e., late investors can "free ride" on early entrants' investment in product and process innovation adaptable to the local conditions and in costs for learning how to deal with local governments, customers, suppliers, competitors and other stakeholders in the value chain. Obviously, the advantages of early investors are the disadvantages of late movers and vice versa. The combination of these advantages and disadvantages has an impact on foreign venture's market growth, risk reduction, asset efficiency, and accounting return. The magnitude of this impact is an empirical question that will be addressed later on based on the Chinese investment environment.

As mentioned earlier, a potential stakeholder of FDI weighs the expected benefits against the cost of market entry, and would enter the market only if expected benefits outweigh the potential costs. Basing decision on rigorous cost-benefit analysis, having a realistic strategy, and prudently timing its market entry is crucial to the potential stakeholder's success. However, timing of market entry is only one of many factors one has to consider in formulating a FDI strategy. Other factors include: 1) a transnational investor's resources and capabilities in technology, production, marketing, capital and organization; 2) the host country environment in terms of technology, customer needs, industry structure, market demand, and its government's FDI and industrial policies; 3) potential competitors from the same or different foreign countries and the host country. A timing strategy formulation framework is presented in Figure 4.2.

The distinctive resources and capacities of a transnational investor determines its competence in the FDI market, its capability of risk reduction, and its ability to seize preemptive investment opportunities. A pioneer entrant of FDI must wait for a feasible opportunity of investment to present itself. The appearance of such an opportunity depends not only on the investor's own foresight, skills, resources, and good fortune, but also on its competitors. The resource-based theory suggests that when environmental uncertainty is high, the necessities of distinctive competence for a firm's pursuit of sustained economic rents are reinforced. In a dynamic and complex emerging economy as in China, the investor's distinctiveness of resources in technology, product and process innovation, capital, interna-

Figure 4.2 Timing of FDI - Strategy Formulation Model

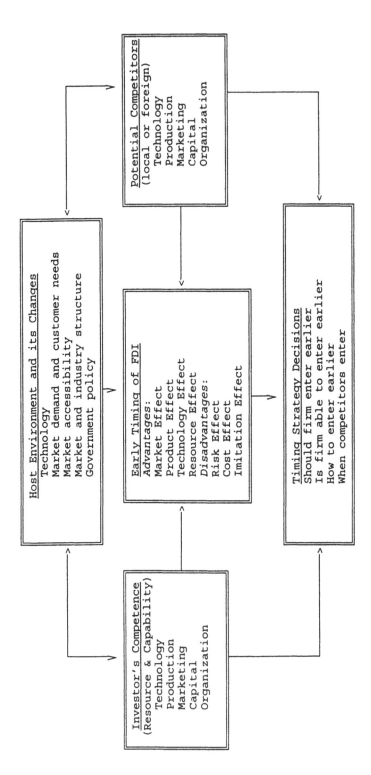

-tional distribution and promotion, and organizational and managerial skills is a prerequisite for accessing, surviving and expanding in this context. The investor's ability to allocate and utilize its distinctive resources is another necessary condition for maximizing the benefits of entering a FDI market.

The market expansion effect, operational risk effect, and economic efficiency effect of FDI timing at the business unit level largely depend on the particular characteristics of the investment environment in the host country. The investment environment, especially in the areas of technological level, customer needs, market demand, industry structure, and government policy, is likely to affect the interrelationship between FDI timing and the venture's profitability and stability. Moreover, first-mover opportunities are often generated by environmental changes in the host country. Mainly because of the transformation of national economies and market structures, government policies in emerging economies are often so uncertain that this factor must be given the highest priority in the process of making decisions on FDI timing.

A firm's opportunity to be a first mover is not under the control of the firm itself. Preemptive investment opportunities in the host country are perceived not only by the potential investor, but also by its local rivals as well as by other foreign competitors. The responses and actions by its competitors toward pioneering opportunities need to be carefully examined. The transnational investor must study the strengths and weaknesses of its potential rivals in areas such as technology, production, marketing, capital, and organization.

When an opportunity presents itself, the investor must then answer the questions of whether it should enter the foreign territory as the first mover or early entrant and whether it has the capacity to become the first entrant and build a sustainable advantage. If the answers are yes, the firm must decide how to enter the host market and best exploit the opportunity. During this process of strategic moves, many factors need to be considered and analyzed, which include entry mode (joint venture vs. wholly owned), sharing arrangement, selection of project location (open areas vs. closed areas), etc. These factors will either facilitate or inhibit the form or strength of the relationship between timing strategy and foreign venture performance, since they influence the venture's vulnerability to external context and ability to control the venture. Once a pioneering strategy is chosen, the investor must react faster than its rivals, contribute proactively to its own pioneering opportunities, and take measures to keep its first-mover advantages. If the investor chooses not to be an early mover, or if a rival has preempted this position, then the investor must decide whether, how, and when to follow.

4.5 Survey Results from China

Lessons from Top-30 FIEs in China

A national survey on the ranking of foreign-invested firms in China clearly supports some of our conclusions. As shown in Table 4.1, all of the top-30 foreign-invested manufacturing firms, measured by revenues, are very early movers. According to Luo (1997), these FIEs established their operations before 1984. This list of largest foreign-invested enterprises includes some of the best-known joint ventures in China, such as Shanghai Volkswagen, Beijing Jeep, and Fujian Hitachi. Moreover, these entrants have all become leaders in their respective industries. For instance, in the automotive industry, Shanghai Volkswagen and Beijing Jeep occupy the top spots among the top-30; in the electronics industry, Shenzhen Gangjia, Huaqiang Sanyo, Shunde Huabao, Beijing Matsushita, and Fujian Hitachi are primary leaders ranked within the top-20 list; similarly, in the electrical machinery industry, Jiangsu Chunlan Refrigerators, Shanghai Mitsubishi Elevator, and China Tianjin Otis Elevator are the top-three industry leaders.

It is worth noting that two automotive joint ventures (Shanghai Volkswagen and Beijing Jeep) are currently the top-two largest foreign-invested firms in China. These high-profile foreign investors, Volkswagen and AMC/Chrysler, have deliberately taken a first mover strategy attempting to acquire and sustain advantages in China's emerging market. When entering, each of them publicly acknowledged the difficulties and risks in China, and announced that their entry decision was motivated by the long-run prospects instead of short-run profits. During the course of their operations, each of them ran into various sorts of difficulties, ranging from product quality to foreign exchange shortage. For example, at one point, Beijing Jeep was close to the point of bankruptcy had there not been the last-minute bail out efforts by the Chinese government. While early movers gained their experience and achieved learning in China, their global competitors (late movers) watched, unable or unwilling to enter. As the Chinese economy seems to come of age by the mid-1990s, numerous late movers have decided to join the competition, and a new wave of FDI have come from players such as General Motors and Mercedes-Benz. However,

Table 4.1 Top-30 Foreign-Invested Manufacturing Firms in China in 1993

Rank and Company	FDI Origin	Industry	Sales (¥mil.)
1 Shanghai Volkswagen AG	Germany	Automotive	10,529
2 Beijing Jeep Corp.	USA	Automotive	3,275
3 Shanghai Bell Telephone	Belgium	Telecom equipment	2,826
4 Guangzhou Peugeot Motors	France	Automotive	2,536
5 Chongqing Qingling Motor	Japan	Automotive	2,290
6 Shenzhen Gangjia Electr.	Hong Kong	Electronics	2,203
7 Nanhai Oils & Fats Ind.	Malaysia	Food processing	2,000
8 Fujian Yongen Group	Unknown	Unknown	1,867
9 Huaqiang Sanyo	Japan	Electronics	1,865
10 Shunde Huabao Electric	Hong Kong	Electronics	1,776
11 Shenzhen Zhonghua Bike	HK	Automotive	1,755
12 1st Auto Volkswagen	Germany	Automotive	1,655
13 Shanghai Phoenix Bicycles	Unknown	Automotive	1,554
14 Beijing Light Automobile	Hong Kong	Automotive	1,513
15 Beijing Matsushita TV	Japan	Electronics	1,504
16 Fujian Hitachi TV	Japan	Electronics	1,441
17 Guangdong Jianlibao	Macao	Food processing	1,397
18 Shanghai Ciba-Geigy	Switzerland	Pharmaceutical	1,397
19 Shenyang Jinbei Minibus	Hong Kong	Automotive	1,377
20 J.S Chunlan Refrigerators	HK	Electrical machinery	1,352
21 S.H. Mitsubishi Elevator	Japan	Electrical machinery	1,329
22 Shanghai Ek Chor Motor	Thailand	Automotive	1,296
23 Wuyang-Honda Motors	Japan	Automotive	1,292
24 Sanyo Electrical Machinery	Japan	Electrical Machinery	na
25 Huafei Color Kinescope	Netherlands	Electronics	1,148
26 Beijing Int'l Switching Sys.	Germany	Telecom equipment	1,103
27 China Tianjin Otis Elevator	USA	Electrical machinery	1,084
28 China-Schindler Elevator	Switzerland	Electrical machinery	1,070
29 Shenzhai Saige Hitachi	Japan	Electronics	1,067
30 Shanghai Yongxin TV	HK	Electronics	1,064

Source: Adapted from Luo (1997).

as of this writing, while annual sales of the two early movers, Volkswagen and Chrysler, reach approximately 400,000 and 60,000 cars, respectively, late movers such as General Motors and Mercedes-Benz have yet to produce a single car in China. It seems clear that early entrants have built up enviable market share positions in China through years of sustained efforts. This advantage may be particularly strong for Volkswagen, which currently has two successful joint ventures and occupy 60 percent of the Chinese automobile market.

In summary, this evidence, drawn from a national survey conducted independently and from a detailed look at one of the most visible FDI-active industries strengthens the theme of our study that timing of FDI does matter significantly. Overall, the lessons from FDI in China seem to indicate that while facing operational risks and low profitability, early movers are able to build strong market share positions that late movers will find difficult to compete away.

Timing Effect During the Early Period of FDI

In order to determine whether early movers and late entrants differ significantly in economic return and operational risk *during the early period* of investment in China, a univariate analysis of the data obtained from Jiangsu Provincial Commission of Foreign Economic Relations and Trade was employed whereby the difference in group means for each dimension of performance was tested using the t-test statistics. This analysis included seven early foreign entrants (established in 1980 and 1981) and twenty four late foreign movers (established in 1989 and 1990) in light industries in the province. The economic return effect comprised of return on investment, sales growth, and asset turnover. All these indicators referred to foreign ventures' *first three year* performance after formation. The operational risk effect was measured by the geometric average of standard deviations of a venture's above three economic indicators. The test results are revealed in Table 4.2.

As shown in Table 4.2, early entrants are significantly superior to late entrants in terms of sales growth. Although the context of emerging economy is dynamic, complex, and uncertain, the promising market provides early entrants of FDI with many preemptive investment opportunities and commercial potentials on which they can capitalize. As a result of deliberate investment through contributing competencies, early investors achieve greater market power in the host market than late entrants.

Table 4.2 Mean Difference Tests Between Early Entrants and Late Entrants

Variable	Early entrants	Late entrant	*t* statistics
ROI	0.08	0.13	1.91*
SALES GROWTH	26.78	15.28	-4.27**
ASSET TURNOVER	4.94	3.30	-3.31**
RISK	87.66	53.34	-6.23**

* ** denote 5% and 1% significance level respectively.

It is also found that early foreign entrants face enormously more operational risks than late movers in the start-up phase of international expansion in the Chinese context. In other words, the superiority of early investor's market growth effect accrues at the expense of high operational risk in the indigenous setting.

This test also observes that late investors have higher performance in terms of the first three year's ROI than early entrants. In another respect of accounting performance, however, the *t*-test shows that early entrants outperform late movers with regard to asset turnover. The finding of high asset turnover but low ROI for early investors suggests that early movers entering a frontier territory such as China have a low level of capital contribution commitment at the initial period of operation. This complies with the transaction cost perspective which argues that when uncertainty is high, the firm should commit itself to the environment at a minimum because of high switching, start-up and anti-imitation costs.

Timing Effect During the Late Period of FDI

Recently, Luo and Peng (1998) have examined the timing effect on FDI performance during the late period of investment in China. The two major findings follow:

First, they demonstrate that the later the FDI entry, the worse the financial and market performance. By implication, the earlier the entry, the better the FDI performance during the late period. Specifically, earlier entry is superior with respect to return on sales, return on equity, and sales growth.

Second, earlier entry outperforms later investment in asset turnover, competitive position, and risk reduction. This evidence demonstrates that entering earlier into a transitional economy such as China leads MNEs to gain more *over time* in terms of profitability, market expansion, asset efficiency, competitive position, and risk reduction. Early timing presents a favorable influence on both market performance (sales growth and competitive position) and financial performance (profitability, asset turnover and risk reduction).

In summary, their analysis finds noticeable first mover advantages for early investors in China over time. Specifically, this test finds that early investors have superior performance in profitability, sales growth, asset turnover, competitive position, and uncertainty reduction relative to late entrants in the *late* operation period. These results, in addition to the evidence presented earlier, yield a number of important implications for foreign investors.

4.6 Implications and Guidance for Foreign Investors

Taken together, the above discussions provide a clear answer that there are noticeable first mover advantages during the late phase of FDI in the Chinese market. On the other hand, first movers face substantially high operational risk and low profitability during the initial phase of operations. These findings suggest a number of implications for both first movers and late movers.

First Movers

A foreign investor's competence influences its capability of risk reduction and its ability to seize upon preemptive investment opportunities in the host market. In order for an investor to become a pioneer entrant of FDI, a feasible first mover opportunity must be present. The identification of such an opportunity depends upon the investor's own foresight, skills, resources, and good fortune, as well as that of the competitors. Once such an opportunity is identified, the next strategic question immediately emerges for the foreign investor: whether it should exploit this opportunity and enter the transitional economy as a first mover.

The lessons from the timing of FDI in China based on the two tests reported here suggest that the potential investor should articulate its strategic objectives that it intends to achieve before making the entry timing decision. It is well-known that transitional economies are not "easy" markets to enter. Even China, the most sophisticated transitional economy in terms of FDI absorption to date, presents a harsh environment that is unfamiliar to most foreign investors. If the objectives for FDI entry are to diversify the global business portfolio and reduce the operational risks quickly, then becoming a first mover in high-risk transitional economies is definitely not advisable. Instead, a high level of operational risks should be expected in these countries during the early stage of local operations. Likewise, if the objectives are for immediate short-run profits, it is not a good bet to become a first mover in these countries.

However, if the objectives are to build up strong market share positions and develop local markets over the long run, then early FDI entry is strongly advisable. Since major FDI players in China have all entered in the early 1980s with a large number of preemptive investments, they have effectively accumulated a significant amount of learning and erected high entry barriers. As a result, late entrants may have a hard time catching up. For example, in the automobile industry in China, late entrants are likely to find that the domestic market is already carved up by early movers such as Volkswagen and Chrysler, and that it is very difficult to sell 100,000 or so vehicles a year which is generally the point at which car plants start to be profitable. Indeed, this study confirms that, in the long run, early movers can accomplish more not only in profitability and stability but also in market expansion and competitive position.

Early timing is significantly favorable to the first mover's late stage performance such as return on sales, return on equity, sales growth, asset turnover, competitive position, and risk reduction. Despite the sacrifice of higher operational uncertainties during the early phase of investment, first movers are better off over time from superior market positions, localized organizational learning, better relationship with governmental authorities and business community, and established organizational reputation and product image. It has been long advised that foreign investors entering into transitional economies need more 'patience'. The above evidence confirms the necessity of patience and long range planning in such a transitional environment.

Some tactics for this purpose may include: i) preempting potential opportunities through obtaining patents or copyrights or filling positioning gaps on the marketing side in the host territory; ii) minimizing technological leakage to rivals in the local settings by retaining employees, limiting access or developing organizational capabilities, and iii) avoiding excessive inertia by tracking the evolution of indigenous customer needs, being willing to cannibalize and keeping operational flexibility in the host country context.

Late Entrants

As noted above, late movers have a better early-stage performance in accounting return and risk reduction than first movers do. This advantage may derive from (1) organizational learning from early movers; (2) more stabilizing regulatory environment in the host country; and (3) improved investment infrastructure. This implies that late investment is an appropriate strategic choice for those investors who pursue short term profitability or risk aversion in China. If market expansion and asset efficiency are sought, even in the short term, however, late entry becomes disadvantageous choice.

In the long run, late entry is less advantageous than early investment in both market and financial arenas. The survey results suggest that late entrants have a lower performance in major aspects of operations than early movers when comparing their *late stage* outcomes. Today, late foreign entrants are competing with not only early foreign investors but also local firms. In China, an increasing number of firms, especially township and village enterprises, have mushroomed in every economic sector. As a result of structural reform and industrial deregulation, these local businesses are much more strategically flexible, organizationally autonomous, and technologically proactive and innovative than Chinese companies under 'old' regime. Therefore, the later the entry into this market, the more competitive pressure the entrant would encounter.

For late movers in search of market expansion in China, some strategies available for them to opt for include i) entering through a market niche: heterogeneous-to-home industry and market structures in China provide them with much more business opportunities which enable them to find it profitable, feasible, and preferable to avoid direct confrontation with a strong pioneer through tactically focusing particular segments in which they have competitive advantages; ii) purchasing or acquiring a pioneer firm, either local or foreign business, if the pioneer firm is capital-constrained, lacks resources, and has not yet achieved its market potentials. Very recently some emerging economies such as China have allowed transnational investors to purchase or acquire indigenous state-owned enterprises, many of which are local pioneer firms in the industry but immensely lack capital, technological, or organizational resources, and iii) learning from early entrants of FDI in the host country: late investors can reduce the contextual risks and operational uncertainties and enhance the cross-margin rate by studying early investors' behavior in dealing with the local governments, supplies, customers, and other stakeholders in the value chain.

4.7 Conclusion

While the timing of FDI is an important dimension that affects the entry decisions, it is important to caution that such a dimension is not the sole determinant of FDI decisions. Premature entry, in the interest of obtaining first mover advantages, will only backfire. FDI decisions in general are made in connection with other strategic considerations such as global positioning, organizational learning, and the MNE's own advantages. Moreover, the impact of government policy on FDI decisions is significant. This is true not only in the context of China but other transitional economies. For example, despite its adoption of "free market" principles, the Russian government has repeatedly attempted to encourage early movers and threaten late movers. In a meeting with U.S. executives in 1990, Mikhail Gorbachev remarked: "Those companies who are with us now have good prospects of participating in our great country .... whereas those who wait will remain observers for years to come - we will see to it" (Luo and Peng, 1998). Foreign investors have to seriously consider such credible commitments to help first movers and equally credible threats to contain late entrants when making FDI timing decisions.

While the outcome of such a "carrot-and stick" policy in Russia and Eastern Europe is not clear due to the relatively short period of absorbing FDI, in China a large number of early movers have been rewarded handsomely due to their collaboration with the government. Perhaps the foremost example is Volkswagen, which currently operates the largest foreign-invested firm in China, the Shanghai Volkswagen, as well as a number of other joint ventures. Since the Chinese government regards the automobile industry as one of the "pillar" industries earmarked for strong support, Volkswagen has been identified as a key player with annual sales of 400,000 cars and 60 percent of the lucrative Chinese market. In contrast, late movers such as General Motors, Ford and Mercedez-Benz have had a hard time in gaining government approval for their FDI projects.

In summary, while the timing of FDI entry is an important dimension in contemplating such decisions, foreign investors have to consider other important dimensions as well. In addition to traditional criteria such as global strategy and organizational resources, foreign investors also have to pay careful attention to government policy in transitional economies which tend to encourage early entrants.

In the course of formulating FDI timing strategy, both early and late entrants (particularly early movers) should attach the utmost importance to the integration of timing strategy with other investment strategies such as entry mode and location selection. In the joint venture entry mode, a good local partner can spur an early mover's market expansion and enhance its market power against rivals in the host environment because of the effect of operational synergy between a local partner's existing market power and a foreign partner's technological and organizational competencies. Moreover, when early investors are treading unchartered waters, local partners can greatly assist the ventures in reducing contextual or transactional risks using their country-specific knowledge. In a similar fashion, open area location in emerging economies is able to foster risk reduction for early investors. Indeed, relative to non-open regions, open areas provide international firms with a better business atmosphere and a superior investment infrastructure that are conducive to the operational stability and risk reduction for early movers.

In recent years China's remarkable economic progress has led transnational investors, particularly those early movers, to revise radically their view of the country's opportunities and redouble their efforts to capitalize on its potential. As the senior managers of many early movers originated from North American, European, and Asian MNEs come to believe that the forces working to open up China's economy are irreversible, they are hastening to expand the scale, scope, and structure of their activities in the country. These early investors are there for the long haul and they have already figured out how to make profits and sustain them over time, and are working to lock out late-moving competitors. Indeed China is - and will long remain - a difficult and uncertain operating environment for transnational investors, however, the long-term economic opportunities China offers are so remarkable that senior managers will find it prudent to pay attention to the experiences of those companies most active there to date. Most of early movers began with one or two small ventures - small both in financial commitment and in scale relative to the parent's global business lines - as a way of putting an opportunistic toe in the water. Many of these pioneers are now moving, purposefully and aggressively, into a distinct second generation of business activity in China. Most successful pioneering ventures took frustrations in stride, viewing them as an unavoidable part of the learning process in a complex and unfamiliar environment. A few years later, these early entrants made explicit and strategic decisions to move beyond the experimental stage. For most of early entrants of FDI in China, experimentation is no longer the goal; the new objective is to build and hold a dominant share of the Chinese market, and to preempt, if possible, entry by other MNEs, while making good profits. For late movers, being left behind by early entrants has become a real and urgent risk. If China is indeed of strategic importance to them, such companies must act quickly and draw on the lessons learned by pioneering or more aggressive players in the Chinese market.

Bibliography and Further Readings

Aliber, R.Z. (1970). 'A Theory of Foreign Direct Investment'. In Kindleberger, C.P. (ed.), *The International Corporation*, Cambridge, Mass: MIT Press.

Anderson, S.P. & Engers, M. (1994). 'Strategic Investment and Timing of Entry'. *International Economic Review*, vol.35, pp. 833-853.

Beamish, P.W. (1993). 'The Characteristics of Joint Ventures in the People's Republic of China'. *Journal of International Marketing*, vol.1, issue 2, pp. 29-48.

Brewer, T.L. (1993). 'Government Policies, Market Imperfections, and Foreign Direct Investment'. *Journal of International Business Studies*, vol.24, pp. 101-120.

Brown, C.S. and Lattin, J.M. (1990). *The Head-Start Effect as a Source of Pioneering Advantage*. Working paper, Stanford University.

Buckley, P.J. and Casson, M. (1981). 'The Optimal Timing of a Foreign Direct Investment'. *The Economic Journal*, vol.91, pp. 75-87.

Caves, R. E. (1982). *Multinational Enterprise and Economic Analysis*. New York: Cambridge University Press.

Chang, S. (1995). 'International Expansion Strategy of Japanese Firms: Capability Building Through Sequential Entry'. *Academy of Management Journal*, vol. 38, pp. 383-407.

Cohen, M.D., March, J.G. and Olsen, J.P. (1972). 'A Garbage Can Model of Organizational Choice'. *Administrative Science Quarterly*, vol. 17, pp. 1-25.

Conner, K.R. (1988). 'Strategies for Product Cannibalism'. *Strategic Management Journal*, vol.9, pp. 9-26.

Davidson, W.H. (1980). 'The Location of Foreign Direct Investment Activity: Country Characteristics and Experience Effects'. *Journal of International Business Studies*, vol.12, pp. 9-22.

Freeman, J. and Hannan, M.T. (1983). 'Niche Width and the Dynamics of Organizational Populations'. *American Journal of Sociology*, vol. 88, pp. 1116-1145.

Hannan, M.T. and Freeman, J. (1977). 'The Population Ecology of Organizations'. *American Journal of Sociology*, vol. 82, pp. 929-964.

Lambkin, M. (1988). 'Order of Entry and Performance in New Markets'. *Strategic Management Journal*, vol. 9, pp. 127-140.

Lieberman, M.B. and Montgomery, D.B. (1990). 'To Pioneer or Follow?: Strategy of Entry Order'. In H. Glass (ed.), *Handbook of Business Strategies*, (2nd edition), New York: Warren, Gorharm and Lamont.

Lieberman, M.B. and Montgomery, D.B. (1988). 'First Mover Advantages'. *Strategic Management Journal*, vol. 9, pp. 319-332.

Lilien, G.L. and Yoon, E. (1990). 'The Timing of Competitive Market Entry: An Exploratory Study of New Industrial Products'. *Management Science*, vol. 38, pp. 568-585.

Luo, Y. (1998). 'Timing of Investment and International Expansion Performance: A Case of China'. *Journal of International Business Studies*, in press.

Luo, Y. (1997). 'Pioneering in China: Risks and Benefits'. *Long Range Planning*, vol. 30, pp. 768-776.

Luo, Y., Peng, M. and Tan, J. (1997). 'Timing of Foreign Direct Investment'. *1997 AIB Asia Pacific Conference Proceedings*, 193-198.

Luo, Y. and Peng, M. (1998). 'First Mover Advantages in Investing in Transitional Economies: Two Tests from China'. *The International Executive* (in press).

Mascarenhas, B. (1992). 'Order of Entry and Performance in International Markets'. *Strategic Management Journal*, vol. 13, pp. 531-543.

McCarthy, D.J., Puffer, S.M. and Simmonds, P.J. (1993). 'Riding the Russian Roller Coaster: U.S. Firms' Recent Experience and Future Plans in the Former USSR'. *California Management Review*, vol. 36, pp. 99-115.

Mills, D.E. (1988). 'Preemptive Investment Timing'. *Rand Journal of Economics*, vol. 19, pp. 114-122.

Mitchell, W. (1990). 'Dual Clocks: Entry Order Influences on Incumbent and Newcomer Market Share and Survival When Specialized Assets Retain Their Value'. *Strategic Management Journal*, vol. 12, pp. 85-100.

Mitchell, W., Shaver, J.M. and Yeung, B. (1993). 'Performance Following Changes of International Presence in Domestic and Transition Industries'. *Journal of International Business Studies*, vol. 24, pp. 647-669.

Rivoli, P. and Salorio, E. (1996). 'Foreign Direct Investment and Investment Under Uncertainty'. *Journal of International Business Studies*, vol. 27, pp. 335-358.

Robinson, W.T. (1988). 'Sources of Market Pioneer Advantages: The Case of Industrial Goods Industries'. *Journal of Marketing Research*, September, pp. 47-67.

Sharma, A. (1995). 'Entry Strategies of U.S. Firms to the Newly Independent States, Baltic States, and Eastern European Countries'. *California Management Review*, vol. 37, pp. 90-109.

Teece, D.J. (1987). 'Profiting from Technological Innovation: Implications for Integration, Collaboration, Licensing, and Public Policy'. In D. J. Teece (ed.), *The Competitive Challenge*. Cambridge, MA: Ballinger.

Vernon, R. (1985). 'Comment on Chapter by J. H. Dunning and G. Norman'. In A. Erdilek (ed.), *Multinationals as Mutual Invaders*. London: Croom Helm.

5 Project and Location Selection in China

Chapter Purpose

This chapter covers two issues: project selection and location selection. These issues are important because they influence the effectiveness and efficiency of international investment in China. This chapter begins with an introduction of conceptual foundations on the issues, followed by governmental policies on project orientation and locational preference. Managerial guidelines on selecting appropriate locations and the right type of projects are reiterated.

5.1 Conceptual Foundations

Project Selection

A host government indirectly influences FDI flow through the granting of subsidies for certain types of projects and the imposition of restrictions on others. Policy preferences are reflected in differentiated rules and regulations being applied to different categories of projects. Although the actual categories may vary across countries, a broadly defined classification may distinguish between those which are oriented on technological advancement, exports, domestic markets, import-substitution, or infrastructure. Faced with the need for foreign exchange earnings, product and process innovations, and infrastructure improvement, most developing countries provide preferential treatment to technologically-advanced, and export and infrastructure-oriented ventures. Macroeconomic priorities are reflected not only in tax policies, foreign exchange provisions, financing, and access to other production factors, but also in variable market entry barriers.

An MNC's selection of technologically-advanced or infrastructure-oriented projects is of the utmost importance. This is especially true for

116

those ventures that pursue market growth, risk reduction, and economic efficiency. An export-oriented strategy is a major means for achieving cost-minimization and efficiency, while domestic-oriented and import-substitution strategies are ways to accomplish local market expansion.

Export-oriented FIEs tend to have an internal strategic orientation. They attempt to lower their manufacturing cost through exploiting lower labor or other direct costs in the host country. Their market focus is not on the local market but rather on home or international markets. This manufacturing-export pattern of operations emerges in many FIEs operating in newly emerging market economies. These internally-oriented FIEs emphasize high-capacity utilization, low advertising and promotion, low product R&D efforts, and low manufacturing direct costs in the local market. They utilize the host country as an export platform to manufacture a product for resale outside the host country.

Local market-oriented FIEs tend to have an external strategic orientation. They value product innovations meant to improve their output. They are less critically concerned with manufacturing expenses or relative direct costs. They put their focus on local market expansion rather than on home or international markets. Large market share, great market power and high market growth in the host country are the long-term strategic goals of these FIEs.

Technologically-advanced FIEs tend to have a dual-emphasis orientation. They maintain a stable domain wherein they not only operate with efficiency but also identify emerging opportunities through market scanning and research. In other words, dual-emphasis oriented FIEs seek benefits accrued from business opportunities in the local market and their efficiency-generating competencies gained through either market expansion outside the network or business integration within the network. In general, such FIEs emphasize output improvements and differentiation through product, process or managerial innovation. Businesses that combine efficiency with improvements or innovations may have levels of return higher than the industry average. There is no strictly limited market focus for dual-emphasis FIEs. They can sell in the local market or export to home or third countries. Rather, the clear-cut feature of this type of FIE is the high intensity of R&D in product, process and market. In order to attract a greater number of technologically-advanced FIEs that are not solely focused on the local market, host governments of emerging economies often provide them with preferential treatment. This is of great value to their overall performance.

Selecting the type of project is important for both parent firms and FIEs. The project type can influence efficiency, risk reduction, local market growth, and cost-minimization of both parent firms and their overseas subunits. Previous studies have suggested that the host market environment influences the incentive effectiveness. For example, Guisinger (1985) concluded that commodity-based incentives, such as tariff and quota protection, were of dominant importance to twenty-four out of thirty-six domestic market-oriented investors surveyed in his study. In contrast, only one export-oriented investor out of a total of twelve was influenced by commodity incentives; financial incentives were far more important. Similarly, Reuber (1973) concluded that protection of local markets in a developing country was critical to market development and government-initiated projects. Tax preferences may be more important for export-oriented investors because they are searching for an export platform from which to manufacture for resale outside the host country. In recent years, Rolfe and White (1992) and Wells (1986) have further confirmed that export-oriented investors are more likely to be influenced by tax holidays and reductions than are host market-oriented investors.

In China, after expiration of the terms of income tax exemption and reduction, export-oriented and technologically-advanced ventures are levied an income tax at half the rate stipulated for other types of projects (e.g., domestic-oriented and import-substitution). In addition, export-oriented FIEs are exempted from paying import duty on inputs used to produce exported products. Since a large amount of product value in export-oriented manufacture is made of imported components, incentives related to import duties can be very important. Moreover, according to the new Chinese turnover tax law which took effect on January 1, 1994, the value-added tax (17%) paid by FIEs is refundable if the final goods are exported to foreign markets.

Income or turnover tax preferences and import duty exemptions appear to have a strong effect only when a majority of the nontax factors (e.g., infrastructure quality) are also favorable. If none of the nontax factors are favorable, it is unlikely that tax holidays and import duty exemptions can alone attract foreign investment. Although technologically-advanced projects also receive tax preferences, this treatment is likely to be offset by the disadvantages of non-tax factors. As the National Council for US-China Trade reported (1990), despite recent improvements, many U.S. investors still complain about the poor quality of the Chinese infrastructure.

Operational dependence on the local environment leads to greater exposure to uncertainties and risks. FIEs established to exploit the local market and take advantage of cheap labor are subject to uncertainty in both the local input and product markets. Export-oriented operations, on the other hand, can be run independently of local markets; their exposure to country-specific risks are kept at a minimum. Discrepancies between actual investments and what host governments desire also exposes FIEs to uncertainty and risk.

In accordance with Chinese industrial policy, foreign investors are encouraged to invest in (i) high export ratio projects; (ii) new equipment or new technologies that correspond to domestic needs; (iii) energy, transportation, telecommunications, and other infrastructure-related industries. FIEs investing in these types of projects are provided with further preferential treatment including: (a) reduction in land-use fees; (b) exemption from the profit remittance tax; (c) priority in obtaining water, electricity, transportation, and communication services. Thus, other things being equal, FIEs investing in projects favored by the government have a higher performance in terms of risk reduction than do FIEs investing in other projects.

Different types of projects carried out by MNC foreign subsidiaries have varying market performance (Kobrin, 1988). Despite higher risks and uncertainty, domestic-focused and import-substitution projects benefit from more opportunities in local market growth than do others. Many developing and transitional economies have a high demand for imports. This fact will lead to greater opportunities for import-substitution when the government tightens import control as the result of a foreign exchange shortage. Developing and transitional economies also present more business opportunities than do developed markets. Opportunity does not guarantee venture success, however. A FIE's experience in the host market, ability to reduce local risks, and bargaining power vis-a-vis local authorities are all necessary for achieving and maintaining market power and growth.

Location Selection

Foreign manufacturers must also consider location characteristics. Transaction cost theorists view production site specificities as fundamental to choosing where to invest. The interaction between location-specific factors and investor competence as a source of competitive advantage has recently attracted research interest (Rugman and Verbeke, 1993). In general, the optimum location of production depends on plant economies of scale, transportation costs, tariff and nontariff barriers, relative production costs, and presence of long-standing customers in the foreign market. Friedman, Gerlowski, and Silberman (1992) also demonstrate that the local market conditions are significant factors affecting location choice.

Production location in the FDI literature is usually defined in terms of national markets. However, conditions also vary widely within national borders, especially in large or less developed countries or in the presence of transitional economics. Luo (1997) has provided evidence that location decision within a country is significantly influenced by the host-government's policies and preferences toward foreign direct investment. Indeed, in many newly emerging open economies such as China, different regions and even different areas within a region have varying treatments in tax, foreign exchange, and tariffs, and local market conditions. Many developing countries have designated special areas as open economic zones to encourage or facilitate FDI operations. These zones benefit from better facilities, privileged policies, an international business atmosphere, and better investment infrastructure, which positively affect FDI performance. Region-specific and zone-specific locational strategies thus constitute important means for achieving risk reduction, cost-minimization, and efficiency.

For FDI in newly opened market economies in transition, location strategy is even more crucial to venture success. It has been found that, in this context, cultural distance, business atmosphere, government policies, foreign business treatment, stage of economic development, and degree of openness vary substantially across different regions, and between open economic zones and other areas.

The influence of cross region location on FIE performance is an environment-specific issue. In fact, neither the level of economic development nor the stage in the economic reform process is even across different regions in China. The open coastal cities and open economic regions have historically been more developed economically and contain better infrastructure (transportation, communication, production and business service, etc.) than do other areas. Moreover, the open areas have been provided with greater autonomy and authority to conduct their economic affairs. Open areas generally provide more Western-style business facilities and a cultural atmosphere conducive to international activities. Finally, FIEs located in open areas benefit from preferential treatment in terms of income tax and other fees. For instance, income tax on FIEs established in the open cities along the coast is levied at the reduced rate of 24%; ventures located in non-open areas have a rate of 33%. Besides, FIEs in open areas are exempted from paying the Industrial and Commercial Consolidation Tax (ICCT) for their (i) imported production equipment, business facilities, building materials, and vehicles; (ii) raw materials, spare parts, components or packing materials imported for producing export products; and (iii) export products. In sum, the open areas are likely to be perceived as less risky and more efficient locations than non-open areas.

According to the National Council for US-China Trade, Washington, D.C. (1990), investors from the U.S. and other Western countries are more likely to locate their operations in open areas than those from Asian territories and countries (Hong Kong, Taiwan, Singapore, Thailand, etc.). For instance, until 1989, 95% of US-origin FDI flows into China targeted metropolitan and major cities of open coastal provinces with the remaining 5% establishing operations in non-open areas. In contrast, about 43% of Asian investment is located in inland provinces and non-open regions or small cities in coastal provinces. The major factor contributing to this lack of symmetry is the greater cultural affinity amongst business people from the Asian sphere, particularly from the other Chinese commonwealth and their local counterparts. The Chinese commonwealth area nurtures a network of entrepreneurial relationships and an array of political and economic systems that are bound together not by geography but rather by shared tradition. Since less open areas in China are generally more tradition-bound, Asian investors may experience less difficulty in adapting to these environments. Another major factor contributing to this distribution pattern of FDI is the sectoral difference between investors from Asian areas other than Japan and those from the U.S. and European countries. In recent years, many production bases for traditionally labor-intensive industries such as textiles and light industries have shifted from coastal areas to inland regions or from large open cities to small non-open areas. This movement reflects the need to control costs in these industries, where Asian investors have had a dominant presence. The key profile of each major location is detailed in Table 5.1.

One of China's most remarkable efforts to attract FDI was the promulgation of the Provision to Encourage Foreign Direct Investment ("the 22 Articles") initiated by the State Council in October 1986. In addition to offering a series of preferential policies, this provision encouraged each region, down to the county level, to set up one Economic and Technological Development Zone (ETDZ) in its territory. Hence, any geographical region

Table 5.1 Major Locations at a Glance (1993)

Province	Population (mil.)	GDP (¥bil.)	Imports ($mil.)	Exports ($mil.)
Heilongjian	36.4	103	1,001	1,831
Jilin	25.6	67	640	1,307
Liaoning	40.4	181	2,230	6,210
Hebei	63.0	18	360	1,990
Beijing	11.0	85	1,380	1,700
Tianjin	9.3	50	5,900	6,600
Shandong	86.4	270	1,520	5,900
Jiangsu	69.6	276	2,741	5,959
Shaghai	13.0	151	16,950	13,980
Zhejiang	43.4	170	2,410	4,320
Fujian	31.5	95	4,042	5,825
Guangdong	66.0	314	19,900	27,000
Inner Mongolia	22.3	46	550	650
Shanxi	30.1	65	203	634
Henan	89.5	158	559	1,366
Anhui	59.0	98	324	964
Jiangxi	39.7	70	228	884
Shaanxi	34.4	62	500	990
Hubei	56.5	108	1,340	1,686
Hunan	62.5	115	739	1,610
Guangxi	44.4	9	726	1,325
Hainan	7.0	20	1,667	902
Ningxia	5.0	10	32	111
Gansu	23.5	35	200	280
Sichuan	112.5	187	1,266	1,650
Guizhou	34.1	41	118	245
Yunnan	38.0	66	317	523
Qinghai	4.5	11	14	90
Xinjiang	16.0	48	417	495
Tibet	2.6	3	80	20

Source: China Statistical Yearbook, 1994.

can generally be divided into two parts: the ETDZ and the rest. The ETDZ is often located near a harbor. It is designed to provide the basic infrastructure for the establishment of new ventures. ETDZ emergence became a magnet for FDI over the past few years. In these zones, FIEs benefit from preferential treatment on various taxes and fees such as the Enterprise Income Tax (EIT), Customs Duties, the Industrial and Commercial Consolidation Tax (ICCT), and land rent. For instance, EIT is 15% for FIEs in ETDZs while 24% in other locations, unless the enterprise is export- and technologically-oriented. Consequently, FIEs located within ETDZs are in a better position to achieve profitability than are FIEs located outside ETDZs.

According to the Provisions for the Encouragement of Foreign Investment, FIEs in ETDZs can attain further preferential treatment if they produce either technologically-advanced or export-oriented products. The Instrument of Ratification Needed for Joint Venture, Cooperative Ventures, and Wholly Foreign-Owned Ventures promulgated by Ministry of Foreign Trade and Economic Cooperation (MOFTEC) on June 16, 1986 stipulates that if a firm fails to conform with this policy, all the privileges based on its location in an ETDZ and the type of projects will be revoked. This suggests that a firm's zone location is correlated with its type of project. In other words, among FIEs in ETDZs, those investing in export-oriented or technologically-advanced types of projects are in a better position for cost reduction than are those investing in other types of projects, other things being equal.

5.2 Governmental Policies on Project and Location Selection

Locational Policies

In July 1979, Guangdong and Fujian were granted special policies and flexibility in their foreign economic activities by the central government. These include: (i) increased local power to invigorate their economic development; (ii) more flexibility in opening up economically, developing international business and trade, attracting foreign investment, and introducing technology, under the guidance of state planning; and (iii) more financial support, with the two provinces free to utilize most of the added revenue over the next 10 years.

In August 1980, the Standing Committee of the National People's Congress approved the establishment of four special economic zones (SEZs), namely, Shenzhen, Zhuhai, Shantou, and Xiamen. In April 1988, the 7th National People's Congress at its first session approved Hainan as China's largest special economic zone. The local government of these SEZs are granted provincial-level power in economic administration. There are specific favorable policies, such as increased credit loans, retaining all newly increased revenues including those from foreign exchange earnings, for a certain period of time, and exemption from tariffs for materials needed for construction within the zones. To be more specific, FIEs located in these five SEZs enjoy: (1) a reduced 15 percent rate on corporate income tax; (2) exemption of income tax for the first two years and a 50 percent reduction of income tax during the third to fifth years, starting from the first profit-making year, for manufacturing FIEs with a term of business over 10 years, upon approval by tax authorities; (3) an extended three-year, 50 percent reduction on corporate income tax for FIEs using advanced technology; (4) a reduced rate of 10 percent of income tax for FIEs exporting their own products, if their yearly export volume reaches 70 percent or more of the total output value; (5) exemption from export tariffs and value-added tax on export products manufactured by FIEs; (6) exemption from import tariffs and value-added tax on importing equipment or raw materials needed in the manufacturing of exporting products by FIEs or office equipment for use by the FIEs themselves; and (7) favorable rates for land usage.

In April 1984, 14 coastal port cities were opened and granted more autonomy to attract FDI. These cities include: Tianjin, Shanghai, Dalian, Qinhuangdao, Yantai, Qingdao, Lianyuangang, Nantong, Ningbo, Wenzhou, Fuzhou, Guangzhou, Zhanjiang, and Beihai. FIEs located in these coastal cities are entitled to the following preferential treatment: (1) a 24 percent corporate income tax levied on manufacturing FIEs in general; (2) a 15 percent corporate income tax for those FIEs which are technologically-intensive, have a project with over $30 million in FDI, are infrastructure-oriented or state-encouraged; (3) a 50 percent reduction of the 24 percent corporate income tax if 70 percent of output is exported; (4) manufacturing FIEs with a business term of over 10 years are entitled to a two-year exemption from and a subsequent three-year 50 percent reduction of the corporate income tax, starting from the first profit-making year; (5) EJVs investing in port construction and having a minimum 15 year business term, are entitled to a five-year exemption from and a subsequent five-year 50 percent reduction of the corporate income tax; (6) FIEs are exempt from tariffs and value-added tax for equipment and materials imported for production, and exempt from value-added tax for their exported products.

Since 1984, the State Council has approved the establishment of 32 national-level ETDZs. They are located in Dalian, Qinhuangdao, Tianjin, Yantai, Qingdao, Lianyuangan, Nantong, Caohejing, Minhang, Hongqiao, Ningbo, Fuzhou, Guangzhou, Zhanjiang, Weihai, Yingkou, Kunshan, Wenzhou, Rongqiao, Dongshan, Shenyang, Hangzhou, Wuhan, Changchun, Harbin, Chongqing, Wuhu, Xiaoshan, Nansha, Dayawan, Beijing, and Urumqi. FIEs investing in the above ETDZs enjoy the following privileges: (1) a 15 percent corporate income tax for manufacturing FIEs. If the project will be over 10 years in duration, it enjoys a two-year exemption from and a subsequent three-year 50 percent reduction of corporate income tax; (2) a 10 percent corporate income tax for FIEs with 70 percent of output exported, after a stipulated term; (3) a 50 percent reduction of the 15 percent corporate income tax for an extended three-year period; (4) exemption from tariffs and value-added taxes for imported materials, equipments, parts and accessories that are used in production and operations; (5) exemption from export tariffs and value-added tax on export products.

In February 1985, the State Council approved the establishment of open coastal economic regions including Pearl River Delta, Yangtze River Delta, and South Fujian-Xiamen-Zhangzhou-Quanzhou Delta, covering 51 cities and counties. In March 1988, the State further approved Liaodong (East Liaoning) Peninsula, Shandong Peninsula, and several cities and counties in other coastal regions as open coastal economic regions. This makes almost all coastal cities and counties open to foreign investment. The following preferential policies are applicable to FIEs in these regions: (1) a 24 percent corporate income tax; (2) a 15 percent corporate income tax for those FIEs that are either technologically-advanced, have over $30 million in FDI, or are infrastructure-oriented; (3) favorable corporate income tax, tariffs, value-added tax, and other benefits for export-oriented and technologically-advanced FIEs.

In April 1990, the State Council opened the Pudong New Area of Shanghai, which is a triangular area to the east of the Huangpu River, southwest of the Yangtze River mouth, and next to downtown Shanghai. The area covers 518 square kilometers, with a population of 1.38 million. Bordering on the East Sea and nestled against the Yangtze River to the north, the Pudong New Area is situated at the joint of the so-called golden seacoast and golden waterway of China. The central government gives Shanghai greater power to approve the formation of FDI projects. FIEs in the Pudong New Area have the following privileges: (1) a 15 percent corporate income tax in general, and two-year exemption and a subsequent three-year reduction by 50 percent of the tax rate if the project duration is over 10 years; (2) a five-year exemption from and a subsequent five-year reduction by 50 percent of the corporate income tax when investing in energy and communication projects such as building of airports, harbors, railways, highways, and electric power stations; (3) FIEs are allowed to set up tertiary-sector projects such as department stores and supermarkets; (4) FIEs are allowed to set up financial institutions such as banks, accounting and auditing firms, and insurance firms. International trading companies are also permitted to be established and conduct import and export business; (5) no tariffs or value-added tax on imported machines, equipments, vehicles, materials, and the like used in production and operations; (6) the land use right can be transferred within the area with up to a 70 year grace period; and (7) all the income obtained by the government in the area will be used for further development and improvement of the area's infrastructure.

In May 1988, the first of China's New and High-tech Industrial Development and Experimental Zones was established in Beijing. Emulating the 'electronics street' of Zhongguanchun in Beijing's Haidian District, this industrial park, also called China's 'Silicon Valley', covers an area of 100 square kilometers. China has since approved the establishment of over 50 more High-Tech Zones. FDI projects in these zones enjoy even more favorable treatment than those in ETDZs, according to the Interim Regulations on Certain Policies of the State New and High-Tech Industrial Development Zones, issued by the State Council, and Taxation of the State New and High-Tech Industrial Development Zones, regulated by the State Tax Bureau.

China has also approved 14 bonded areas in Pudong (Waigaoqiao Bonded Area), Tianjin, Futian (Shenzhen), Shatoujiao (Shenzhen), Dalian, Guanzou, Qingdao, Zhangjiagang, Ningbo, Fuzhou, Zhuhai, Hainan, Shantou, and Xiamen. Bonded areas serve mainly to initiate entrepot trade and offer export services such as processing, packaging, storage, and exhibition. FIEs located in these bonded areas are allowed to act as agencies for other FIEs in the same area that need to import raw materials or parts used in their production. FIEs in these areas are not required to obtain import or export licenses or permits for imported machines, equipment, and materials necessary for the construction of infrastructure facilities and production. These imported items are also free from tariffs and value-added taxes.

Project-Related Policies

Project orientation affects the FIE's eligibility for preferential treatment from the government and its vulnerability to governmental intervention. An export-oriented project is defined by MOFTEC as one which exports at least 70 percent of the total product manufactured in China. The definition of "technologically-advanced project" is, however, obscure. In practice, foreign investors need to check with the local authorities about whether or not their technology is considered advanced before making any commitments. If less than 70 percent of total output is exported but sold domestically in the Chinese market, it is considered by the government as a local market-oriented project. Infrastructure-oriented projects, in general, refer to those invested in energy, transportation, telecommunications, power generation, and other infrastructure-related sectors which bring in new technologies. Import-substitution projects means those which produce products within China that previously had to be imported to meet domestic demand. These products are generally sold in China in foreign currency instead of Renminbei (RMB). In recent years, the number of import-substitution projects has been decreased drastically as a result of the rising quality of goods now produced by many local firms and FIEs.

5.3 Finding a Home: Some Advice

A recent survey reveals that Shanghai and Shenzhen are home to China's most profitable first-generation American joint ventures, with returns on investment at 16.2 percent and 13.6 percent, respectively. Western companies in the inland cities seem to be less profitable than those in eastern coast provinces. Nearly half of the executives reporting on inland investment projects responded that their joint ventures have not met expectations due to poorly-developed infrastructures and transportation networks, and uncertain raw material supplies (Stelzer et al., 1991).

Nevertheless, being in an inland town or province with a committed municipal or provincial leadership can have some unusual benefits. Because there are fewer ventures in many inland cities, FIEs there can get more personal attention and support from the provincial governor or mayor. Closer personal interactions with top local decision-makers can be more frequent. These interactions have become increasingly important during the past decade as the Chinese economy has become decentralized, shifting substantial power to local governments.

There are many cases where foreign ventures in some small inland cities have managed to overcome mounting obstacles due to direct involvement by local governments. This is not normally expected from the municipalities of big cities. Many local officials are zealous supporters of Deng's reforms and are eager to attract foreign direct investment. In order to compete for foreign investment with coastal areas, some of them adopt aggressive policies to offset their disadvantages in terms of geographical location. Commitment from local governments is often indispensable to the success of a foreign business in China.

Foreign investors in China have access to a broad range of special incentives, depending on the location of their venture, the nature of the project, and how the FIE project is classified. As noted earlier, FIEs located in different areas and with different project types are treated idiosyncratically by the Chinese government. Any foreign investor looking at opportunities in China needs to understand exactly which preferential policies may apply to a particular project. However, getting a firm handle on this is not always easy. Local government officials who are eager to entice foreign investment may exaggerate the incentives in a particular locale. In recent years, the explosion of 'special areas' has left many investors wondering how to choose one locale over another. Foreign investors should check out whether or not the 'special area' is approved to offer preferential investment policies. If so, they should find out what level of the government (central, provincial, or city-level) holds the authority to implement these policies. A thousand ETDZs at various levels have been established, ranging from state-level ETDZs to county or even township-level small ETDZs. In general, preferential policies offered by low-level ETDZs are very unstable. In fact, many of these small, lower-level ETDZs have been recently shut down by the central government.

Geographic affinity represents an important factor contributing to the phenomenal growth of FDI initiated by investors from Hong Kong, Taiwan, Macau, and Singapore. Hong Kong and Macau are adjacent to Shengzhen and Zhuhai, both among the first four special economic zones opened in 1979. Similarly, Taiwan is just opposite Xiamen, another special economic zone located in Fujian province. Although Singapore is not as close to China as Hong Kong and Taiwan, it enjoys strong geographic advantages, not only due to its proximity to the mainland but also its international air and sea routes, which straddle the time zones of Asia and Europe. It is at the heart of the economically dynamic Asia-Pacific region. These geographic advantages reduce transportation costs and turnaround time for mainland production, obviously crucial in vertically integrated manufacturing.

The opening of China coincided with the emergence of severe labor shortages in Hong Kong, Singapore and Taiwan and the need for restructuring within these three economies. There has been a large-scale movement of export-oriented, labor-intensive industry from Chinese community territories, particularly Hong Kong, to such mainland coastal areas as Guangdong, Fujian, Jiangsu and Zhejiang. In addition, although international investors from Hong Kong, Taiwan, Singapore and Macau are the major source of FDI in China, in a broad sense, they are moving relatively labor-intensive activities into China in an attempt to escape rising labor costs and space constraints at home. Many Chinese community investors, particularly those from Hong Kong and Taiwan, have been operating in the same labor-intensive industries such as textiles, garments, electronics, electrical goods, metal, plastics and toys - most have mature technologies which comprise most of their prior exports. As the tightening labor market has raised wage costs in their home territories and economic expansion has made factory sites more and more expensive, moving production to China, where wage levels are fundamentally lower, becomes immensely attractive. Today, it is rare to find a single Hong Kong-owned electronics company that does not have at least one factory in Guangdong, the huge province that borders Hong Kong.

In the past, foreign companies, whether from Asian territories or from the Western world, have mostly gone to coastal areas where they were attracted by preferential tax policies, easy access to trained labor, and the region's rapidly developing infrastructure. To encourage FDI in the interior regions, the central government has recently introduced measures to enhance border trade, open inland infrastructure and oil and gas projects to foreign participation, and improve tax incentives for foreign investors in major inland cities, among others. These changes have already made the interior more attractive to foreign investors and may generate even better investment opportunities in the future.

The Chinese government, well aware that further disparities between coastal and inland economic growth rates could pose long-term risks to social stability, has prescribed a number of policies to give the inland economy a boost. First, the government has extended the open city concept to selected locations in the interior. Some inland cities are now able to offer the same or even better investment incentives than in SEZs, ETDZs, or coastal cities. Local government have been given broad discretionary authority to enact legislation to encourage foreign investment. As a result, thousands of cities all over China are vying to attract FDI.

Second, China has opened up sectors or areas previously off-limits to foreign investment. For example, foreign companies can now pursue offshore oil and gas drilling opportunities in the Tarim Basin and other inland areas. Moreover, central authorities have sought to encourage trade between inland provinces and countries on China's borders by reducing tariffs and re-establishing transport links.

Third, China announced in April 1994 that the three specialized banks would prioritize loans and allocations of funds to the interior. As the State Planning Commission recognizes that the inflow of foreign capital to China will be insufficient to fund all of the country's infrastructure needs, China's new State Development Bank plans to focus on the inland provinces, leaving the wealthier coastal areas to rely on commercial funding sources. It is reported that the bank will prioritize loans to four sectors: infrastructure such as railways, highways, and communications; raw materials industries such as steel, coal, chemicals, and oil; new industries such as electronics; and agriculture and forestry.

Fourth, foreign investors in inland regions such as Changchun, Changsha, Chengdu, Chongqing, Guiyand, Hefei, Hohhot, Lanzhou, Kunming, Mudanjiang, Nanchang, Nanjing, Shenyang, Shijiazhuang, Taiyuan, Urumqi, Wuhan, Xian, Xining, Yanchun, and Zhengzhou now enjoy a 15 percent tax rate for general enterprises, with a full or partial tax holiday of 3-10 years. FIEs established in remote economically undeveloped areas can also qualify for a further 15-30 percent tax reduction for an additional 10 years.

Lastly, more than 25 high-technology zones, mostly in the interior, are allowed to offer technologically-advanced projects tax advantages similar to those provided by the SEZs. These high-tech zones are located in Changchun, Changsha, Chengdu, Chongqing, Fuzhou, Harbin, Hefei, Lanzhou, Nanjing, Shijiazhuang, Weihai, Wuhan, Xian, Zhengzhou, and Zhongshangang. FIEs in these zones are eligible for a reduced tax rate of 15 percent. EJVs with terms of over 10 years, designated as high-tech enterprises, are also entitled to a two-year tax holiday, starting with the first profitable year.

At present, the interior's major strengths are its low land and labor costs and proximity to natural resources. Foreign companies looking to set up enterprises utilizing low to medium technologies and requiring a considerable labor force will find the interior most suitable. As the infrastructure and available labor skills in the interior improve, medium and high-tech industries will also find suitable investment sites there. Even if a prospective foreign investor prefers the coast, he should examine the inland areas to see how they compare before deciding on a final project location.

To summarize, foreign investors should consider at least five aspects of location before making a decision. First, prospective foreign investors should find out about all the local policies relevant to FDI project approval, taxation, financing, land use, infrastructure accessibility, and industry priority. They should also consult MOFTEC's list of officially approved special industrial zones or ETDZs to avoid getting caught in unofficial 'pseudo' economic zone. In early 1994, the State Council closed 1,000 of the 2,700 special industrial zones which had been set up by local governments to attract foreign investment.

Second, as noted earlier, prospective foreign investors should thoroughly examine infrastructure conditions. For example, lack of deep-water ports in certain regions can pose a problem for import or export. FIEs located too far from a railroad terminal may have high transportation costs. Foreign investors should also ensure that the existing water supply, electricity grid, and telecommunication systems can meet the needs of the proposed plant.

Third, foreign investors should consider local living conditions and the influence on the expatriate life of their staff. Important factors may include housing, transportation, communication networks, health care facilities, international schools, and cultural distance.

Fourth, foreign executives should evaluate the local government, and find out if municipal and provincial officials will be accessible, whether they are inclined to provide assistance, and how efficient they are.

Finally, investors should study the accessibility and quality of production factors such as local labor, capital, natural resources and raw materials, and technology. Labor skills and the ability of local firms to absorb new technologies are particularly influential to venture success.

Location selection is often interrelated with such decisions as project selection, industry selection, timing decision, and partner selection. For instance, export-oriented projects should be located in areas which supply superior labor skills, transportation conditions, and the local materials needed for production. Projects in capital-intensive or technology-intensive industries might be better situated in cities with a strong infrastructure and absorptive capabilities. The first mover in a newly opened sector should choose a site which is developed economically, has connections with the western business culture, and is promoted by the government. Late entrants already familiar with the Chinese market may consider an interior area where market demand is high and industrial competition is weak. A foreign investor launching a joint project with a local partner who already maintains superior organizational and technological skills and relationships with external stakeholders (such as suppliers, customers, distributors, and government officials), is not limited to coastal regions.

5.4 Choosing the Right Project: Some Advice

Recently, some researchers examined the effect of project type selection on FIE performance based on the analysis of the data collected from Jiangsu province (Luo, 1997; 1998; Luo and Sadrieh, 1996). The primary findings suggest that there exists a systematic association between project type and FIE performance; different project orientations influence FIE performance idiosyncratically. FIE success hinges on a good fit between the strategic objectives of the parent firm and the strategic orientations of its overseas projects. Maintaining market orientation flexibility and contributing distinctive competencies are imperative for overall success.

Export-oriented projects are found to favorably influence FIE risk reduction. Most export-oriented FIEs are satisfactory with their export growth. Indeed, export-oriented projects in a global environment can enable FIEs to accomplish their strategic tasks by taking advantage of the internalized transnational networks of MNCs. This internalization advantage effectively assists FIEs in achieving economic rents derived from comparative advantages across national boundaries. Today, country-specific comparative advantages in certain factors are not quickly dissipated due to the existence of trade barriers across borders and mobility barriers within the border. Under these conditions, globally integrated network can enable the internally-oriented FIEs to take advantage of transaction costs economies and internalization advantages. Moreover, an internally-oriented strategy can help the investor reduce operational risks and attain preferential treatments by the host government in emerging economies. It is hence advisable that export orientation is an appropriate strategic choice for those transnational investors who seek risk diversification, short-term financial return, global integration advantage, or production factors exploitation in host countries.

Local market-oriented projects are found to be significantly correlated with FIE sales growth but have high operational risks. In other words, FIEs seeking market growth in China appear to have accomplished their goals in local market expansion but have encountered high instability and uncertainty. By focusing on identifying and capitalizing on emerging market opportunities in China, local market-oriented FIEs help MNCs attain internationalization advantages by geographically expanding foreign markets and transnationally increasing product scope. With increasing familiarity with the Chinese environment, more and more MNCs have in recent years entered this market in pursuit of local market shares. Indeed, when government-instituted controls over industry supplies are lifted during transition, the explosion in the number of participants, both foreign and local, in newly competitive industries does not exhaust its potential. The rapidly expanding Chinese economy together with the existence of a pent-up demand spurs MNCs to search for local market growth using innovative, risk-taking, and proactive strategies. For large diversified MNCs which are long-sighted, technologically competitive, and adaptive to the local environment, external orientation would be a right choice for them to preempt emerging product or market opportunities.

Technologically-advanced projects tend to have a dual-emphasis. That is, their market domain is in both the Chinese domestic and international markets. This dual orientation is the only one of the three types of projects which positively relates to profitability. Market orientation flexibility (i.e., not focused solely on the local market) and advanced technological skills are major reasons why a dual orientation relates to overall success. Market orientation flexibility not only mitigates a FIE's dependence on local settings thus reducing firm's business uncertainties, but also enables the firm to quickly respond to changing conditions in the host, home and international markets. Additionally, keeping a certain degree of market orientation flexibility is commonly encouraged by host governments, particularly in transitional economies. This encouragement supports all major aspects of FIE performance. Another reason for the superiority of the dual-emphasis orientation lies in the fact that parent firms of this type of FIE contribute rent-generating competence (e.g., advanced technology) to the venture. While market structural potentials are a necessary condition for corporate success, distinctive competencies are a sufficient condition for achieving sustained economic benefits.

The analysis also demonstrates that the relationship between project type and sales growth is moderated by investment size. Local market-oriented projects with a greater investment size are more likely to succeed in achieving market growth than those with smaller investments. Thus, an appropriate fit between project type and investment size can contribute to high efficiency. Economies of scale and investment commitments seem important for market expansion in China.

To sum up, prospective foreign companies should consider several factors before choosing a type of project. First, they should check out the Chinese governmental policies regarding different types of projects. These policies include taxation, financing, infrastructure access, foreign exchange balance, local content requirement, and industrial regulations concerning entry barriers, regional restrictions, distribution channels, and partner selection. Second, prospective investors should integrate project selection with the strategic goals of the parent companies and corresponding orientations of the FIEs. Moreover, they should consider their own ability to reduce risks and uncertainty in the local context and their strengths in financial, technological, operational, marketing, and managerial arenas. Next, investors must be able to maintain an appropriate balance between the local responsiveness of their FIEs in China and the global integration requirements of their entire network. The density of interactions between their FIEs in China and other subsidiaries as well as the parent within the network should be viewed as crucial to project selection. Finally, prospective investors should opt for projects which are not only financially profitable but also strategically flexible. Strategic flexibility has been proved to increase both profitability and stability. Keeping the project flexible in terms of market orientation is particularly essential for projects invested in the highly uncertain and complex environment of China.

Bibliography and Further Readings

Brecher, R. (1995). 'Considering the Options', *China Business Review*, May-June, pp. 10-19.

Friedman, J., Gerlowski, D.A. and Silberman, J. (1992). 'What Attracts Foreign Multinational Corporations? Evidence From Branch Plant Location in the United States', *Journal of Regional Science*, vol.32, pp. 402-418.

Guisinger, S. (1985). 'A Comparative Study of Country Policies', In S. Guisinger (ed.), *Investment Incentives and Performance Requirements*. New York: Praeger.

Kobrin, S.J. (1988). 'Trends in Ownership of U.S. Manufacturing Subsidiaries in the 1980s', in Contractor, F.J. and Lorange, P. (eds.), *Cooperative Strategies in International Business*, pp. 129-142, Lexington, MA: Lexington Books.

Luo, Y. (1997). 'Strategic Traits of Foreign Direct Investment in China: A Country of Origin Perspective', *Management International Review*, in press.

Luo, Y. (1998). 'Great China Multinationals in the PRC: A Comparative Analysis of Their Investment Behavior and Performance Relative to Western Multinationals, *International Business Review*, in press.

Luo, Y. and Sadrieh, F. (1996). 'An Empirical Analysis of Strategic Orientation in International Strategic Alliance Performance in a Transitional Economy', Paper presented at 1996 Academy of International Business Annual Meeting, September, 1996, Banff, Canada.

National Council for US-China Trade (1990). *Special Report on US Investment in China*. Washington, D.C.: Department of Commerce.

Ness, A. (1995). 'Shifting the Center', *China Business Review*, September-October, pp. 43-46.

Reuber, G. (1973). *Private Foreign Investment in Development*, Oxford, UK: Clarendon Press.

Rolfe, R. J. and White, R. (1992). 'The Influence of Tax Incentives in Determining the Location of Foreign Direct Investment in Developing Countries', *Journal of the American Taxation Association,* vol.13, pp. 39-57.

Rugman, A.M. and Verbeke, A. (1993). 'Foreign Subsidiaries and Multinational Strategy Management: An Extension and Correction of Porter's Single Diamond Framework', *Management International Review*, Special issue, vol. 33, pp. 71-84.

Stelzer, L. et al. (1991). 'Gauging Investor Satisfaction', *China Business Review*, November-December, pp. 54-56.

Verma, S. (1995). 'Looking inland', *China Business Review*, January-February, pp. 19-25.

Wells, L. (1986). 'Investment Incentives: An Unnecessary Debate', *CTC Reporter*, Autumn, pp. 58-60.

6 Partner Selection in China

Chapter Purpose

This chapter discusses partner selection and its impact on venturing success in China. It begins with an introduction of conceptual foundations for partner selection in an overseas market, followed by an illustration of partner selection criteria for foreign investors entering China. The next section summarizes the empirical evidence pertaining to local partner attributes in relation to FDI performance in China. The following section reiterates managerial implications for international executives active or interested in the Chinese market. Finally, sources and guidance for identifying appropriate Chinese partners are provided.

6.1 Conceptual Foundations

A major challenge for global management has been searching the way that MNCs become competent and attain sustained superior performance. In an attempt to expand globally, MNCs have in recent years turned increasingly to the use of international joint ventures (IJVs) or alliances. However, the intercultural and interorganizational nature of IJVs results in enormous complexity, dynamics, and challenges in managing this cross-border, hybrid form of organization. One popular argument is that inter-partner comparative or configurational features, variously termed as strategic symmetries (Harrigan, 1985), interfirm diversity (Parkhe, 1991), or complementary resources and skills (Geringer, 1991), create inter-partner 'fit' which is expected to generate a synergistic effect on IJV performance (Luo, 1997a).

IJVs have widely been considered vehicles for joining together complementary skills and know-how. The IJV form of organization does, however, entail additional costs due to shared decision-making and the need for coordination among partners. Therefore, it is assumed that firms establish IJVs only when the perceived additional benefits of exercising the IJV option outweigh its expected additional costs. One of the key notions in the IJV literature is that these additional benefits will accrue only through the retention of a partner who can provide complementary skills, competencies, or capabilities that will assist the firm in accomplishing its strategic objectives (Hamel, 1991). Partner selection determines an IJV's mix of skills, knowledge, and resources, its operating policies and procedures, and its vulnerability to indigenous conditions, structures, and institutional changes (Luo, 1997b). In a dynamic, complex, or hostile environment, the importance of local partner selection to IJV success is magnified because the right partner can spur the IJV's adaptability, strategy-environment configuration, and uncertainty reduction.

During the process of IJV formation, foreign parent firms must identify appropriate criteria for local partner selection as well as the relative importance of each criterion. They are divergent depending on firm, setting, and time. Broadly, the criteria can be classified into three categories: (i) task or operation-related; (ii) partnership or cooperation-related; and (iii) cash flow or capital structure-related. Operation-related criteria are associated with the strategic attributes of partners including absorptive capacity, product relatedness, market position, corporate image, strategic orientation, and industrial experience. Cooperation-related criteria often mirror in the organizational attributes such as inter-partner collaboration in the past, foreign experience, leadership, organizational form and size. Cash flow-related criteria are generally represented by financial attributes exemplified by profitability, liquidity, leverage, and asset management. A partner's strategic traits influence the operational skills and resources needed for the joint venture's competitive success, organizational traits affect the efficiency and effectiveness of inter-firm cooperation, and financial traits impact the optimization of capital structure and cash flow.

Conceptually, strategic, organizational, and financial attributes are all crucial to IJV performance. A partner with superior strategic traits, but lacking strong organizational and financial characteristics, results in an unstable joint venture. The possession of desirable organizational attributes without corresponding strategic and financial competence leaves the joint venture unprofitable. A partner with superior financial strengths without strategic and organizational competencies can lead to an unsustainable venture. From a process perspective, the mid-range linkage between partner selection and IJV success lies in inter-partner fit. While strategic attributes may affect strategic fit between partners, organizational traits are likely to influence organizational fit, and financial attributes will impact financial fit. Figure 6.1 schematically summarizes these relationships.

Figure 6.1 Partner Attributes and IJV Success

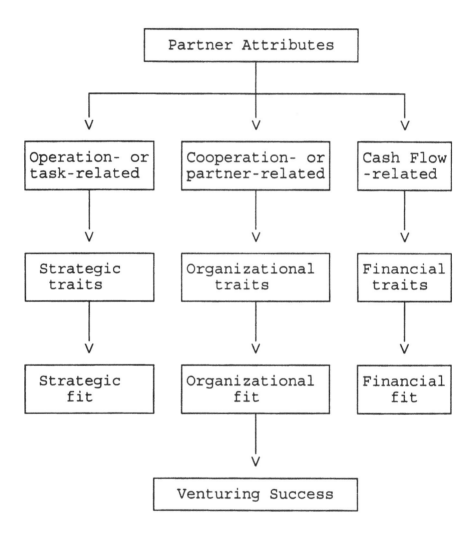

A consideration of partner attributes is only one of the critical factors behind partner selection. Other related factors underlying this decision include the four 'Cs': (i) *Compatible goals*; (ii) *Complementary skills*; (iii) *Cooperative culture*; and (iv) *Commensurate risk*. A firm must be willing to give as much as it gets. IJVs in which one party is out to take as much as possible without giving anything in return are bound to fail. As in any kind of relationship, an IJV is a two-way street in which both sides are complementary. Similarly, an IJV is more likely to fail if it does not advance both firms' strategic goals.

Goal assessment is particularly important when a firm is searching for a partner. Each company should evaluate the objectives of the partner and identify whether or not they are compatible with its own. The situation that holds the most promise for compatibility is one in which strategic goals converge while their competitive goals diverge. In addition, complementary management styles and cooperative culture influence significantly mutual trust, which in turn affects venture success. Symmetry must exist at the top level of management. Peer relations between the top executives of joint venture partnerships should be established. These relationships are especially important in IJVs that are dissimilar in size. Lastly, a commensurate level of risk is needed to act as glue to hold the IJV together. If nothing is at risk, there is less of an incentive to stay together. This risk can be either financial or operational or both. Risk sharing is becoming increasingly necessary in certain industries which move faster than individual firms can keep pace. In situations where technology is changing rapidly, a firm could be exposed to a major failure unless it spreads the risk across a consortium. However, if a firm views risk only in terms of initial investment, the IJV may become simply a tool to be used and then discarded. The fact that successful ventures must share risks, also means that this sharing and equality of risks must be maintained. If one firm learns substantially more than the other firm, risks will no longer be in balance and the venture will quickly dissolve, leaving one firm at a substantial disadvantage over the other in the marketplace.

A firm entering into a joint venture must consider all of the above four 'Cs', taking full advantage of what the other firm has to offer. This is particularly important in newly emerging economies such as China, where business opportunities are promising, but also quite challenging. MNCs entering these economies are likely to face higher barriers and more uncertainty than when entering other, more familiar environments. The more promising the industry appears, the more restrictions or interventions the host government is likely to make. It has been argued that MNCs investing in such economies need to collaborate with local partners in order to facilitate market access, improve government relations, acquire culture-specific knowledge, and gain access to scarce resources. Careful partner selection is therefore vital.

In newly emerging economies, even where some economic sectors have been decentralized and privatized, governments still hinder industrial and market structure adjustments. Indeed, the 'invisible hand' in the reform process often causes unexpected social, political or economic turmoil that may go beyond the tolerance level of the government or society. Under these circumstances, the visible hands of administrative, fiscal, and monetary interventions are called to the rescue. The administrative option is often the most expedient, allowing for swift action which will be promptly reflected in the market. In this situation, local partners can be of great value to the foreign firms. They can make investing in restricted industries possible and help MNCs gain access to marketing channels, while meeting government requirements for local ownership. In addition, having recourse to an IJV as a means of reducing political risks or achieving political advantages is a logical choice for many MNCs operating in strategic sectors in such economies. Moreover, local partners can assist foreign partners in obtaining insightful information and country-specific knowledge concerning governmental policies, local business practices, operational conditions, and the like. Furthermore, the form of IJV helps MNCs gain access to, or secure at a low cost, locally-scarce production factors such as labor force, capital, or land. Among these various needs, some are unique to emerging market economies while others are applicable to all contexts. In market economies, for example, local partners also assist MNCs in gaining local knowledge, meeting human resource needs, sharing costs and risks, and getting access to the market.

In sum, local partner selection is critical to the success of IJVs investing in newly emerging economies. On the one hand, such economies have in recent years become major hosts of MNCs' direct investment because these rapidly expanding economies, characterized by an exploding demand previously stifled by ideologically-based government interventions, provide tremendous business opportunities which MNCs can preempt. On the other hand, transnational investors in such economies face the challenges of structural reform, combined with weak market structure, poorly specified property rights, and institutional uncertainty. Local partners can then be of utmost value to foreign investors in addition to providing benefits commonly recognized in any context: they help boost market expansion, obtain insightful information, mitigate operational risk, and provide country-specific knowledge.

6.2 Strategic Attributes of Local Partners in China

It is important to note that different strategic, organizational, and financial traits may have a heterogeneous effect on overall and unidimensional IJV performance. That is, each trait may affect different aspects of IJV performance idiosyncratically. MNCs need to discern not only important partner selection criteria in general but also which are crucial to their specific strategic goals. The strategic traits of local partners in China include the following attributes.

Absorptive Capability

It has been noted in the IJV literature that complementary needs create interpartner 'fit' which is expected to generate a synergistic effect on IJV performance. However, complementarity is not likely to materialize unless a certain threshold of self-skills is in place. Local partners in emerging economies generally seek technological and innovational skills from foreign partners. The success of an IJV's local operations and expansion in these economies will largely depend upon its local partner's absorptive capability, or its ability to acquire, assimilate, integrate, and exploit knowledge and skills. The firm's ability to process, integrate, and deploy an inflow of new knowledge and skills closely depends on how these relate to the skills already established. This skill base is expected to influence strategic fit and organizational fit between IJV partners, which in turn influence the IJV's accomplishment in economic rent. This rent contains both financial synergies and operational synergies. As a result, a local partner's absorptive capability is likely to contribute to the IJV's profitability and sales growth. Since absorptive capability is more important in capital- or technology-intensive projects, which are often oriented towards the local market in China, the sales growth effect is likely to be revealed in local market expansion rather than exports by the IJV.

Market Power

Because a major objective of foreign investors in emerging economies is to preempt market opportunities and business potential, a local partner's market power is a key asset for IJV development. The market power is often represented by the local partner's industrial and business background, market position, and established marketing and distribution networks.

Market power also enables the firm to effect some industry-wide restriction on output, increase its bargaining power, and offer the advantages of economies of scale. Over the last few years, the Chinese government has relinquished control over a growing number of industries. The rapidly expanding Chinese economy, together with high market demand, has made market position extremely important for the success of any business in the country. In such circumstances, a local partner's market strength is key to the IJV's financial return and indigenous market growth. Moreover, strong local market power can strengthen the IJV's commitment to local market expansion. This commitment will make the IJV less inclined to increase exports in its business operations. Furthermore, strong market power can lead to greater bargaining power against the government. This can help the IJV reduce political risks and business uncertainties.

Product Relatedness

The product diversification relationship between a local partner and the IJV in which it participates can influence the venture's economies of scale, economies of scope, and efficiency of transaction costs. This relationship may also affect the IJV's ability to develop the market and products in the host country because product relatedness between the local firm and the venture implies the extent to which the joint venture can utilize the existing distribution channels, product image, industrial experience, and production facilities already established by the local partner. Although a Chinese partner can help the IJV better its relationship with the government, gain access to scarce production factors, increase administrative efficiency, and reduce financial and operational risks with either related or unrelated product diversification, there are some unique values or synergies in related diversification (vertical or horizontal). Economic rents arising from economies of scale and from a local partner's existing distribution channels, marketing skills, consumer loyalty, and production facilities are predicted to be greater in a related product linkage than in an unrelated one. In the Chinese industrial environment, competitors, buyers, suppliers, and various governmental institutions interact with each other in extremely complicated ways. The related product link between a local partner and the venture can be very helpful in building up long term stable relationships with suppliers, buyers, local government, and other entities in the IJV's value chain.

Industrial Experience

When operating in a transitional economy characterized by weak market structure, poorly specified property rights, and institutional uncertainty, an IJV seeking efficiency and growth needs an adaptive orientation, a solid supply relationship, comprehensive buyer networks, and a good organizational image. The local partner's market experience and accumulated industrial knowledge are of great value for the realization of these goals. A local partner's established history and strong background in the industry often result in a good reputation or high credibility in the market. Lengthy industrial/market experience signifies that the local firm has built an extensive marketing and distribution network, a badly needed competence for IJV market growth in China. In addition, since China has a stronger relationship-oriented culture compared to industrialized market economies, the business activities of IJVs in China can be greatly facilitated by local partners' connections in the domestic business scene and good relations with influential persons. Local firms with longer market experience are expected to have developed a better business relationship network. Goodwill and superior contacts constitute country-specific knowledge or what the resource-based view calls the 'resource position barrier' (Wernerfelt, 1984) which enhances an IJV's competitive advantage, economic efficiency, and risk reduction capability.

Strategic Orientation

Strategic orientation (i.e., prospector, analyzer, defender, or reactor) of local firms is important to venture success because the degree of match in strategic orientation influences inter-partner consistency in terms of strategic goals, cooperative culture, investment commitment, and strategic behavior. These in turn affect the formulation and implementation of technological, operational, financial, and managerial strategies or policies at various levels including corporate, business, functional, and international. As strategic orientation determines organizational adaptability and innovativeness, it may affect not only the strategic behavior of local firms in the above domains, but also organizational behavior such as managerial philosophy, futurity, and style, which may in turn influence mutual trust and collaboration between parties.

In order to reap benefits from the market demand, a defensive orientation may be too conservative for firms seeking market expansion in

China. However, it is also not realistic to orient Chinese firms in a highly proactive direction because this orientation could lead to vast operational and contextual risks and enormous innovative and adaptive costs in a complex, dynamic and hostile environment. An analyzer orientation fits the environmental traits in a transitional context where environmental sectors are fundamentally complex and dynamic, information is not codified, and regulations are not explicit. Under this orientation, the partner candidate should be innovative and adaptive but not extremely aggressive and risk-taking when the market changes. They should allocate most of their resources to a set of reasonably stable environments while at the same time conducting somewhat routinized scanning activities in a limited product-market area. They monitor market situations in the host country, and carefully apply product and market innovations previously developed. This analyzer strategy reduces the likelihood of outright failure and creates upper limits to success. In general, Chinese firms with the analyzer orientation are ideal candidate partners for foreign companies pursuing both profitability and stability. This was empirically supported by Tan and Litschert (1994).

Corporate Image

A superior corporate image usually implies a superior product brand, customer loyalty, or organizational reputation. Corporate image may be unusually critical in China because Chinese consumers are particularly loyal to the products made by the companies maintaining superior image in the market. For instance, when purchasing various household appliances, Chinese people tend to attach more importance to corporate image than to the physical attributes of the products. In deciding whether to buy a joint venture's products, they are used to evaluating not only the reputation of the joint venture itself but also the goodwill of Chinese partners in the past. Therefore, it is essential for foreign investors to collaborate with those Chinese businesses that have maintained a good organizational reputation and product image, as perceived by most Chinese consumers. This selection will significantly benefit the market power and competitive position of the joint venture in the relevant industry.

A superior company image in China also implies better relationships with the local government, as well as suppliers and distributors. These relationships are crucial for firms pursuing a market share and competitive position in the industry. Recently, the State Council of PRC has decided to form business groups as part of the reform focus for the next five years. It is deemed that a firm with a superior corporate image will be more likely to be the leading or core unit in the group. Such business groups, which will soon become new market-driven oligopolists in related industries, will become the ideal local partners for MNCs in the future.

6.3 Organizational Attributes of Local Partners in China

Organizational Form

Economic transition has given birth to a new diversity of organizational forms. The spectrum spans the continuum from state-owned to non-state-owned (private and collective) businesses. A local partner's organizational form influences not only its motivation behind the formation of an IJV but also its commitment and contribution to the operation of the IJV, which in turn affects the IJV's local performance. During structural reforms in the Chinese economy characterized by weak market structure, poorly specified property rights, and strong governmental interference, state-owned firms have the advantage in gaining access to scarce resources, materials, capital, information, and investment infrastructure. In addition, state-owned organizations usually have an advantage over privately or collectively-owned firms in terms of industry experience, market power, and production and innovation facilities. Moreover, it is fairly common for state-owned enterprises to have privileged access to state-instituted distribution channels. These channels play a dominant role in product distribution in the Chinese market. State-owned businesses are also treated preferentially by the government in selecting market segments. This organizational form may hence facilitate the market growth in new domains. Finally, given that they are state-owned, hierarchical state firms tend to have a better relationship with various governmental institutions. This relationship is expected to result in greater problem-solving capacity for these firms. For all these reasons, state-owned organizations are likely to contribute more to an IJV's local market expansion than non-state-owned organizations.

Private or collective enterprises are typically operated and managed by entrepreneurs. They have fewer principle-agent conflicts and greater strategic flexibility. The existence of many unfulfilled product and market niches in the Chinese economy increases their chance for survival and growth. Their simple structure and small size have positioned them for speed and surprise, giving them a greater ability to react quickly to opportunities in the environment and proactively outmaneuver more established firms. In addition, private and collective businesses are pressed by 'a hard budget', forcing them to be more efficient and profit-oriented. In contrast, state firms lack self-motivation and operational autonomy, while being highly vulnerable to bureaucratic 'red tape'. It is reported that over sixty percent of state-owned enterprises in China have shown a loss whereas private or collective businesses have been showing continuous profit (Jefferson, Rawski and Zheng, 1992). IJVs with efficiency-oriented private or collective partners are thus likely to enjoy a superior return on investment. This proposition has been supported by a recent analysis of China's top 100,000 companies which finds that firms with defined property rights (collective or private firms) are more productive and profitable than state-owned enterprises (Li, Gao and Ma, 1995).

Organizational Size

A local partner's ability to contribute to its IJV's survival and growth is positively associated with its organizational size (Luo, 1997a). Organizational size with respect to the number of employees or total assets makes an important contribution to economies of scale, market power, process innovation, and organizational image. It also influences an IJV's ability to overcome entry barriers stemming from minimum efficiency scale, a factor which is critical to IJV profitability and market growth. Organizational size may also affect the degree of organizational fit between two partners, which in turn impacts the magnitude of the synergistic effect (financial and operational) for the IJV. Moreover, greater organizational size implies higher capability to reduce risks and mitigate uncertainty. Organizational size in a given Chinese firm is positively linked with its bargaining power in the course of negotiations with local authorities (Luo, 1996), which may also be conducive to risk reduction. Furthermore, a larger local partner can lower the cost of financing and lead to better access to the capital markets for the joint venture.

International Experience

A local partner's previous foreign experience is critical to the success of intercultural and cross-border ventures. Foreign experience affects the organizational fit between partners in the early stages of the joint venture and the changes of fit as the venture evolves over time. Because the business atmosphere and commercial practices in emerging economies such as China are quite different from those in developed countries, mistrust and opportunism have often taken place in the course of IJV operations. A local firm's foreign experience, through import and export business or cooperative projects with other foreign investors, proves to be a very desirable attribute since this experience represents superior knowledge, skills, and values regarding modern management methods. Contact with foreign companies and business people can sharpen sensitivity toward competitiveness in the international market. A long history of business dealings with foreign markets can increase receptivity toward maintaining quality standards, customer responsiveness, and product innovation. As foreign experience is accompanied by exposure to foreign (Western) values, it also increases a local firm's ability to effectively communicate with its foreign partner. This acquired knowledge stimulates the trust and collaboration between partners. As a consequence, a local partner having international experience is likely to contribute more to the IJV's financial return, risk reduction, and sales growth in the domestic as well as export markets.

Organizational Collaboration

As the length of the interaction between partners increases, the economic transactions become increasingly embedded within the social relations of the two partners, which in turn deters opportunism. Previous contact between partners leads to the development of specialized skills and routines adapted to the exchange. These include specific knowledge about the structure and operation of the partner organization, and increased abilities amongst the personnel within each of the partner firms. Such skills and routines constitute an investment in specific assets adapted to the interpartner cooperation; the investment is at risk if cooperation breaks down. Hamel, Doz and Prahalad (1989) assert that the operation and management of IJVs involve daily interactions which can be greatly facilitated if the partners have correctly assessed each other's strengths and weaknesses. Past and existing long-term relationships between partners, based on previous import/export, investment, or even on private interactions, can therefore prove to be a fine asset to economic efficiency and export growth (Luo, 1996). Such relations also foster a climate of openness which is essential for discussing behavioral problems that may be a barrier to learning. This type of background is especially important in newly emerging economies where a relationship-oriented culture is more prevalent than a task and job-oriented culture. It is hence expected that the length of past collaboration between partners has a favorable effect on risk reduction.

Organizational Leadership

Leadership in Chinese state-owned businesses is a fairly complicated issue because top-level management positions are assigned by the upper level government authorities. Moreover, the communist party representatives in the firm, normally remaining out of sight, are politically the real bosses of the firm. On the other hand, leadership is fundamental to venture success in China. The relationships with leader often outweigh the contractual terms and clauses precedingly agreed upon by both parties to an IJV, because law enforcement in China has been weak for many decades as a result of the tradition, the public's poor concept of law, and habitual working practices. The leadership of the Chinese partner also critically influences the cooperative culture between the two partners, which in turn affects their mutual trust. In addition, the partner's relationships with various governmental authorities are largely determined by the interpersonal relationship between its management and in-power governmental officials. These personal connections, or guanxi, can be the most important factor for a joint venture's competitive edge, especially if the venture has to rely upon the government in acquiring approvals, materials, capital, and other resources or in securing various kinds of support and assistance such as dispute resolution, infrastructure access, distribution arrangements, and taxation holidays or allowances. As a result of continuous industrial decentralization and economic reforms, which further increase the autonomy and authority of corporate-level managers, the effect of a Chinese partner's leadership appears to be even more fundamental to the joint venture operation today. To evaluate the leadership of Chinese businesses, foreign investors should scrutinize such areas as educational background, relationship with governmental authorities, innovativeness, international experience, managerial skills, length of previous leadership, and foreign language skills.

Organizational Rank

Organizational rank includes both business level and class in China. Chinese organizations, including state-owned and collectively-owned enterprises, are generally ranked by their upper level governments into the following levels: national, provincial, city, county, and so on. At each level, especially the national and provincial levels, firms may be further classified into different classes. For instance, the Panda Electronics Group in Nanjing, Jiangsu Province, is a national-level first-class company, while the Nanton Bicycle Factory in Nanton, Jiangsu Province is a provincial-level first-class business. In general, different levels of firms imply various kinds of autonomy and authority offered by the government. The higher the organizational level, the greater the power delegated to the firm and the greater the support it attains from the government. However, these are often achieved at the expense of more governmental interference. For foreign partners, the solution to this trade-off largely depends upon their strategic goals and organizational capabilities in the strategy-environment alignment in the host country. Unlike organizational level, business rank by class is more associated with the efficiency and effectiveness of the company. The higher class firms generally present superior product quality, better internal management, quicker customer responsiveness, and superior organizational performance. Thus, foreign companies seeking high financial and market outcomes in China should examine closely the organizational level and class of potential Chinese partners.

6.4 Financial Attributes of Local Partners in China

Profitability

A local partner's profitability will directly influence its ability to make a capital contribution, fulfill financial commitments, and disperse financial resources to the joint venture. These in turn affect the joint venture's profit margin, net cash inflow, and wealth accumulation. The profitability attribute will also indirectly influence the joint venture's capital structure, financing costs, and leverage. As in developed countries, less profitable firms usually have to pay higher interest rates or on shorter terms to attain bank loans in China. In recent years, a sustained tight monetary policy, reflected in increased interest rates and reduced bank lending and money supply (a situation of 'credit crunch') has resulted in liquidity problems for many Chinese businesses, particularly those heavily relying on bank loans. Moreover, in a recent step, the Chinese government is separating bank functions from policy directing. This measure led banks to more strictly control loans to less efficient, less profitable firms. As a large proportion of capital contribution by Chinese partners to joint ventures comes from bank loans, this new measure substantially confines the capacity of Chinese partners to meet their financial commitments.

Viewed from the operational perspective, a less profitable business often implies organizational weaknesses in the technological, operational, and managerial spheres. To Chinese consumers, a non-profitable business normally means poor product quality, poor management, and/or slow customer responsiveness. If this poorly performing business is a state-owned enterprise, reasons may extend to a 'class struggle' within management, organizational rigidity, and/or conservative leadership. If the poorly performing business is a collectively-owned or privately-owned enterprise, the underlying factors may also include weak competitive advantage, little market power, underdeveloped distribution channels, and/or lack of guanxi with the business community or governmental authorities. In sum, lack of profitability of local partners can be symbolic of internal weaknesses in financial, technological, operational, organizational, and managerial arenas. Foreign investors should be wary when scrutinizing a possible local partner's ability to make profits. The indicators for this ability include gross profit margin, net profit margin, return on assets, and return on equity, among others. Table 6.1 lists all the profitability ratios widely used in China.

Liquidity

A local partner's liquidity is critical to the IJV operations because it directly affects the venture's ability to pay off short term financial obligations. In the international business literature, it is commonly understood that foreign investors attain financial synergies from the optimization of operational cash flows. Foreign venturing can reduce the default risk and uncertainty of operational cash flow; this reduction depends on the correlation of the pre-cooperation cash flow of the two firms. As a result of greater size, the joint venture will have better access to capital markets and lower financing costs, other things being equal. Given the partial segmentation of national economies and markets, this benefit is even greater for IJVs than for domestic joint ventures. Ideally, in an attempt to achieve the maximum financial and operational synergies, two partners should be complementary not only in capital structure but also between one's financial strengths and the other's competitive strengths.

Table 6.1 Major Indicators of Financial Attributes

Indicators	Definition
1. Profitability	
a. Gross profit margin	Total margin available to cover operating
(sales - cost of goods sold)/sales	expenses and yield a profit
b. Net profit margin	Return on sales
Profit after taxes/sales	
c. Return on assets	Return on total investment from
Net return/total assets	both stockholders and creditors
d. Return on equity	Rate of return on stockholders'
Profits after taxes/total equity	investment in the firm
2. Liquidity	
a. Current ratio	The extent to which the claims of short-
Current assets/current liabilities	term creditors are covered by ST assets
b. Quick ratio	The firm's ability to pay off ST debts
(current asset-inventory)/current liab.	without having to sell its inventory
c. Inventory to net working capital	The extent to which the firm's
Inventory/(current assets-current liab.)	working capital is tied up in inventory
3. Leverage	
a. Debt-to-assets ratio	The extent to which funds are used
Total debt/total assets	to finance the firm's operations
b. Debt-to-equity ratio	Ratio of funds from creditors to
Total debt/total equity	funds from stockholders
c. Long term debt-to-equity ratio	The balance between debt and equity
Long-term debt/total equity	
4. Activity	
a. Inventory turnover	The amount of inventory used by
Costs of goods sold/inventory	the firm to generate its sales
b. Fixed-asset turnover	Sales productivity and plant utilization
Sales/fixed assets	
c. Average collection period	The average length of time required
Accounts receivable/average daily sales	to receive payment
d. Total asset turnover	Total assets productivity and efficiency
Total sales/total assets	

Liquidity is extremely low in most Chinese firms, particularly state-owned enterprises. Many firms have a current ratio even lower than 1. In harsh contrast to the equity status in Western businesses, the initially contributed capital and accumulated retained earnings, so called 'retained funds' in China, account only for a very small percentage of the capital resources needed for operations. Consequently, most Chinese firms have to depend heavily on short and long term loans. This is the major reason why Chinese firms are so vulnerable to changes in governmental monetary policy and the 'credit crunch'. International investors should realize that the poor liquidity of Chinese firms and the tight monetary policy will be sustained for a long time during the economic transition. This is inevitable because the pressure of high inflation and necessity to maintain social stability during a time of economic boom and transformation leave no option but a more tightly controlled monetary supply and vigorously confined capital reinvestment for state-owned businesses. Foreign partners seeking cost and risk sharing or pursuing the reduction of operational cash flow uncertainties should be particularly cautious to ensure that they have a thorough grasp of their Chinese partners' liquidity.

Leverage

As a consequence of the fundamental lack of equity necessary for many business activities, the leverage level of most Chinese firms is markedly low. This is reflected in the high level of various leverage ratios such as debt-to-assets ratio, debt-to-equity-ratio, or long term debt-to-equity ratio (see Table 6.1). It is well known today that many Chinese firms are encountering a 'triangular debt' problem, whereby the firms owe large sums of money to each other but have no cash with which to settle their accounts. Accounts receivables open more than 180 days are very common, often representing a substantial part of a Chinese company's liquid resources. Apart from the aforementioned 'credit crunch', this situation can be attributed to cultural factors as well. Preferential terms of payment, particularly temporal extension of payment deadlines, are widely used in China as a primary marketing tool. In a country where guanxi is painstakingly nurtured and the maintenance of harmony is of paramount importance, sellers will do their utmost to avoid embarrassing customers who may be temporarily unable to pay.

In selecting local partners in China, foreign investors should choose those who are less vulnerable to the 'triangular debt' and have a strong leverage position. This superior position often implies that the firms (i) are more conscientious about credit screening and investigations, and thus have maintained a network of customers/buyers with a superior leverage position; (ii) have better asset management or superior organizational skills. It is essential for the firms in China to establish clear-cut working policies, both internal and external, that will promote the best cash turnover possible and maximize benefits from the economics of accounts receivable. Because these issues significantly influence growth and survival in the Chinese market, foreign investors should attach utmost importance to the leverage level of local firms during the selection process.

Asset Efficiency

Asset efficiency of a local partner is critical to the efficiency and effectiveness of the joint venture because it is a mid-range construct for maximizing return on investment. The net gains from resource contributions depend in large part on the management of assets, especially inventory, accounts receivable, and fixed assets. A partnership with a local firm which manages total assets skillfully and efficiently is surely beneficial to the foreign investor pursuing either short term profitability or a long term competitive position in the market.

Asset efficiency has become particularly important for the evaluation of Chinese business performance in recent years. Prior to the economic reform, a firm's economic incentives to enhance asset efficiency were rather low because of blurred intellectual property rights and a rigid central planning system. Today, however, firms have much higher autonomy in allocating and utilizing various assets. Thus, the level of asset management mirrors the degree of advancement of managerial skills and the extent of effectiveness of corporate administration. Although a large local firm helps the joint venture increase the economy of scale and gain better access to capital markets or commercial loans, the net size effect on the firm's financial and market performance virtually relies on asset turnover. Foreign investors should research and analyze a local partner's asset efficiency indicators such as inventory turnover, fixed-assets turnover, accounts receivable turnover, and total assets turnover (Table 6.1). Additional insights may be obtained by comparing these indicators longitudinally to see how much improvement the local partner has accomplished over time, and by comparing the indicators with those of other local firms in the industry to see to what extent the partner outperforms its major competitors.

6.5 Empirical Evidence

My recent studies (1996; 1997a; 1997b; 1997c) on partner selection have examined various strategic and organizational attributes of Chinese partners in relation to IJV performance in China. The key results can be summarized as follows:

First, product relatedness and market position are critical strategic traits affecting all the major dimensions of IJV performance. Related product linkage between local partners and IJVs outperforms unrelated diversification in terms of both financial return and sales growth. The local partner's superior market position is an essential determinant for IJV success in accomplishing economic efficiency, risk diversification, and market growth.

Second, the strategic fit between partners depends not only upon the resource complementarity they actually contribute, but also on the absorptive capabilities of both partners. A local partner's high capacity to absorb and assimilate its counterpart's tacit knowledge will lead to better overall performance in general and better ROI and local sales in particular for the IJV.

Third, a local partner's organizational experience is of utmost importance in facilitating strategic or organizational fit between partners and hence contributing to the IJV's efficiency and effectiveness. A local firm's industrial and foreign experiences are found to have a favorable influence on risk reduction, market development, and accounting return for the IJV.

Fourth, greater length of inter-partner collaboration in the past leads to superior overall performance and, in particular, to risk reduction, export sales, and profitability. This collaboration spurs fruitful interfirm trust and mutual forbearance, in turn resulting in a better operational outcome and stabilization of venture activities in a dynamic, complex environment.

Finally, organizational form and size are not found to be significant for overall IJV performance. Nevertheless, hierarchical state enterprises can assist IJVs greatly in enhancing market power and facilitating market development. Organizational size in terms of the number of employees positively influences an IJV's local sales.

In sum, the above findings suggest that partner selection criteria are important not only for the overall performance of international expansion by foreign businesses (multivariate effect), but also for several aspects of IJV performance taken separately, such as financial return, local market expansion, export growth, and risk reduction (univariate effect). The results indicate enormous differences in the effects that different criteria have on an IJV's overall and unidimensional performance. Each selection criterion differently affects individual dimensions of IJV performance. Cooperation-related criteria, or organizational traits, such as past collaboration and foreign experience, are found to be important to the IJV's overall performance and have a positive effect on uncertainty reduction and profitability. Operation-related criteria, or strategic traits, such as absorptive capacity, product relatedness, and market power, are found to be more important to an IJV's sales growth and financial return. Some country-specific criteria such as organizational form are also linked with some aspects of IJV performance.

6.6 Implications for International Executives

Based on the aforementioned empirical evidence, MNCs will be able to determine which criteria they should use in choosing local partners and which criteria are vital to their goal accomplishment. For example, those investors seeking local market expansion should select local partners that have rich industrial experience, a superior market position, high absorptive capacity, and/or related product diversification. Those seeking profitability and stability should select local firms which have superior foreign experience, longer past inter-partner collaboration, and/or greater market power. From the standpoint of MNCs, the critical partner-selection criteria can ensure partner-traits that are favorable for the achievements of their strategic goals. The host government or local partners, on the other hand, can try to make these traits available to attract more stable and profitable foreign direct investment.

Doing business in China is not easy. It is both a science and an art. Each deal is unique and has its own difficulties, with different investment structuring and business and legal considerations. To complicate matters further, Chinese government policies, the business environment, and laws and regulations are constantly changing. Nevertheless, some considerations always require special attention; one of these is finding the right partner.

After many years of reform, there are a lot of enterprises in China that do not belong to the government and are operating on their own. These enterprises may be good candidates, as they can have stronger incentives to make the joint venture work than would state-owned enterprises. On the other hand, they may not have as much government support, which may or may not be important to a particular foreign business. A related issue here is whether you need an active partner or a somewhat passive one in terms of management. This will depend on, among other things, the foreign investor's familiarity with China and how much of its technology or intellectual property rights the firm wants to disclose or prefers to keep within the organization.

Before travelling to China, obtaining as much information as possible about the potential partner is well advised. Get a copy of its business license, which will tell you about its legal capacity to contract with a foreign investor, its registered capital, its business scope, and the name of the legal representative who is legally authorized to sign any joint venture contract. It is also necessary to obtain a copy of the company's brochure and find out about the industry and the candidate's competitors (this can be another good source for potential partners). It the candidate received any award from the upper level government authorities, the foreign investor should get a copy. Such an award may include the Chinese party's ranking in terms of size, production, quality, reputation, or economic efficiency as recognized by the industry in a particular province or in the nation.

Site visit is imperative. Social activities, which almost invariably will be pressed on investors during the visit, should be better left until the deal is signed, sealed, and delivered. Politely rejecting such offers will not, as many Westerners mistakenly believe, hurt the relationship or cause your potential partner to lose face. It might even earn you respect for taking your business seriously. Diligent work is more, not less, important for IJVs in China than for those in other countries. Reliable information can often be obtained only from such a visit. During the site visit, investors should try to observe employee attitudes and talk to management, from the lowest to the highest ranks. Don't shy away from asking questions about the operation, employees, finance, technologies, cash flow, and other relevant matters.

It is always important to check whether or not your Chinese partners share your investment objectives, or at least be able to reconcile his objectives to yours. If your partner puts his own interests, benefits, and political advancement above those of the joint venture's, or if his management style differs substantially or completely from yours, or if he wishes to base the venture's potential success on his political clout, you have cause for concern.

It is often said that the key element for success for IJVs in China is the Chinese partner's *guanxi*. This is not true. Guanxi is not a substitute for basic organizational fundamentals such as the various strategic and organizational attributes examined in my study. Guanxi won't make customers buy the IJV's products; it cannot make the quality of those products acceptable to overseas buyers; it cannot increase the productivity of workers. If guanxi is improperly used to obtain approvals or resources, and if the impropriety is discovered, there may be negative repercussions resulting in revocation of the approvals and a taint on the foreign investor's reputation which will affect his future investment opportunities. All in all, do not place undue reliance on guanxi and particularly beware of someone who claims nothing but guanxi in China.

In recent years, a number of common pitfalls in locating a suitable Chinese partner have become apparent. One is that some potential candidates are in serious financial trouble; they perceive joining forces with a foreign partner as a way to rejuvenate their dying organization. William Mallet of Tianjin Otis Elevator, China, advises that, "foreign investors should not try to resurrect worthless organizations. They should link with ones that were strong financially, because that will provide a solid investment foundation" (Goldenberg, 1988).

Another problem lies in differences of priorities. In general, foreign partners are interested in market access, cheap labor, and lax rules on pollution control; the Chinese side is interested in capital and technology as well as promoting their exports. When these priorities are at odds, coordination between the joint venture partners becomes very poor. As the Chinese phrase goes, they are "sleeping in the same bed but having different dreams". Beijing Jeep typified one of these clashes over priorities between foreign and Chinese partners. With a strong interest in absorbing technology, the Chinese felt that AMC had reneged on the terms of their contract, which called for joint design and production of a new Jeep, when exhaust system, noise controls, and speed failed to meet international standards.

Nevertheless, there are many success stories of MNCs finding suitable Chinese partners. A good Chinese partner can be very helpful in a number of ways. They can significantly cut the cost of production, help break entry barriers to the targeted market, and even enhance the technology of the parent company. The operations of the McDonnell Douglas cooperative venture and the Johnson & Johnson venture in Shanghai are two notable examples of success. In both cases, the Chinese partners played a key role in promoting their products in the Chinese market.

6.7 Sources for Identifying Chinese Partners

Different sources are available to help identify potential Chinese partners; foreign companies should explore as many avenues as possible before making a decision.

First, home-country foreign embassies and consulate offices, which are located in many major Chinese cities, are a good source. From time to time, they publish project lists that contain useful information, such as the type of industry, nature and location of the project, investment amount, partners involved in the project, and the status of the financing. Foreign firms in China should visit the foreign commercial officers at their embassies to find out more about the country or region and about the investment potential in particular industries. These offices also publish articles and reports relevant to various businesses and industries.

Second, information on potential partners can also be obtained from various Chinese government departments such as the Ministry of Foreign Trade and Economic Cooperation (MOFTEC) and its provincial and municipal offices. The State Planning Commission at different localities also distributes lists of potential projects and partners. Foreign investors need to keep in mind that these government departments, in playing the role of introducer, usually have objectives and motivations of their own, different from the foreign company's. Their main objective is to bring investments into certain factories that need capital investment or technology. They are not there to find your firm the best possible partner. However, some of the information they provide can be useful. This is also true of the different international trust and investment companies (ITICs), which are established in almost all provinces in China, and of some Chinese engineering consulting companies.

Third, Chinese management consulting companies and investment advisors in Hong Kong and many major cities in the Unites States and other countries can also source projects and potential partners. Some consulting companies are better than others, and some are more experienced and knowledgeable in a particular industry than others. These companies usually charge commissions or consulting fees for assisting with the establishment of a joint venture. Foreign firms interested in using these companies should ask about their track record, experience, fee arrangement, and other relevant information.

Fourth, established business contacts in China, such as distributors, importers, or buyers, may be suitable partners or be able to introduce you to another local company. In fact, many foreign companies often enter joint ventures with those Chinese firms with which they have already collaborated in the past in other businesses such as import and export, counter-purchase, offset, compensation trade, and the like. Amongst the numerous local businesses they may have previously cooperated with, a foreign investor can choose a local company which is the best for the accomplishment of their investment objectives. This evolutionary approach is advisable for most foreign investors because it is likely to minimize financial and operational risks, reduce transactional and inter-partner learning costs, and mitigate inter-partner misfit and opportunism.

Lastly, foreign companies may contact Chinese import and export corporations, trade delegations from China, and their friends and business contacts in their own country who have experience in China. Foreign investors can also identify possible local partners in various Chinese foreign trade and investment fairs, exhibitions, trade talks, and news conferences held in China or elsewhere.

6.8 Conclusion

To conclude, it is essential to venture success in China that the potential partner possess complementary skills and resources, and share compatible goals and a cooperative culture. Using reliable sources of information, foreign companies should examine the following attributes of a local partner candidate:

(i) *Strategic traits*, including absorptive capacity, product relatedness, market power, industrial experience, strategic orientation, and corporate image;

(ii) *Organizational traits*, including organizational form, organizational size, organizational leadership, previous collaboration, international experience, and organizational rank;

(iii) *Financial traits*, including profitability, liquidity, leverage, and asset efficiency.

The foreign company should ask the following crucial questions:

(1) Can the Chinese partner successfully absorb and assimilate transferred or contributed foreign technology?

(2) Does the venture product lie at the core business of the local partner?

(3) What is the competitive position of the Chinese partners in the industry? Is this position dynamically sustainable? Does the Chinese side have the political and economic clout necessary to maintain a dominant position in its field?

(4) How strong are the Chinese partner's industrial experience and reputation? How strong are its marketing, distribution, and promotional strengths? How good are its business relationships and guanxi with suppliers, buyers, distributors, and other entities in the value chain?

(5) What is the strategic orientation of the partner? Is it reasonably innovative, proactive, and adaptive?

(6) Is the customer loyalty to the Chinese partner's products or services high? What is the image level of the company, brand, and product in the market?

(7) What kind of ownership does the Chinese partner have? Is it state-owned, collectively-owned, or privately-owned?

(8) Does the Chinese partner receive strong backing from its overseeing governmental agency, which will have a stake in the prospective joint venture project? How strong is its relationships with other governmental authorities such as taxation bureau, state bank, foreign exchange administration bureau, industrial and commercial administration bureau, local commission of foreign economic relations and trade, industrial department, and local economic or planning commission, among others?

(9) How much authority does the partner have in obtaining essential suppliers, raw materials, and infrastructure support? What is the level or rank of the firm? Is it one of the nation's first-class enterprises?

(10) How big is the partner's firm size in terms of number of employees and asset size? How productive are its employees and assets?

(11) Is the partner's leadership professionally competent and devoted? Does the top management get along well with the Communist party representative(s)? Does top management have international experience?

(12) How good has previous collaboration between the two parties been? If not so good, what is the major reason? Are the two parties culturally cooperative?

(13) Does the Chinese side have the autonomy to independently deal with international trading and investment with foreign companies? How long has the partner had experience dealing with foreign businesses?

(14) What is the financial situation of the Chinese partner? What is the previous level of profitability, liquidity, leverage, and asset efficiency? Do you believe that the partner will not only be profitable but also stable in the

long run? Is the partner able to overcome its financial weaknesses and maintain its financial strengths over time, along key financial ratios?

Bibliography and Further Readings

Barney, J. B. and Hansen, M.H. (1994). 'Trustworthiness as a Source of Competitive advantage'. *Strategic Management Journal*, vol.15 (Winter Special Issue), pp. 175-190.

Beamish, P. W. (1987). 'Joint Ventures in LDCs: Partner Selection and Performance'. *Management International Review*, vol.27, pp. 23-37.

Buckley, P. J. and Casson, M.C. (1988). 'The Theory of Cooperation in International Business'. In F. Contractor and P. Lorange (eds.), *Cooperative Strategies in International Business*, 31-34, Lexington, Mass.: Lexington Books.

Contractor, F. and Lorange, P. (1988). 'Why Should Firms Cooperate? Strategy and Economic Basis for Cooperative Ventures'. In F. Contractor and P. Lorange (eds.), *Cooperative Strategies in International Business*, 31-34, Lexington, Mass.: Lexington Books.

Geringer, J. M. (1991). 'Strategic Determinants of Partner Selection Criteria in International Joint Ventures'. *Journal of International Business Studies*, First quarter 1991, pp. 41-62.

Goldenberg, S. (1988). *Hands Across the Ocean: Managing Joint Ventures*. Boston: Harvard Business School Press.

Hamel, G. (1991). 'Competition for Competence and Inter-Partner Learning Within International Strategic Alliances'. *Strategic Management Journal*, vol.12 (Special issue), pp. 83-104.

Hamel, G., Doz, Y. L. and Prahalad, C.K. (1989). 'Collaborate With Your Competitors- And Win'. *Harvard Business Review*, vol.67, pp. 133-139.

Harrigan, K. R. (1985). *Strategies for Joint Ventures Success*. Lexington, MA: Lexington Books.

Jefferson, G.H., Rawski, T.G. and Zheng, Y. (1992). 'Growth, Efficiency, and Convergence in China's State and Collective Industry'. *Economic Development and Cultural Change*, vol.40, pp. 239-266.

Kogut, B. (1988). 'Joint Ventures: Theoretical and Empirical Perspectives'. *Strategic Management Journal*, vol.9, pp. 319-332.

Kumar, B. N. (1995). 'Partner-Selection-Criteria and Success of Technology Transfer: A Model Based on Learning Theory Applied to the Case of Indo-German Technical Collaborations'. *Management International Review*, vol.35 (special issue), pp. 65-78.

Li, S., Gao, Y. and Ma, G. (1995). 'Picking the Winners in Profitability and Productivity'. *China Business Review*, July-August, pp. 31-33.

Luo, Y. (1996). 'Partner Selection and International Joint Venture Performance: Chinese Evidence'. *Academy of Management Best Papers Proceedings*, 1996, pp. 161-165.

Luo, Y. (1997a). 'Partner Selection and Venturing Success'. *Organization Science*, vol.8, pp. 493-509.

Luo, Y. (1997b). 'Performance Effects of Local Partner Attributes: An Empirical Analysis of Strategic Alliances in an Emerging Economy'. *Journal of International Management*, vol. 2, pp. 293-316.

Luo, Y. (1997c). 'Partner Selection and Venturing Success: Additional Thoughts and Implications'. *Organization Science Electronic Letters* (in press).

Morris, D. and Hergert, M. (1987). 'Trends in International Cooperative Agreements'. *Columbia Journal of World Business*, vol. 22(2), pp. 15-21.

Parkhe, A. (1991). 'Interfirm Diversity, Organizational Learning, and Longevity in Global Strategic Alliances'. *Journal of International Business Studies*, vol.22, pp. 579-601.

Porter, M. E. (1986). *Competition in Global Industries*. Boston, Mass.: Harvard Business School Press.

Tallman, S. and Shenkar, O. (1994). 'A Managerial Decision Model of International Cooperative Venture Formation'. *Journal of International Business Studies*, vol.25, pp. 91-114.

Tan, J. and Litschert, R. (1994). 'Environment-Strategy Relationship and Its Performance Implications: An Empirical Study of the Chinese Electronics Industry', *Strategic Management Journal*, vol. 15, pp. 1-20.

Wernerfelt, B. (1984). 'A Resource-Based View of the Firm'. *Strategic Management Journal*, vol. 5, pp. 171-180.

Yan, A. and B. Gray (1994). 'Bargaining Power, Management Control, and Performance in United States-China Joint Ventures: A Comparative Case Study'. *Academy of Management Journal*, vol. 37, pp. 1478-1517.

Zeira, Y. and Shenkar, O. (1990). 'Interactive and Specific Parent Characteristics: Implications for Management and Human Resources in International Joint Ventures'. *Management International Review*, vol. 30 (special issue), pp. 7-22.

7 Network Cultivation in China

Chapter Purpose

This chapter centers on the issue of managerial network (interorganizational guanxi) in China. Specifically, it addresses the importance of guanxi in influencing investment and operation of foreign companies in China, provides definition and principles of guanxi, and presented social roots and philosophies of guanxi. The economic rationale of guanxi and its difference from Western networking are also discussed. The relationships among organizational dynamics, managerial network, and firm performance are explored. Practical guidance to guanxi construction and cultivation is offered.

7.1 Understanding Concept and Importance of Guanxi

The Chinese word guanxi refers to the concept of drawing on connections in order to secure favors in personal relations. It is an intricate and pervasive relational network which Chinese cultivate energetically, subtly, and imaginatively. It contains implicit mutual obligation, assurance and understanding, and governs Chinese attitudes toward long-term social and business relationships. Guanxi relations are delicate fibers woven into every Chinese individual's social life, and, therefore, into many aspects of Chinese society. Its roots are deeply embedded in the Chinese culture, which has a history of more than 2000 years (Luo and Chen, 1996).

This chapter is concerned about guanxi primarily at the organizational level, that is, interorganizational guanxi, or managerial network. Relationship development or network building between organizations is critical to corporate success everywhere in the world. When a personal relationship is dedicated to and used by an organization, guanxi then works at the organizational level. Inter-organizational guanxi, or *guanxi hu* in Chinese, is first established by and continues to build upon personal relationship. If one attempts to build a good network with another organization, one must first develop fine guanxi with key managers in the organization (Luo and Chen, 1997). Since the 'iron rice bowl' was broken in China in the early 1980s, the application of guanxi at the organizational level has become increasingly pervasive and intensive (Xin and Pearce, 1996). This is because a manager will be rewarded (e.g., with a commission or bonus) or promoted by the organization if he uses his personal guanxi for organizational purposes (e.g., marketing, promotion, and sourcing). This trend has been even more evident since 1985, when the number of township and village enterprises and privately-owned businesses began growing explosively, and state-owned firms started to employ the 'contractual liability lever' in their management and reward systems. When guanxi is addressed at the organizational level, it connotes personal relationships with managers or officials of partner organization. More specifically, when interfirm guanxi is spoken of, it refers to cross-organizational connections among managers. When guanxi between businesses and government authorities is addressed, it refers to the personal relationships between firm managers and government officials.

Guanxi is one of the major dynamics in the Chinese society where business behavior revolves around guanxi. It has been pervasive in the Chinese business world for the last few centuries. It binds literally millions of Chinese firms into a social and business web. It is widely recognized that guanxi is a key business determinant of firm performance because the life blood of the macro economy and the micro business conduct in the society is guanxi network. Any business in this society, including both local firms and foreign investors and marketers, inevitably face guanxi dynamics. No company can go far unless it has extensive guanxi in this setting. In China's new, fast-paced business environment, guanxi has been more entrenched than ever, heavily influencing Chinese social behavior and business practice.

Given the fact that guanxi represents in large part the lifeblood of the Chinese business community as well as institutional context (Kao, 1993), it is important to have guanxi not only with other organizations in the business community such as suppliers, buyers, and competitors but also with various levels of political government and regulatory authorities (Luo, 1997b). In the absence of a stable legal environment, decision making by government officials often includes weighing the impact of guanxi. Personal preferences are exercised in lieu of strict legal interpretations of rules. Rather than subscribing to the abstract notion of impartial justice, the Chinese have traditionally relied on their personal contacts with government officials in order to get things done. For instance, whenever there is resource scarcity, resources are likely to be allocated by guanxi rather than bureaucratic rules.

Although, as a result of reform, the central and local governments in China have relinquished their roles in dictating firm operation and management, they still exercise control over resource distribution, investment size, industry structure, bank loans, and business formation in strategic sectors. Administrative interference often plays the bigger part in monitoring and directing the economic development than fiscal and monetary policies. This provides the bureaucrats at various levels of governments and their regulatory authorities with power to ratify projects, allocate resources and materials, arrange financing and distribution, and provide infrastructure access. From a supply perspective, a firm responds to such bureaucratic control by trying to reduce its quota in government contracts so it can trade more lucratively with other firms directly. From a production perspective, a firm wants to have many of its suppliers secured through government channels at lower costs. Managers also need to maintain good guanxi with bureaucrats as protection against the uncertainty of an environment in which the legal safeguards of a true market economy are still lacking.

7.2 Grasping Principles of *Guanxi*

A realistic understanding of guanxi principles is important, especially for foreign businesses in China. These principles are detailed below:

First, guanxi is *transferable*. If A has guanxi with B and B is a friend of C, then B can introduce A to C or vice versa. Otherwise contact between A and C is impossible. For this reason, formal business correspondence is unlikely to receive a reply until direct personal contact has been established. The success of transferability depends on how satisfactory B feels about his guanxi with A and C respectively.

Second, guanxi is *reciprocal*. A person who does not follow a rule of equity and refuses to return favor for favor will lose his face (*mianzi*) and be defined as untrustworthy. However, exchanges often favor the weaker partner. At the individual level, guanxi links two persons, often of unequal ranks, in such a way that the weaker partner can call for special favors for which he does not have to equally reciprocate.

Third, guanxi is *intangible*. It is established with overtones of unlimited exchange of favors and maintained in the long run by unspoken commitment to others in the web. People who share a guanxi relationship are committed to one another by an invisible and unwritten code of reciprocity and equity.

Disregarding this commitment can seriously damage one's social reputation, leading to a humiliating loss of prestige or face.

Fourth, guanxi is essentially *utilitarian* rather than *emotional*. Guanxi bonds two persons through the exchange of favors rather than through sentiment. This relationship does not have to involve friends, though that is preferred. Guanxi relations that are no longer profitable or based on mutual exchanges can be easily broken.

Lastly, guanxi is virtually *personal*. Guanxi between organizations is first established by and continues to build upon personal relationship; when the person leaves, the organization loses that guanxi as well. In other words, guanxi does not have to have group connotation; the relationship is personal. Although Chinese place great emphasis on rank, guanxi operates essentially on the individual level. However, guanxi utilization at the organizational level has been increasingly pervasive and intensive. This is because an employee will be rewarded by the organization if he uses his personal guanxi for organizational benefits.

Paradoxically, as unabated opening up of Chinese economy results in a tendency of the convergence of the Chinese management philosophies with the modern Western and Japanese ones, the concept of guanxi turns to be laden with even more powerful implications in recent years. A number of new terms associated with guanxi are created and immediately permeated through the society. '*La guanxi*' ('pull' guanxi) means to get on the good side of someone, to store social capital with them, and to carry no negative overtones. '*Gua guanxi*' ('work on' guanxi) means roughly the same but with a more general, less intensive feeling and usually carries negative overtones. '*Guanxi gou qiang*' (guanxi made ruined) means the relationship has gone bad. '*Li shun guanxi*' ('straight out' guanxi) means to put a guanxi back into proper or normal order, often after a period of difficulty or awkwardness. '*Guanxi wang*' ('guanxi net') means the whole network of guanxi within which favors are exchanged and circulated. Finally, '*guanxihu*' ('guanxi family') means a person, an organization, even a government department, occupying a focal point in one's specially connected guanxi network.

7.3 Comprehending Philosophies of *Guanxi*

Guanxi are delicate fibers woven into every Chinese individual's social life, and therefore, into many aspects of the Chinese society. Although the

Chinese cultivation of guanxi becomes the focus of international executives' attention only after the recent decentralization and privatization of the Chinese economy, its roots are deeply embedded in the Chinese culture with a history of more than 2000 years.

Ever since Confucius codified the societal rules, values, and hierarchical structures of authority during the sixth century B.C., the Chinese society has been functioning as clan-like networks. Such networks can be viewed as concentric circles, with close family members as the core and distant relatives, classmates, friends, and acquaintances as peripherals arranged in accordance with the distances of relationships and degrees of trusts. Purposeful investment is frequently made to maintain and extend such networks. When situation arises where one's business undertaking is beyond his individual capacity, the network of guanxi is often mobilized to influence some key persons' decision making to achieve desirable results.

As a social philosophy, Confucianism is concerned with the practical task of trying to establish a social hierarchy strong enough to harmonize a large and complex society of contentious human beings. A Confucianism's key tenet thus holds that man is fundamentally a relation-oriented being in which all relationships fall into two categories: 'predetermined' and 'voluntary.' In a predetermined relationship, behavior expectations are dictated by one's status within and responsibilities to a predetermined group, such as family. Individual desires are heavily down-played. But in many relationships that take place beyond the family, the individual plays an active role in determining the character and tone of the exchange. These are 'voluntary' relationships, in which individuals can define their own role. The individual's dual role - both as passive follower of predetermined relationships and initiator of voluntary relationships - can make the interactions of guanxi very complicated.

Chinese place great stock in the importance of face (*mianzi*). The idea of enjoying the prestige of not losing face and at the same time saving other people's face is a key component in the dynamics of guanxi. According to tradition, 'losing face' socially is comparable to the physical mutilation of one's eyes, nose, or mouth. *Mianzi* is an intangible form of social currency and personal status. Often, it is determined by social position and material wealth. One must have a certain amount of *mianzi* to cultivate and develop a viable network of guanxi connections. *Mianzi* provides the leverage one needs to successfully expand and manipulate a guanxi network.

Another related philosophy is *renqing*, i.e., unpaid obligations to the other party as a consequence of invoking the guanxi relationship. In other words, *renqing* is a form of social capital that can provide leverage during interpersonal exchanges of favors. Developing *renqing* is a precondition for the establishment of guanxi and a consequence of using it for one's advantage. When the Chinese people weave their networks of guanxi, they are also weaving a web of *renqing* obligations that must be "repaid" in the near future. In essence, *renqing* provides the moral foundation for the ideals of reciprocity and equity that are implicit in all guanxi relationships. If you disregard the rule of equity while exchanging *renqing* favors, you may lose face, hurt your friend's feelings, and jeopardize your guanxi network.

7.4 Appraising Economic Rationale of Guanxi

Guanxi connections are often more critical for firm performance than organizational affiliations or legal standards. These connections provide a balance to the cumbersome Chinese bureaucracy by giving individuals a way to circumvent rules through the activation of personal relations. The construction and maintenance of managerial network have become a form of social investment (Wall, 1990). One of the major underlying rationale behind the above peripheral behavior should be contributed to the economic legitimacy for using guanxi.

The institutional uncertainties in the Chinese society, most notably, mainland China, have been considerably high. Under these circumstances, transaction costs are bound to be fairly high accordingly. Thus, such an environment would lead firms to 'internalize' transactions to avoid turbulence. Because generic expansion and acquisitions, an alternative of internalization widely adopted from the West, often bear a high possibility of firm liquidation or spin-off that, if happens, is unacceptable by the social standard. In such case, both parties of acquisition lose 'face', which is immensely harmful for each future business in that kind of environment. As a result, the dominant logic of relying on personalized exchanges leads Chinese firms to choose a guanxi-based strategy of growth, building loosely-structured networks (i.e., *guanxihu*) to facilitate economic exchanges while avoiding the institutionally difficult tasks of ownership transfer (Luo and Chen, 1996).

At the organizational level, as a form that is neither market nor hierarchy and formal interorganization alliance, guanxi-connected business network helps overcome a firm's problem of not having enough resources to accommodate growth, while avoiding substantial bureaucratic costs in internalizing operations. In such a context, firm boundaries are blurred in that multiple network connections can be found, but direct ownership is rare. They engage in extensive networking activities based on guanxi and informal agreements through a great deal of trust building and favor exchanging. Based on these efforts, guanxi partners loosely structured networks on the basis of guanxi to coordinate activities, pool resources, and pursue joint growth (Peng and Heath, 1996).

Information market imperfection in a transitional or uncertain environment also necessitates the emergence of *guanxihu*. Information passed through *guanxihu* from reliable sources is far more trustworthy, richer, and more useful, thus saving search costs and allowing *guanxihu* partners to make more informed decisions. In addition, *guanxihu* connections can provide flexibility of resource allocation in an environment where needed factor mobility is severely constrained and administrative intervention by the government is still immense (Boisot and Child, 1988). By pooling and coordinating resources, organizational learning can occur. For instance, when a *guanxihu* partner have been exposed to Western technology through licensing or joint ventures, it may help diffuse such knowledge throughout the network. As a result, better utilization of excess resources can be accomplished, and more competitive products can be generated.

The nature and pattern of economic transformation in China also lead to the pervasion of guanxi-based business connections. This economy is characterized by undeveloped market structures, poorly specified property rights, and institutional instability which make market exchanges uncertain and costly. The economic transformation has weakened the planning regime and made the macro-economic control more decentralized. However, the necessary formal constraints of a market-based economy, namely, a well-defined property rights-based legal framework, have also been lacking at the same time. This situation has inevitably resulted in a sharp rise in opportunistic behavior, and transaction costs are bound to be high. The lack of a stable political structure and developed factor markets further compounds the volatility and unpredictability which have a strong bearing on the strategic choice of the firm for growth. Under these circumstances, state firms would seek informal constraints characterized by network-based personalized exchanges. At the same time, although with greater operation autonomy, collectively and privately owned firms have more difficulties in gaining access to scarce raw materials and other resources and achieving governmental assistance and support. Good guanxi connections therefore constitute a substitute for institutional support in this circumstance.

Although the central and local governments in the Chinese context have relinquished its dictating role in controlling firm operation and management as a result of reforms, they still exercise control over resource redistribution, investment size, industry structure, bank loans, and business formation in strategic sectors. One of three primary visible hands - the 'administrative' interference (the other two are fiscal policy and monetary policy) often plays the biggest part in monitoring and directing the economic development in recent years. This provides the bureaucrats in the central government and local authorities with power in project ratification, resource allocation, financing arrangement, raw material supply, infrastructure access arrangement, distribution and promotion assistance, and the like. All involved firms have strong incentives to cultivate guanxi with these bureaucrats. The supplier would like to reduce its quota for government contracts so it can lucratively trade with other firms directly at higher prices. The producers want to have much of their suppliers secured through government channels at lower costs. Not only for resources, managers also need to cultivate some guanxi with the bureaucrats to protect against the uncertainty of the environment in which the legal safeguards of a true market economy is lacking. Moreover, managers at recently mushroomed privately-owned and township and village enterprises as well as foreign-invested ventures have stronger incentives to do so as they have more difficulties to get the governmental preferential treatments in various aspects of operations and are more vulnerable to an uncertain environment because of the 'liabilities of newness and smallness.' This is consistent with the resource dependence model in that networks increase the external legitimacy of the firm, thus increasing its chance for survival.

7.5 Appraising the Difference Between Guanxi and Western Networking

Relationship development or networking building between organizations is critical to corporate success everywhere in the world. In recent years Western managers have increasingly seen the management of networks as an important aspect of strategic behavior and the networking paradigm as a means of understanding the totality of relationships amongst firms engaged in production, distribution, and the use of goods and services. Networking can enhance a firm's competitive advantage by providing access to the resources of other network members, and is particularly important in respect of entry into the market that involves the firm's core technologies and competencies. In addition, networking can bridge the gap between business people of different nations and cultures, hence stimulating trade that might not otherwise take place at all. Guanxi, along with its own Chinese characteristics, also includes the above western qualities. Furthermore, both concepts share some common features. In particular, they both emphasize that networks are not discrete events in time, concerning self-liquidating transactions, but are continuous relationships. That continuity requires that activities undertaken by the parties in a relationship cannot be completed without the active and reciprocal involvement of both parties.

However, as stated above, favor exchanges that take place amongst members of the guanxi network are not solely commercial, but also social, involving the exchange of *renqing* (social or humanized obligation) and the giving of *mianzi* (face in the society) or social status. This feature makes guanxi to be often named as 'social capital'. In contrast, networking in the West is the term virtually associated with commercial-based corporate-to-corporate relations. Because of this difference, many Western business people are often in danger of overemphasizing the gift-giving and wining-and-dining components of a guanxi relationship, thereby coming dangerously close to crass bribery or to being perceived as 'meat and wine friends only'. Indeed, guanxi is an investment in a relationship. It is not, however, simply a 'fee-for-service'. Guanxi is given to strengthen personal relationships, which may or may not be called upon in the future. Moreover, when assessing other organization endeavor in developing relationship with them, Western companies tend to emphasize their partner's commitment to the overall market of which they are part (market commitment), commitment to them as individual customers (customer commitment), the perceived adaptability of the partner, and the perceived distance between them. By contrast, firms that belong to a same Chinese guanxi network attach the utmost importance to one another's long term commitment to a partner firm and particularly its key managers's social status through all the possible ways, though firms in the web may actually contribute to one another unequally. Finally, guanxi is essentially personal, not corporate, relations. Whereas Western networking focuses on organizational commitment in the assessment of partner firm's effort to develop the relationship, guanxi emphasizes on personal relationship creation and development. When the personal relationship is devoted to and used by the organization for whatever purposes, guanxi then plays a role at the organizational level. If you seek to build a good network with another organization, you must first develop a fine guanxi with key managers in the organization. This difference underlies the idiosyncratic business behavior in two heterogenous settings: firms in the Chinese society build the relationship first and, if successful, transactions will follow, whereas Western businesses build transactions first and, if they are successful, a relationship will follow.

7.6 Integrating Organizational Dynamics with Guanxi

Firms with different organizational dynamics should utilize guanxi idiosyncratically because a major reason executives seek out connections and cultivate close personal relationships is to obtain resources or protection not otherwise available. Such personal connections are imperative to managers in China given the absence of the stable legal and regulatory environment that would facilitate impersonal business activities. Institutional uncertainty during economic transformation has been quite high. Under such circumstances, transaction costs are bound to be fairly high. Thus, within such an environment, firms tend to 'internalize' transactions to avoid turbulence. According to the resource dependence perspective, when operating in the same cultural environment, the degree of necessity for this internalization is dependent upon an organization's capabilities and skills. Thus, different organizational traits will lead to varying need to 'internalize' transactions. A guanxi-connected business network helps a firm overcome the problem of not having enough resources to accommodate growth, while alleviating substantial bureaucratic costs by internalizing operations and avoiding the institutionally difficult tasks of ownership transfer (Boisot and Child, 1994). Firms therefore tend to opt for a guanxi-based strategy, building loosely-structured networks to facilitate economic exchange. In such a context, firm boundaries become blurred; multiple network connections can be found, but direct ownership is rare. Firm managers engage in extensive networking activities based on guanxi and informal agreements through trust building and favor exchange.

The information uncertainty perspective argues that organizations with distinctive competencies in a dynamic context need to use distinctive strategies to align with internal arrangement and external environment. As market information is greatly distorted in China, information passed through the guanxi network from reliable sources is usually far more trustworthy, richer, and more useful. Networking saves on searching costs and allows guanxi partners to make more informed decisions. Because firms with different organizational dynamics are idiosyncratic in their ability to scan information, control information uncertainty, and benefit from changes in information, they have different levels of need and capacity to build and sustain guanxi network. If guanxi is in fact more important to those managers with a greater need to find a substitute for formal but untrustworthy information, this should be reflected in the magnitude with which these managers cultivate and utilize their network.

Guanxi connections can also provide flexibility in resource allocation in a transitional economy where production factor mobility is severely constrained and there is still an enormous amount of administrative intervention by the government. Organizations with different orientations, skills, experience, size, and the like are treated differentially by various levels of government, leading them to have different institutional advantages and disadvantages. This structural feature is sustained because they are deeply embedded in social, economic, and political systems. The resource dependence perspective argues that firms with different institutional advantages rely on external resources to varying degrees. Although the economic transition has weakened the planning regime, the Chinese economy is still characterized by undeveloped market structures, poorly specified property rights, and a weak production factor market. In this situation, the guanxi network often substitutes for government-instituted, formal channels of resource allocation and dispersal. As a consequence, a different extent of reliance on scarce resources necessitates a different degree of guanxi utilization.

Although guanxi differs from Western networking in that the former is embedded in intricate, informal personal relationships, inter-partner complementarity in strategic needs, organizational skills, and competitive strengths are still imperative to the construction and sustainability of a guanxi network. To a large extent, guanxi is utilitarian rather than emotional. Specific organizational traits affect strategic symmetries, interfirm diversity and reciprocity, and resource complementarity between network partners. In a dynamic, complex environment, a guanxi partner's organizational dynamics are expected to determine the network's mix of skills, knowledge, and resources, and its vulnerability to indigenous conditions, structures, and institutional changes. Thus, firms with different organizational dynamics will create idiosyncratic degrees of guanxi utilization, which in turn may influence organizational performance. A detailed discussion on these dynamics follows:

Strategic Orientation

A key dimension underlying organizational strategies is the relative emphasis an organization places on *market effectiveness* vs. *operational efficiency* as a basis for competition. Prospectors are organizations that value being "first-in" in new product and market areas, and respond rapidly to early signals of opening opportunities in a changing environment. Defenders compete primarily on the basis of operational efficiency, and tend to ignore environmental changes that have no direct influence on their current areas of operation. Analyzers emphasize both market effectiveness and operational efficiency. They are seldom the first to react to changing environmental conditions, but watch their competitors closely for innovation, and then rapidly co-opt those that appear to be the most promising.

Because market effectiveness-seeking organizations are market-driven, innovative, adaptive, and proactive businesses, which concentrate on identifying and capitalizing on emerging market opportunities, they place an emphasis on communicating with local markets and spanning boundaries to accommodate external dynamism and expansion needs, under the relational culture and transitional economy characterized by underdeveloped market structures, poorly specified property rights, and institutional instability. These organizations must rely enormously and proactively upon the guanxi network in dealing with various organizations in their value chains including numerous competitive forces such as suppliers, buyers, and competitors, and government authorities. From an implementation standpoint, vigorous utilization of guanxi with government agencies and competitive forces is a prerequisite for acquiring important resources necessary to implement and realize market effectiveness strategies.

In contrast, operational efficiency-seeking organizations are rigid businesses that are nonadaptive to contextual conditions. They deliberately reduce innovation and adaptive costs and risks by selecting a stable and narrowly defined product or market domain. Operational efficiency is primarily achieved through cost minimization rather than from exploiting emerging opportunities and market demands that were pent up during structural transformation. Such organizations are deemed to have a low level of interaction with environmental forces and government agencies. The operation of these organizations may successfully run without a considerable use of guanxi connections. Moreover, as the money involvement of guanxi cultivation is increasing during transition, relationship construction is becoming very costly (Xin and Pearce, 1996). This further compounds the little use of guanxi by cost-minimization oriented organizations. Therefore, organizations with a greater degree of market effectiveness may need to utilize more guanxi connections with business community and government authorities.

Organizational Size

Guanxi utilization is influenced by organizational size because small businesses need to stress the importance of their personal connections to counteract those liabilities that result from their organizations' smallness. Management researchers have long maintained that smallness presents its own liabilities to organizational survival, because small firms have managers with fewer ties with others before operation commencement. As such ties expand intensively and extensively, organizational performance will improve.

In China's transitional economy, small organizations have institutional disadvantages in both the regulatory and competitive environments. In the former context, the smaller the size of an organization, the less the institutional or regulatory support from the government. The important national resources are dispersed to those organizations that are vital to the national economy and structural economy, as perceived by the government (Rawski, 1994). As a result, small organizations often have less structural protection, regulatory assistance, and economic support from the government than big ones. In addition, small organizations usually have little bargaining power with the government, and are hence subject to more government intervention or hindrance. Under these circumstances, cultivation and utilization of personal connections with government officials appear to be significant to the survival and growth of small organizations.

In the competitive environment, guanxi connections with suppliers, buyers, and even rivals are also imperative to compensate for the liability of smallness. Because small firms are disadvantaged in economies of scale and scope, risk-taking capabilities, and financial strengths, they are not equipped with the organizational capabilities that big firms usually have. Rather, small firms have a distinctive competence in strategic and operational flexibility. In the language of option theory, this flexibility enables small organizations to employ non-market, non-hierarchical inter-firm connections to offset their institutional disadvantages in the course of competition, which in turn adds value to these firms. Thus, while the institutional disadvantages of small organizations imply the great need to use guanxi in the marketplace, their strategic and operational flexibility make them more adaptable and flexible in guanxi utilization, helping ensure their success in constructing and using guanxi. Thus, smaller organizations may need to rely more on guanxi connections with business community and government authorities.

Technological Skills

An organization's technological skills constitute a predominant element of its organizational capability. These skills are a subset of the total competencies that allow the firm to create new products and processes and respond to changing market circumstances. The resource dependence argument suggests that firms with superior capabilities rely less on external resources than those with inferior capabilities. This further suggests that the greater the technological strength, the less the necessity to build and use guanxi for competition and operation. As superior technological skills enhance the institutional bargaining power of the organization with the government in transitional economies, it is less necessary for an organization with stronger technological expertise to cultivate guanxi relationships with governmental and regulatory authorities. Instead of actively interacting with external resources, a technologically superior firm is more likely to create new technological interdependencies between business units within the firm itself. They argue that this interdependence means that such an organization will increase economic gains by leveraging its core competence within the network while preventing divulgence of its capabilities to any outside network.

On the flip side, Chinese firms with poor technological skills have to use more guanxi as a major competitive instrument for obtaining orders from buyers, deals from suppliers, and approvals from the government. When the necessary formal constraints of a market-based economy, namely, a legal framework which clearly defines property rights and a highly developed production factor market, are lacking, guanxi utilization turns to be economically logical and culturally viable for those organizations needing to offset their technological disadvantages. As such organizations are more vulnerable to market changes and environmental uncertainty, their guanxi connections with competitive forces and government agencies may help them maintain a certain degree of operational stability and risk-solving capacity. Therefore, organizations with poorer technological skills may have to construct and cultivate more guanxi connections with business community and government authorities.

Managerial Skills

Resource-based view of the firm argues that sustainable competitive advantages stem from having unique bundles of resources that competitors cannot imitate. Managerial skills are resources which may be especially important because they are often hard to imitate due to scarcity, specialization, and tacit knowledge. Unlike technological skills, managerial skills are causally ambiguous resources embedded in complex social systems, involving many social and cognitive processes not yet well understood. Managerial skills are specialized resources which are difficult to trade or imitate, and bestow competitive advantage on a firm. According to the resource dependence argument, therefore, the tacitness of advanced managerial skills mitigates the necessity to rely upon external resources, although these resources may be useful for every firm.

Because guanxi connections are a substitute for a shortage of firm-specific competitive advantages, organizations with superior managerial skills are likely to depend less on guanxi connections comparative to those with inferior managerial resources and capabilities. It has been reported that organizations lacking skillful management tend to use more guanxi-based business strategies such as sales force marketing and credit liberalization in purchasing. This is because personnel marketing is essentially a reflection of guanxi contacts. Sellers would try not to embarrass customers temporarily unable to pay in a culture where guanxi relationships are painstakingly nurtured and harmony is upheld as a high priority. At the same time, it is observed that organizations possessing advanced managerial skills are more likely to focus on guanxi-free based business strategies such as advertising, R&D, pricing, and product/service quality. Consequently, organizations with poorer managerial skills may have to utilize more guanxi connections with business community and government authorities.

Length of Operations

New organizations may face greater risks than older ones, because they lack external legitimacy and necessary ties with important nodes in the value chain. Empirical studies generally support the idea that newness is a liability for organizations and that firm performance improves as ties increase. To compensate for this liability, new organizations need to be more proactive and aggressive in their search for external resources essential to their survival and growth. Correspondingly, organizations with an established history and long industrial experience enjoy credibility in the industry and market. With experience, an organization will have built an extensive marketing and distribution network, a highly needed competence for market expansion in China. Because business transactions can be greatly facilitated by a firm's guanxi connections with government authorities and competitive forces, the firm which has been operating longer is more likely to have developed a better guanxi network. These superior contacts constitute a firm-specific capability or what the resource-based view calls 'resource position barrier' which enhances the firm's competitive advantage and risk reduction ability. Newer organizations hence struggle actively to build and cultivate guanxi connections with buyers, suppliers, and government institutions. More investment in guanxi establishment and cultivation is imperative for them if they wish to counteract their institutional liability of newness, improve their market position and competitive advantage, and ensure their survival and expansion. Hence, newer organizations may need to build more guanxi connections with business community and government authorities.

Organizational Location

In China, levels of economic development and stages of economic reform are uneven in different locations, especially comparing open vs. non-open economic regions. Cultural environment, business atmosphere, and government policies also vary across them. Open areas generally provide more Western-style business facilities and cultural atmosphere than non-open areas. Moreover, organizations in open areas tend to rely more on an arms-length approach to transactions than those in non-open regions. Because the industrial environment tends to be more competitive as a result of ongoing transition and continuous decentralization, organizations in non-open economic regions use more guanxi connections with other business people and bureaucrats to compensate for their disadvantages and strengthen their competitive position. Furthermore, organizations in non-open regions receive less preferential treatment by the central government in regards to taxation, financing, and resource supply compared to those in open regions. Such a regulatory setting presses them to rely more on guanxi connections as compensation for the constraints in their institutional environment.

Therefore, organizations located in non-open economic regions may need to cultivate more or better guanxi connections with business community and government authorities than those located in open economic regions.

7.7 Aligning Foreign Investment Decisions with Guanxi

The choice of local partner is likely to influence the degree of adaptability of foreign investment to local environment and business practices. As a result, the linkage between guanxi and FIE performance can be affected by the mode of entry. Foreign investors can opt for either the joint venture (equity or contractual) or wholly foreign-owned subsidiary as an entry mode upon entering the Chinese market. Although the wholly foreign-owned subsidiary mode has been gaining popularity in recent years, the joint venture remains the dominant mode of entry and accounts for 71.73 percent of the total value of actual FDI in 1994. In light of the preference for joint ventures, the selection of an appropriate local partner is of fundamental importance to the foreign investor. Indeed, when a foreign firm enters a host country in which the cultural, political and economic systems differ greatly from its own, it is more likely to cooperate with an local partner which has developed unique country- or firm-specific skills and advantages that are very costly, if not impossible, to duplicate by a foreign firm. Moreover, the greater the complementarity or indivisibility between foreign and indigenous firms, the greater the potential for synergistic effects in a joint venture. Foreign investors who have local partners (joint venture participants) are likely to have better access to the powerful Chinese guanxi networks than others (wholly-owned investors). These advantages for joint ventures can be reflected in cheap and reliable material supplies, market access, preferential tax treatment, low land rent, priority in obtaining infrastructure services, and provision of assistance from the authorities when problems arise.

Foreign direct investment in China is originated mainly from two sources: Chinese community investors and Western multinationals. Although more than 40 countries from all over the world have direct investment in China in 1994, however, almost three-quarters (73.29%) of the total foreign direct investment in the country has come from the Chinese community territory - Hong Kong and Macao (59.75), Taiwan (10.04%), and Singapore (3.49%). It is approximately four times as much as FDI undertaken by Western multinationals. One primary factor contributing to this situation is the cultural proximity between these business people and their Chinese counterparts. The Chinese commonwealth area nurtures a network of entrepreneurial relationships and an array of political and economic systems that are bound together not by geography but rather by shared tradition. Guanxi-based business dealings are not foreign to investors from this area. Indeed, for many generations, emigrant Chinese entrepreneurs have been operating comfortably in a network of guanxi, laying the foundations for stronger links among businesses across national borders (Kao, 1993). As a result, an interconnected, yet potentially open system has arisen, which provides a new market mechanism for conducting global business. Through well-established guanxi network within China, foreign investors from Chinese commonwealth territories are likely to more readily gain access to and benefit more from the insightful information, scarce resources, and controlled industries as opposed to other foreign investors. Those Western multinationals unfamiliar in large part with the Chinese market, particularly with the imperative guanxi utilization, can jointly enter the market with overseas Chinese companies, or appoint overseas or local Chinese managers skillful in managerial expertise and guanxi construction to fill in the leading management positions in the Chinese ventures.

Guanxi relationships are highly dynamic and must be continuously reinforced given the mobility of the participant's position or institution. It is a long and challenging task to identify the influential persons and build guanxi with them or their associates. Given this environment, it appears that foreign investors need time to gradually become familiar with local business practices and progressively build their guanxi networks. Those FIEs with a longer presence in the country are likely to have developed a better guanxi network and acquired more experience. Although guanxi may be associated with opportunism, the reciprocity rule precludes the persistence of opportunism in the long run. This is quite analogous to the prisoner's dilemma situation, where opportunism is not the best solution to repeated games with uncertainty in the long term. As a consequence, those FIEs with longer history in China are more likely to experience a lower level of opportunism and a higher level of trust with *guanxihu*. Therefore, those FIEs with greater length of operation in China tend to build a more extensive guanxi network, one which would be, moreover, longer-standing, and of better quality. Foreign businesses newly appeared in China should be active in adapting the new environment, learning from foreign incumbents in China, and building up own managerial network.

7.8 Constructing Own Guanxi Network

Chinese and Western business people approach a new relationship from opposite ends. To a Westerner, starting with a standard contract, altering it up to fit the different circumstances and signing the revised version, seems straightforward. Commercial law is ingrained in our thinking. Traditionally in China, commercial law barely existed and certainly indicated bad faith. The business clauses might form a useful agenda but obligations came from relationships. Judging from this perspective, one should not feel strange when he heard that McDonald's were evicted from a central Beijing building after two years despite having a 20-year contract - simply because the incomer from Hong Kong had strong guanxi with the government whereas McDonald's had not kept its own in good repair.

Many Chinese have developed extremely sophisticated skills that facilitate the development of interpersonal relationships. Shared attributes and affiliations are fundamental to the process. In Chinese society, people use the bonds of shared kinship, locality, work place, or school to make friendly contracts. These shared affiliations can be quite flexible. A shared locality, for example, may be a village, a county, a city, a province, a geographic region, or even an entire country. Shared circumstances, attributes or affiliations are important, so the more attributes an individual has, the more *mianzi* he will enjoy, and the more guanxi he can construct.

It is clear that the China market cannot be tackled effectively today without paying due attention to the construction and maintenance of good guanxi. Business transactions with Chinese individuals and organizations need to be approached with the knowledge that the Chinese will place them in the context of their own guanxi networks, which may require meeting obligations to individuals who have no direct involvement in the matter on hand. In China's collectivist culture, the 'real' decision-maker may be the network as a whole, not some mysterious and unseen individual. It is suggested that Western investors and marketers themselves need to establish guanxi of their own, which requires looking beyond the transaction at hand to its implications for the development of personal relationships. In general, a business person can demonstrate the good faith that forms the basis for a gradual transition from outsider to insider by bestowing favor and face through considerate and sensitive giving of minor gifts, hosting appropriate dinners, and more importantly, giving personal attention.

For new foreign investors in this context, entry mode is deemed to be associated with guanxi. A good local partner in the joint venture model can spur the foreign venture's market expansion and enhance its market power against rivals in the host environment because of the operational synergy effect between a local partner's existing guanxi network and a foreign partner's technological and organizational competencies. As foreign direct investment is an ongoing and sequential process, when early investors who have not yet built their own guanxi with the government, suppliers, customers, and competitors, local partners can greatly assist the ventures in reducing contextual or transactional risks using their country-specific knowledge such as guanxi construction. As a lesson for firms investing and operating in the Chinese society, understanding of the crucial role of guanxi in affecting all the major dimensions of firm performance and knowing the ways of creating and maintaining guanxi network are quite necessary for gaining an edge over their competitors and hence influencing corporate success.

The presence of expatriate in China is an imperative for building the firm's own guanxi network. Regular visiting and meeting customers are essential to creating and maintaining long term guanxi with them. American companies often lose their deals in the final stage of transactions due in large part to the failure of regular visiting local agents and customers. This failure makes the local agents and end-users assume that you are not serious about doing business and maintaining guanxi with them. Therefore, if you wants a real stake in the local market, it is certainly helpful to station expatriate there. Foreign marketing personnel are needed to establish long-term guanxi with customers. Foreign engineering expertise is needed to respond after-sale service and bring the latest engineering know-how which not only enables production to keep pace with international competition but also signals a big favor to the local partners and government agencies because technology constitutes the most badly needed production factor in the country. In other words, the presence of expatriate sales personnel and engineers not only provides for excellent guanxi with local customers, but also provides ready know-how to quickly adjust products and prices to market demands.

All the Chinese entrepreneurs, managers and bureaucrats prefer to do business with people with whom they feel close. It is essential for foreign businesses to spend time in establishing personal relationships with them in a proper manner. By day, local business people there run their business. By night, they do the real work - entertaining their contacts in order to build guanxi that will engender the understanding, flexibility, and trust necessary to make business deals work. Such a night gathering in the place of entertainment would be an ideal opportunity for foreign business people to construct guanxi with local businessmen and government officials. The result will certainly be better in this regard if the foreign merchant hosts a good dinner as well as an immediate entertainment satisfactory to all the guests. More importantly, there are a variety of ways to do favors other than dinner and entertainment. For instance, some assistance in children's education and household appliance or cosmetics purchase, and having a holiday tour together are among these options. It is clear that foreign marketers and investors who have maintained good guanxi with local suppliers, buyers, partners, and government authorities have a competitive edge over those who have not in the smooth running of routine business operations, in securing information about government policies, and in securing various administrative approvals.

The 'visiting abroad' invitation may be the most effective and immediate means to build guanxi with the person you invited. It is reported that many Chinese managers and government officials have had too many dinners hosted by foreign businesses to remember who is whom. Through the invitation for the site visit, the company's technological competencies and organizational skills may be strongly impressed on the Chinese manager or official's memory. Of course, one of the most immediate benefits from the invitation is that you have established a new guanxi with the key executive or official in charge of the projects or the deal. This means, though more or less costly, can engender competitive advantages over rivals and generate sustained economic rents in the long run for the firm.

7.9 Searching Right People

It is not realistic nor necessary to build guanxi with everybody in the partner organizations and government agencies. The selection of right person in the course of guanxi construction is therefore crucial to the sustained effectiveness and efficiency of guanxi. In searching a right person at the top level, a foreign business needs to find who has the dominant power controlling the firm and better relationships with local authorities. A puzzle that foreign businesses often face is the power difference between the general manager and the secretary of the communist party (*shu ji*) in the firm. In general, *shu ji* may not interfere in the firm's routine operations except strategic decisions such as large investment projects. The role he actually plays can be judged from three aspects simultaneously: his influence in the firm, his relations with government officials, and political climate in the country. Apparently, *shu ji*'s power is greater if his internal influence is bigger, relations with authorities is better, and nation's political climate is grimmer. If the *shu ji* and the general manager (could be same person in some firms) get along well with each other, then building guanxi with both are helpful. If not, the foreign business must invest in the one with greater power, and at the same time, maintain a relationship with the other at an acceptable level. Besides, building good relations with deputy general managers in charge of production, marketing, and finance are an essential element of relationship construction. Furthermore, although they do not have authority to make eventual decisions, function-level managers usually have a great influence on top management decisions. Foreign businesses new to the local firm can create guanxi with the partners starting with function-level managers. In many large state-owned enterprises, mid-level managers have authority to make decisions involving small size investment projects and regular import and export deals. Among different level managers, top-level ones should be generally treated as the priority as far as guanxi construction is concerned.

Another major type of guanxi building lies in the relationship with government officials. Foreign businesses often feel perplexed when they deal with bureaucrats at various levels. Several suggestions on the issue are provided as follows. First, it must be known that any business in any industry in China is subject to dual governmental controls: one by a provincial government or its agent in the region and the other by a corresponding ministry or its agent in the region. If a project is of strategic importance to the national economy, foreign businesses also confront the interventions from the central government agencies (e.g., State Economic Commission, State Planning Commission, Ministry of Foreign Trade and Economic Cooperation). It is necessary to first have an overall picture concerning what government institutions at both the central and local levels are involved with the project or deal, and which one of them will make the ultimate decision. Second, the mobility of political figures must be taken into account. The time a political figure in power, your guanxi, leaves the institution, will be the time you lose the good relationship with that institution. Therefore, solely relying on one official in the important governmental institution is not a proper guanxi construction strategy from the long term perspective. Third, a foreign business can find the right top-level person in the institution by contacting or consulting with low-level officials in the institution or those in other government institutions. The person the firm searches must be the one who makes the eventual decision, or at least plays a crucial role in the decision-making process. The head of an institution or a department under the institution may not necessarily be a most powerful person in the corresponding unit. The power in this circumstance largely depends on his guanxi with key persons in higher authorities.

7.10 Linking Guanxi with Performance

Networking can enhance a firm's competitive advantage by providing access to the resources of other network members. It is particularly important in respect to market expansion and firm growth. The delicate fibers of inter-personal networks weave into every Chinese individual's social life and expand into many aspects of Chinese society. Guanxi is critical to the social, economic, and political processes of this society. Lured by various forms of financial encouragement and career promotion, managers devote time and efforts to developing inter-personal guanxi in their search for a superior market performance (e.g., sales growth) and financial outcome (e.g., profitability). Good guanxi with buyers may spur customer loyalty and sales volume, thus reducing transaction costs and business uncertainties. Good guanxi with suppliers helps a firm acquire quality materials, good service, and timely deliveries. Good guanxi with competitors facilitates possible interfirm collaboration and implicit collusion, while mitigating competitive costs and operational variabilities. As a result, good guanxi with business community is likely to boost sales and revenues.

A practical consequence of guanxi is that personal connections and loyalties are often more important than legal standards. Although the Chinese government has enacted thousands of business laws, rules, and regulations, few are completely enforced because personal interpretations are often made in lieu of legal ones. For instance, whenever scarce resources exist, they are mainly allocated according to guanxi relations rather than by bureaucratic rulings. In essence, while the Chinese bureaucracy often inhibits business activities, guanxi facilitates them. Guanxi provides a balance to the cumbersome Chinese bureaucracy by giving individuals a way to circumvent rules through the activation of personal relations. Guanxi ties with government authorities are therefore vital to the effectiveness and efficiency of operations.

Although guanxi is constructed on personal relations and favor exchanges, it brings obligations and costs (*renqing*) to its beneficiary. As guanxi is essentially utilitarian and reciprocal, a favor obtained naturally implies an obligation or a liability that must be repaid sooner or later. This is the key assumption underlying guanxi development since breaking this rule will fundamentally impair one's social status or face. The 'individual attachments' advocates argue that individual attachments or personal ties can lead to maintaining relationships that provide fewer of the needed resources than would impersonal relations. Seabright and colleagues (1992) suggest that personal attachment may sometimes reduce favorable business changes that may boost economic efficiency. Because of these costs, liabilities, and attachment inertia problems, the intensity of guanxi utilization may not be necessarily associated with net profit growth. This problem seems to be compounded during economic reform and structural transformation since monetary investment has increasingly become a part of establishing guanxi ties.

Recently, Luo (1997a; 1997b), Luo and Chen (1996), Luo and Chen (1997) have examined the relationship between guanxi and performance for both Chinese and foreign businesses operating in China. Their findings can be summarized as follows:

First, guanxi connections with the business community as well as with government authorities are favorable only for sales growth, not for profit growth. This implies that the costs of guanxi construction and maintenance are likely to be high; they may even offset the benefits of market expansion. This confirms the reciprocal law of guanxi, that is, favors must be returned in order to maintain trust and 'face'. Such return favors are not necessarily equivalent or occurring at the same time (Luo, 1997b). Sellers often benefit from having guanxi with buyers by boosting sales, while buyers can benefit in return by enjoying low prices or liberal terms of payment (thus reducing profits to the sellers).

Second, good guanxi connections with government officials or partner firm executives do significantly enhance market performance. Due to a lack of reliable legal constraints on opportunistic behavior, guanxi is beneficial as a means for developing market share, improving competitive positions, facilitating interfirm collaborations, and acquiring more support from the government. Transaction cost economy or resource complementarity synergy in guanxi relations are mirrored in the benefits of market expansion.

Third, under the conditions of high complexity, dynamism, and uncertainty typical of China's economic reform period, guanxi proves inadequate to ensure firm success and growth. Technological skills and managerial abilities are important for both sales growth and net profit growth. Strategic orientation, organizational form, and industry growth also present a significant influence on firm performance. This leads us to conclude that having guanxi ties with business associates and government authorities is not the only driving force underlying market growth. Internal strengths, or organizational capabilities, in technology and management prove to be a necessary condition for superior financial and operational outcomes. A good guanxi network boosts a firm's market success while organizational capabilities ensure its effectiveness as well as efficiency.

Fourth, guanxi-based sales force marketing and credit granting on which the decisions are virtually dependent upon guanxi are found to have a systematic and favorable effect on a firm's asset turnover and domestic sales growth. For foreign ventures in China, the linkage between guanxi and firm performance is significantly moderated by entry mode, country of origin of investment, and length of operations. Indeed, the results indicated that joint venture mode, Chinese commonwealth country origin, and long presence in the Chinese environment have a facilitating impact on the relationship between guanxi and venture performance. In sum, guanxi has a significant and positive impact on a firm's efficiency and effectiveness, and this impact is modified by the investing and operating characteristics of FIEs. Foreign investors can gain an edge over their competitors by understanding and incorporating the guanxi factor in their business decisions.

In conclusion, guanxi seems to be the lifeblood of the Chinese business community, extending into politics and society. In the Chinese context, although the government has enacted thousands of laws, rules, and regulations, almost none are completely enforced since personal interpretations are often used in lieu of legal interpretations. Therefore, guanxi ties appear to be very helpful in dealing with Chinese bureaucracy. Rather than depending on an abstract notion of impartial justice, the Chinese people traditionally prefer to rely on their contacts with those in power to get things done. A practical consequence of guanxi is that personal connections and loyalties are often more important than organizational affiliations or legal standards. For instance, whenever scarce resources exist, resources are mainly allocated by guanxi rather than bureaucratic rules. In essence, while the Chinese bureaucracy often inhibits action, guanxi facilitates action. Guanxi provides a balance to the cumbersome Chinese bureaucracy by giving individuals a way to circumvent rules through the activation of personal relations. Developing, cultivating, and expanding one's guanxi has become a common preoccupation and a form of social investment in China.

Bibliography and Further Readings

Alston, J.P. (1989). '*Wa, Guanxi*, and *Inhwa*: Managerial Principles in Japan, China, and Korea', *Business Horizons*, March-April, pp. 26-31.

Boisot, M. H. and Child, J. (1988). 'The Iron Law of Fiefs: Bureaucratic Failure and the Problem of Governance in the Chinese Economic Reforms', *Administrative Science Quarterly*, vol.33, pp. 507-527.

Child, J. (1994). *Management in China During the Age of Reform*. Cambridge University Press, Cambridge, England.

Hwang, E.R. (1987). 'Face and Favor: The Chinese Power Game', *American Journal of Sociology*, vol. 92, pp. 35-41.

Kao, J. (1993). 'The Worldwide Web of Chinese Business', *Harvard Business Review*, March-April, pp. 24-36.

Luo, Y. (1997a). 'Guanxi and International Joint Venture Performance in China: An Empirical Inquiry', *Management International Review*, vol. 37, pp. 20-39.

Luo, Y. (1997b). 'Guanxi: Principles, Philosophies, and Implications', *Human Systems Management*, vol. 16, pp. 43-51.

Luo, Y. and Chen, M. (1996). 'Managerial Implications of Guanxi-Based Business Strategies', *Journal of International Management*, vol. 4, pp. 293-316.

Luo, Y. and Chen, M. (1997). 'Does Guanxi Influence Firm Performance', *Asia Pacific Journal of Management*, vol. 14, pp. 1-16.

Nee, V. (1992). 'Organizational Dynamics of Market Transition: Hybrid Forms, Property Rights, and Mixed Economy in China', *Administrative Science Quarterly*, vol. 37, pp. 1-27.

Peng, M. W. and Heath, P.S. (1996). 'The Growth of the Firm in Planned Economies in Transition: Institutions, Organizations, and Strategic Choice', *The Academy of Management Review*, vol. 21, pp. 492-528.

Rawski, T. G. (1994). 'Chinese Industrial Reform: Accomplishments, Prospects, and Implications', *American Economic Review*, vol. 84, pp. 271-275.

Reddings, S.G. and Ng, M. (1982). 'The Role of "Face" in the Organizational Perceptions of Chinese Managers', *Organizational Studies*, vol. 3, pp. 204-209.

Seabright, M. A., Levinthal, D. A., and Fichman, M. (1992). 'Role of Individual Attachments in the Dissolution of Interorganizational Relationships', *Academy of Management Journal*, vol.35, pp. 122-160.

Wall, J. A. (1990). 'Managers in the People's Republic of China', *Academy of Management Executive*, vol.4, pp. 19-32.

Tsui, A. S. and Farh, J. L. (1997). 'Where Guanxi Matters: Relational Demography and Guanxi in the Chinese Context'. *Work and Occupations*, vol. 24, pp. 56-79.

Wank, D. L. (1996). 'The Institutional Process of Market Transition: Guanxi and Private Business in a South China City. *The China Quarterly*, vol. 3, pp. 820-838.

Xin, K. R. and Pearce, J. L. (1996). 'Guanxi: Connections as Substitutes for Formal Institutional Support', *Academy of Management Journal*, vol. 39, pp. 1641-1658.

Yang, M. M. (1994). *Gifts, Favors and Banquets: The Art of Social Relationships in China*. New York: Cornell University Press.

Yeung, I. Y. and Tung, R. L. (1996). 'Achieving Business Success in Confucian Societies: The Importance of Guanxi', *Organizational dynamics*, vol. 3, pp. 54-65.

8 Entry Mode Selection and Sharing Arrangements in China

Chapter Purpose

This chapter illustrates various entry modes of investment available at present to foreign companies entering China. These entry modes include equity joint ventures, wholly foreign owned subsidiaries, contractual joint ventures, umbrella companies, acquisitions, representative offices, branches, build-operate-transfers, licensing and franchising. The merits and limitations of each entry mode are discussed. This chapter provides some practical advice on entry strategies for international executives active in the Chinese market. A comparison of financial and operational characteristics between joint ventures and wholly foreign owned subsidiaries is also presented. Finally, sharing arrangements are discussed, with a focus on the impact of equity distribution on the performance of international expansion in China.

8.1 Introduction

China's astounding economic growth rates over the past years have lured many foreign companies to set up operations there. China's special economic, cultural, and political context is, however, unfamiliar territory to many executives. The rules of the game are often dissimilar to those in market economies. Choosing the right entry mode is therefore crucial to the success of the joint venture. This chapter assesses entry modes and sharing arrangements for international investment in China.

For both the new investor beginning to explore the Chinese market and incumbents with multiple investments in China, entry modes have expanded in recent years. Entry modes available to international trading businesses include conventional import and export, flexible trade (i.e. processing imported materials or foreign samples and assembling imported parts and components), international leasing, and counter-trade (i.e. barter, counter-purchase, offset, switch trading, compensation trade, or buybacks). For international investment, entry modes include equity joint ventures, wholly foreign owned subsidiaries, contractual joint ventures, umbrella companies, acquisitions, representative offices, branches, build-operate-transfers, licensing, and franchising. This chapter is designed to only assess the entry modes for international investment in China. At present, almost half of all FDI in China uses equity joint ventures (EJVs), although wholly foreign-owned enterprises (WFOEs), contractual joint ventures (CJVs), and other options are also available.

In general, foreign investors are free to choose from several entry modes. These include: 1) equity joint ventures (EJVs), the most favored mode, accounting for 49.97 percent of the total amount of actual FDI in 1996. An EJV is a limited liability company with equity and management shared in negotiated proportions by foreign and Chinese partners; 2) wholly foreign-owned enterprises (WFOEs), which represented 29.85 percent of the total value of FDI in 1996. According to China's Law on Wholly Foreign-owned Enterprises, promulgated in April 1986, a WFOE is a foreign company using entirely its own capital, technology, and management while operating in China. The enterprise manages its operations independently and is responsible for all risks, gains, and losses; 3) contractual (or cooperative) joint ventures (CJVs), which constituted about 20.81 percent of actual FDI in 1994. The CJV refers to a variety of arrangements and a loose association of partners that agree to pursue a joint undertaking (which may include a limited liability company). The Chinese and foreign partner cooperate in joint projects or other business activities according to the terms and conditions stipulated in the venture agreement; 4) Other options include the establishment of representative offices, branch offices, umbrella companies; the acquisition of existing firms; licensing and franchising, and build-operate-transfer (BOT) operations.

8.2 Entry Mode 1: Equity Joint Ventures

The most common entry for MNCs into the Chinese market has been through EJVs. As an alternative to either full integration or simple market exchange, the EJV facilitates inter-firm learning and transfer of intangible assets while mitigating incentives for opportunism by creating interdependence between the transacting parties. If the benefits derived from joint efforts, minus the transaction costs specific to the formation and operation of an EJV, are greater than the sum of benefits obtained from exploiting firm-specific advantages separately, an EJV creates synergies which enhance economic rents to the partners. These synergies can be the result of risk reduction, economies of scale and scope, production rationalization, convergence of technologies, and improved local acceptance.

Synergistic effects increase the greater the indivisibility or complementarity between foreign and indigenous firms. Therefore, when a foreign firm enters a country in which the cultural, political and economic systems differ greatly from its own, it is more likely to cooperate with an indigenous firm which has developed unique country-, industry- or firm-specific skills and advantages. These types of skills would be very costly, if not impossible, to duplicate by a foreign firm. In less developed and transitional non-market-driven economies, in which requirements for adaptation and information are greater due to market structure imperfections, cultural change, idiosyncratic investment laws, and different economic stages, the appropriateness of forming EJVs is reinforced. Under the right conditions, the EJV can be the best first choice.

In other respects, however, EJVs are the most difficult option. EJV performance depends greatly upon qualitative variables such as individual personalities, organizational cultures, administrative styles, and management philosophies. Moreover, an EJV is neither an external, market-based method of organizing economic activity, nor a traditional intra-firm structure. Instead, it is a hybrid that does not comply to the rules of either pure form of business administration. Given these considerations, the EJV is likely, but not certain, to offer greater revenues, lower costs, and less risk than other modes.

The EJV form provides foreign companies with long-term connections to the Chinese market. The EJV's ability to sell through the local partner's established marketing channels seems especially attractive to manufacturing businesses looking to penetrate the domestic market. The Chinese government normally favors this mode because it often involves significant technology transfer to the Chinese partner. When EJVs enter industries in compliance with governmental plans, they are more likely to receive special access to utilities and critical input than other entry modes such as WFOEs.

To set up an EJV, each partner contributes cash, facilities, equipment, materials, intellectual property rights, labor, or land-use rights. According to EJV law, a foreign investor's share must be at least 25 percent of total equity. Generally, there is no upward limit in most deregulated industries. However, in governmentally-controlled or institutionally-restricted sectors, such as automobile and telecommunications, foreign investors are often more confined with respect to equity arrangements.

According to recent EJV regulations, there is no maximum term of operation for EJVs, although most are granted up to 50 years. This duration can be extended any time depending upon the agreement of the partners. Chinese approval authorities generally encourage these extensions.

EJVs are notoriously hard to sustain even in the relatively stable environments of the United States and Europe. Investment in China is even more difficult because the country is vast and varied, its culture and traditions are profoundly different from those of the West, and its social, governmental, and economic systems are particularly complex. Today foreign investors must contend with several additional factors when considering investment in China.

First, the marketplace in China is rapidly evolving, fragmenting, and becoming more competitive as more foreign companies set up operations there. Many new entrants are vying for first-mover advantages. Top-level players in some of the most promising industries (e.g., consumer packaged goods, infrastructure, construction, chemicals, pharmaceuticals, and electronics) are pursuing aggressive growth strategies with a focus on gaining market share. Some companies are willing to sustain losses in order to establish beachheads in China, be they in the form of manufacturing plants, distribution networks, or consumer awareness of their products.

Second, the distribution system in China is quite chaotic and undergoing fundamental changes. The traditional three-tier (national, provincial, and local) distribution system in China is crumbling, giving way to various parallel channels that charge different fees and provide different services in every geographic area. These changes indicate that getting your product into the Chinese market can be daunting. Expanding the scope of operations can be even more so. Every Chinese company belongs to and operates under some combination of local, provincial, and central government authority, each with its own agenda. Hence, there are many conflicting interpretations of rules and regulations. If your EJV partner tries to do business outside its authorized territory, it is apt to run into trouble.

Third, negotiations on the joint venture contract can be lengthy and complicated, with a tendency to negotiate in a style described by one veteran China trader as "a blend of the Byzantine and evangelical" (Tateisi, 1996). Chinese negotiators often frustrate Western business people unused to their tactics. Many foreign negotiators leave the table feeling pessimistic about their future partnership. They may attempt to control meeting locations and schedules, take advantage of perceived weaknesses, use shame tactics, pit competitors against each other, feign anger, rehash old issues, and manipulate expectations. Often negotiation continues even after the signing of the joint venture contract. Therefore, a foreign company should choose effective negotiators, prepare for time-consuming meetings, and develop a sophisticated strategy before starting negotiation.

Fourth, foreign companies often find themselves in a dilemma when the Chinese partners demand technology that is 'state-of-the-art'. Chinese negotiators routinely request the most advanced technology from foreign suppliers during initial negotiations, though they may lack sufficient foreign exchange and an adequate infrastructure to utilize complex technology and trained personnel. To ensure a better chance of success, foreign companies are strongly advised to provide the most appropriate, price-competitive technology.

Finally, it is often difficult to decide the contribution made to the venture by each partner. The Chinese side normally prefers to contribute non-cash items such as land use, existing buildings and construction materials, all of which are easy for the Chinese to overvalue due to the difficulty in assessing prices accurately. In order to avoid such complications, foreign investors should have assessments made by independent professional consulting or accounting firms.

8.3 Entry Mode 2: Wholly Foreign-Owned Enterprises

The WFOE form offers foreign investors increased flexibility and control. Within the constraints of the Chinese system, WFOEs allow managers to expand as quickly as they want and where they want, without the burden of an uncooperative partner. WFOEs also allow foreign investors to set up and protect their own processes and procedures, which leads to more careful strategic and operational oversight. Moreover, they can be established more quickly than EJVs; local Chinese authorities are required to respond to initial project proposals within 30 days.

WFOEs offer new hope for a more effective way to work in China. But in any competitive market, turning dreams into reality is challenging. China's complexities double that challenge. However, foreign investors who can let go of the conventional wisdom that joint ventures are the only way to do business in China have a new way to take advantage of the country's vast opportunities. For companies willing to accept the challenge, WFOEs may be ideal.

WFOEs have traditionally been viewed by the Chinese government as offering little in the way of technology transfer or other benefits to the Chinese economy. Recently, the attractiveness of this entry mode to the government has gradually increased. Nevertheless, the governmental support of WFOEs still trails far behind that of EJVs. When domestic credit is tight, however, WFOEs provide China with a means of attracting foreign investment.

WFOEs today operate in many areas where EJVs are currently approved. In some sectors, such as automotive and telecommunications industries, heavy regulations apply, which implies that EJVs are a safer bet. Exceptions always abound in China, however, as Motorola proved in Tianjing and General Motors in Guangzhou. From the Chinese government's perspective, investment form is negotiable; WFOEs are possible even in regulated industries. The real key to the entry mode regulation is not what the rule book says, but instead whether or not a foreign company will bring something of value to the Chinese government.

Some notes of caution should be stated. First, WFOEs must still handle guanxi relations. Many foreign investors need to rely on Chinese agents to make liaisons on their behalf and to help procure land, materials, and services. WFOEs should identify exactly which connections will help and who has them, and then engage with those Chinese individuals and organizations that have access to decision-making authorities to act as advisers.

Second, WFOEs are not allowed to invest and operate in certain industries that are vital to the Chinese economy (see Chapter Three). Nevertheless, the Chinese regulatory environment is evolving; more industries, including some service sectors, are opening up to foreign investment. Although it will be a gradual opening, China will eventually grant WFOE investment access to increasingly more industries.

Third, as WFOEs operate without the control of a Chinese partner, investment approval authorities often hold them to higher standards, including stricter foreign exchange balance requirements. If a WFOE is profitable, the Chinese government may encourage it to find a Chinese partner, in the hope of getting the foreign party to share its profits and pass along technological and management know-how. Alternatively, a Chinese business may try to form an EJV with another foreign party to produce similar goods in competition with the existing WFOE.

Lastly, WFOEs are more vulnerable to criticism relating to cultural and economic sovereignty. Naturally the Chinese do not want foreign companies taking advantage of their country. WFOE managers should recognize and address this concern. One way to do so is to localize production, that is, to buy as many parts and components as possible from local Chinese suppliers. Another way is to hire Chinese managers. Motorola, for example, employs only Chinese managers, very few of whom hold U.S. passports. Foreign companies can also be active in socially responsible projects, such as financing schools, sports events, the arts, public safety, or other community service projects. For instance, some foreign companies recently bought new cars and jeeps for local policy departments. WFOEs can also nurture local brands. Coca-Cola, for example, recently transferred the trademark of its new Tian Yu Di fruit drink to a local producer, Tianjin Jinmei Beverage Company. This move was warmly received as an example of the company's sensitivity to the Chinese value of reciprocity.

8.4 Entry Mode 3: Contractual Joint Ventures

Unlike an EJV, in which profit distributions and management of the venture are determined by the proportion of total registered capital contributed by each partner, the CJV (as governed by the Law of the People's Republic of China on Sino-Foreign Cooperative Enterprises) is an investment vehicle in which profits and other responsibilities are assigned to each party according to the joint venture contract. These are not necessarily in accordance with the percentage of each partner's share of total investment. A CJV is a business partnership in which each party cooperates as a separate legal entity and bears its own liabilities. The two firms entering into a CJV have the option of forming a limited lability entity with legal person status, similar to that of an EJV.

In China, joint exploration projects (e.g., offshore oil exploration consortia), which represented about 1 percent of the total amount of FDI in 1996, are a special type of CJV. Under these arrangements, the exploration costs are borne by the foreign partner, with development costs later shared by a Chinese entity. Although such explorations allow the foreign firm to manage specific projects, this type of FDI does not necessarily result in the establishment of new limited liability enterprises.

Major features of CJVs include:

(i) Liability. A CJV is allowed to adopt non-legal person status. The liability of investors in a venture with non-legal person status is unlimited, while the liability of investors in a joint venture with legal person status is limited to the amounts they have invested. Legal person status is automatic for EJVs. CJVs may elect either status. CJV investors in China may be able to use the unlimited liability conferred on non-legal person status in the tax structure for their PRC venture.

(ii) Capital Requirements. Foreign investors in CJVs with legal person status are required to contribute 25 percent or more of the venture's total registered capital. This requirement does not apply to CJVs that adopt non-legal person status. In practice, 25 percent was generally assumed to be the minimum amount that a foreign investor could contribute to a CJV with non-legal person status.

(iii) Import Tax Exemptions. Like EJVs, CJVs are exempt from paying transfer taxes and duties on imported equipment used as part of the foreign partner's investment in the enterprise, provided the equipment is required for the operation of the joint venture and is valued at no more than the total investment amount specified in the CJV contract.

(iv) Strategic Flexibility. There are no limits on the duration of the contract or prohibitions for withdrawal of registered capital during the countracted term. CJVs have great freedom to structure their assets, organize their production processes, and manage their operations. This flexibility can be highly attractive for a foreign investor interested in property development, resource exploration, and other production projects in which the foreign party incurs substantial up-front development costs. A CJV, for example, can build an accelerated return on its share of investment into the contract to allow it to recoup its equity share by the end of the term. Further, CJVs can be developed quickly to take advantage of short-term business opportunities and dissolved when they complete their assigned task.

Contractual joint ventures differ from EJVs in several following ways. First, profit distributions among parties to a CJV need not be in strict proportion to their registered capital contributions. The foreign party may recover its investment earlier than the Chinese partner upon meeting certain conditions, including reversion of all fixed assets to the Chinese partner. In contrast, the parties to an EJV can distribute profits only in strict proportion to their contributions to the EJV's total registered capital. Moreover, a CJV may distribute profits both in cash and in venture output, while an EJV is restricted to making cash distributions.

Second, as noted above, the CJV's ability to adopt non-legal person status also distinguishes it from an EJV. Besides affecting the liability of the joint venture partner, non-legal person status may allow foreign CJV partners to contribute less than 25 percent of the total registered capital of the joint venture. Foreign partners in an EJV must contribute a combined minimum of 25 percent of a venture's registered capital.

Third, CJVs are not required to survey Chinese sources before importing supplies or raw materials from abroad, while EJVs must give first priority to Chinese suppliers.

Because of their ability to provide foreign investors with returns in excess of their proportional contributions to the venture's total registered capital, CJVs have been the vehicles of choice for build-operate-transfer (BOT) infrastructure projects. The CJV option is expected to continue to be useful in BOT projects and, as a result of the new regulations, will become a more popular option for other types of ventures as well, especially those in which foreign investors seek a preferential return.

8.5 Entry Mode 4: Umbrella Companies

Many foreign companies are now seeking greater flexibility of operations in China's market. A growing number are interested in establishing fully integrated companies that can combine sales, procurement, subsidiary investment, manufacturing, and maintenance service for a broad range of products. Foreign investors interested in the concept include those new to China as well as established firms seeking to unite various existing investments in China under a parent company. The growing complexity of operations of many MNCs in China, and the need to more closely coordinate numerous joint ventures and/or wholly owned subsidiaries, has led several firms to set up holding companies in recent years. The 'umbrella' enterprise, also known as 'investment company' (*touzi gongsi*) or 'holding company' (*konggu gongsi*), has emerged for this purpose.

In contrast to joint ventures, which can manufacture and market only approved product lines, a holding company is able to unite existing investments under one umbrella to combine sales, procurement, manufacturing and maintenance. It can also help balance foreign exchange reserves between joint ventures, act as a clearing house for intra-group RMB financing and smooth the establishment of new investments.

Du Pont was an early convert to the holding company format in the late 1980s, although Philips is credited with having started the concept - apparently after the company's CEO met with Li Peng in 1989 and received the Premier's endorsement. By the end of last year, the Chinese government had approved more than 25 holding companies, both in wholly owned and joint venture form, involving foreign multinationals. One of the MNCs which recently set up a holding company in China is CIBA, the Swiss pharmaceutical and chemical giant. The group's wholly owned umbrella company, CIBA China, employs approximately 30 people in its Beijing office and has branches in Shanghai and Qingdao. It was set up in 1993 and is now capitalised at US$30M. In total, CIBA boasts 15 equity joint ventures in China, has a handful of non-equity ventures and one wholly owned subsidiary, and has US$260M worth of investments in the country.

The umbrella model is especially useful for companies that are multi-divisional, where each division enters and runs differently while the holding company coordinates them. This also suits the way the company is run worldwide, preferring individual businesses so as to avoid building up reserves which would limit the volume of cash that can be cycled on a global basis. With a holding company in China, profits can be more easily transfered among different strategic business units (SBUs) and taken out of the country.

A foreign investor may consider establishing an umbrella enterprise to achieve some or all of the following objectives: (1) Investment in subsidiary projects; (2) Manufacturing products; (3) Faciliting foreign exchange balance for all China activities; (4) Centralized purchase of production materials for subsidiary projects; (5) Provision of product maintenance service and technical support; (6) Training for subsidiary project personnel and end users of products; (7) Coordination and consolidation of project management. Currently, each FIE has a separate company structure; an umbrella enterprise can centralize management and streamline the subsidiaries as operating units; (8) Marketing subsidiary products. Usually, each manufacturing FIE in China has to set up its own sales capability; an umbrella enterprise can achieve greater efficiency by establishing one marketing entity; and (9) Conversion of representative offices into umbrella or subsidiary branch offices, thus removing many operating restrictions such as the need to hire personnel through labor service companies.

An umbrella company may provide a range of services to its subsidiaries including: (1) Assisting personnel recruitment; (2) Providing technical training, market development, and consulting assistance; (3) Assisting borrowing funds, including providing guaranties; (4) Acting as an agent for subsidiaries in the procurement of machinery and equipment, including office equipment, and raw materials, components, and spare parts necessary for production processes; (5) Acting as an agent for SBUs in the sale of products and providing after-sales service; (6) Balancing foreign exchange among SBUs, with the approval of the foreign exchange administration authorities; and (7) Providing financial support to subsidiaries, with the approval of the People's Bank of China. Without special approval from MOFTEC, these services can only be provided to SBUs in which the investment company holds at least a 25 percent equity.

At present, the allowed scope of operations for umbrella enterprises includes manufacturing, investment in subsidiaries, purchase of inputs and raw materials for SBUs, sale of SBU output, and marketing and operational services. An umbrella enterprise cannot act as a general trading company. That is, it cannot import finished product lines and sell them in China. Its business license must state the industries, projects, or products in which it will invest; it does not have an open license to engage in whatever business it wants. If the umbrella enterprise later wishes to engage in an activity not listed in the license, the change must be approved by MOFTEC and the license amended.

Foreign companies wishing to establish an umbrella enterprise usually must have at least two FIEs in China. Internationally known firms are given preference when applying to establish umbrella enterprises. Like all FIEs, an umbrella enterprise has Chinese legal person status.

According to MOFTEC regulations, Chinese partners in prospective joint investment companies must have a minimum total asset value of RMB100 million. Foreign applicants for wholly owned or joint investment companies must meet one of two sets of criteria. In one set, the foreign company must have had a minimum total asset value of $400 million in the year prior to its application, have established one or more FIEs in which it has contributed at least $10 million in registered capital, and have obtained approvals for three additional FIE project proposals. Applicants meeting this first set of conditions have the option of establishing an investment company in the name of a wholly owned subsidiary rather than in their own names, which may offer some comfort to foreign investors who want to insulate corporate headquarters from direct exposure to liabilities in China.

The second set of conditions stipulates that the foreign investor must have established a minimum of 10 FIEs in China, engaged in manufacturing or infrastructure construction to which it has contributed at least $30 million in registered capital. Presently, the investment company itself must have a registered capital of at least $30 million.

An umbrella company and its various FIEs are each treated by Chinese tax authorities as separate entities; consolidation of revenue and expenditures for tax purposes is not allowed. Subsidiary profits that are remitted to the umbrella enterprise as dividends will not be taxed, however. On the other hand, an umbrella enterprise with no manufacturing of its own will be taxed at 33 percent with no tax holidays. Like all other FIEs, an umbrella enterprise must balance its foreign exchange.

8.6 Entry Mode 5: Acquiring Existing Firms

The quickest way to expand one's investment in China is to acquire an existing Chinese firm or another foreign company with local ventures. This mode is particularly useful for entering sectors formerly restricted to state-owned enterprises. The Chinese government now permits foreign investors to buy all or part of the ownership interests of a wholly Chinese owned or Sino-foreign joint venture. China lacks sufficient capital, technology, and management knowhow to meet the needs of industries that are not deemed priorities. Foreign acquisition of Chinese firms gives newly privatized and growing Chinese enterprises easier access to much-needed capital for expansion while under-utilized assets can be put to profitable use. For these reasons, it is expected that this will remain a long-term governmental policy.

Since 1992, China has allowed 31 state-owned firms to be listed on international stock exchanges, which denote the shares by different names according to the bourse: N shares are listed on the New York Stock Exchange, while H and S shares are listed on the Hong Kong and Singapore exchanges, respectively. Foreign investors looking to acquire a piece of Chinese industry can now establish a joint venture company limited by shares (limited company), buy 'B' shares (in hard currency) of one of the 300 or so state-owned enterprises listed on the Shanghai and Shenzhen stock exchanges, or directly acquire a Chinese firm or other joint venture. These may be listed on sale in property rights markets that have sprung up throughout China. Foreign investors can also buy into a Chinese business by participating in its conversion into a foreign-invested joint stock company.

For a foreign investor, the main advantage of entering the China market through acquisition is that many state-owned firms, although in the red, have the potential to operate profitably if provided with the right mix of capital, management, and technology. Though the Chinese government has declared that ownership of some 1,000 key state firms will remain in government hands, this still leaves a huge number of enterprises to be cut loose from state support. Foreign companies will have many opportunities to buy into enterprises in different sectors and regions.

Investing in China through acquisitions offers other advantages as well. The investor may choose to attend to the target firm's operations, as in the case of EJVs and WFOEs, but the investor does not have to do so. As a result, acquisitions not only allow corporate investors to enter China, but also allow general investors, through holding companies, to gain entry, as in the case of many Hong Kong-based companies. Second, cash flow may be generated in a shorter time than in the case of an EJV or WFOE, since the acquired firm, by definition, does not have to be built from scratch. Finally, acquisition deals may be more attractive than EJVs or WFOEs because acquisitions offer immediate access to resources such as land use, ready-made distribution channels, and skilled labor, even when targeted firms have been losing money.

Foreign investors generally target those enterprises with strong market niches in sectors with potential for growth. Foreigners are most likely to be interested in, and permitted to exercise management control over, medium-sized firms which are collectively-owned enterprises, Sino-foreign joint ventures, or even state-owned, regionally based companies. Many state enterprises have been restructured into limited companies, allowing foreign investors to buy into these firms by purchasing company shares. But restrictions remain. The restructuring of each state firm and its subsequent listing is subject to Chinese government approval. Chinese authorities usually stipulate a ceiling to the extent of foreign ownership interest in state-owned businesses.

A foreign company acquiring a local firm should be familiar with two types of limited companies - those that issue privately held shares and those that issue publicly traded shares. Which form the company takes depends upon the percentage of shares held by the founding parties, who must be legal persons. To set up a private limited company, the firm issues shares which it, or its sponsor, buys back and maintains full ownership. By contrast, in publicly traded limited companies, the founding companies may purchase only 30-35 percent of the venture's shares and the rest is sold to the public at large. If at least 25 percent of a limited company is foreign owned, it is considered a FIE and is therefore accorded preferential treatment. Foreign-funded limited companies require at least RMB30 million in registered capital. Dividends are distributed in proportion to equity shares. Existing joint ventures may be converted into limited companies, pending approval by MOFTEC and the original approval authority.

Investors buying a stake in a Chinese company must first evaluate various risks. Gaining government approval for the transfer of ownership and clearance of property titles is often a difficult hurdle. Foreign investors should be careful to obtain accurate information when buying into a Chinese entity, particularly concerning existing liabilities. Analysis of investment risk should also take into consideration the locality, including the workings of the local bureaucracy, transportation links, and other infrastructure issues, since regional rivalries and an aged and inadequate infrastructure often hamper the efficient movement of goods, information, services, and labor throughout many parts of China.

Foreign companies who choose to invest in Chinese companies by buying shares alone should not be deluded that they will have a significant voice in running the company. Because foreign investors in a large Chinese enterprise are limited to a minority shareholding position, either in practice or by law in some sectors, they lack the ability to challenge decisions made by the Chinese shareholders on the board of directors. The Company Law in China lacks any provision for minority shareholders to challenge the decisions of the board, as they are able to do in the United States.

While the transformation of China's state businesses can happen on paper overnight, the culture of state domination remains strong, thwarting the implementation of efficient business practices. In China, a fundamental ambiguity remains between 'shareholding' and 'control'. Many Chinese shareholders are typically agents of the state or state-owned enterprises, making it less likely that they will prioritize maximization of profits. The term 'red capitalist' refers to the majority of Chinese shareholders who claim to be committed to the bottom line but are reluctant to reduce the numerous welfare benefits of Chinese employees or lay off redundant workers.

8.7 Entry Mode 6: Representative Offices

Although technically not considered a FIE, a representative office is a quick and relatively simple way to become acquainted with the Chinese market. It is widely used by many foreign companies which are new to China. This helps foreign companies test the waters before taking the plunge of formatting a FIE within China's complex economy.

Representative offices allow firms to establish contacts with key industrial ministries and begin to build their company's reputation in China.

By law, representative offices are prohibited from engaging in direct, profit-making business activities in China. They are allowed to undertake non-commercial activities including business communication, product promotion, market research, contract administration, and negotiations, on behalf of the head office. Equally important, they can also act as liaison to potential Chinese trading partners, as well as to various Chinese commercial and government offices, and can lay the foundation for further investment by promoting the foreign company's name and reputation. Corporate giants like Bechtel Corp. and Apple Computer Inc. had representative offices in China for at least 10 years before building legal-person status FIEs.

The most apparent advantages the representative office has over other entry modes are its simplicity and flexibility. Unlike an EJV or WFOE, a representative office gives a foreign company a formal presence in China without the complications of an unfamiliar local partner or hefty financial commitment. A representative office, unlike other investment vehicles, has no minimum registered capital requirements. Many foreign businesses find the establishment of representative offices, although not cheap, an excellent way to become familiar with Chinese business environment before making a major commitment.

One flexible feature of representative offices is the lack of restrictions on the line of business in which the company can engage. Other entry modes, by contrast, can only participate in sectors and industries designated by governmental authorities. For example, the government discourages foreign participation in media communications, except for representative offices. Foreign companies in restricted industries such as insurance, banking, trading, also have found that the establishment of representative offices offers them a platform from which to try to convince Chinese government officials to open these sectors for foreign activity.

As the representative office operates independently, it can proceed with liaison, market research and consulting activities in whatever fashion it sees fit. Closing down a representative office is also relatively easy compared to terminating a joint venture. It is also relatively easy for representative offices to hire talented Chinese college graduates or managers who see employment at a representative office as a way to gain exposure to the world of international business, or even as a springboard to working at the head office in future. Such benefits make the representative office an ideal means to explore further investments in China, establish a presence in other regions of China, or arrange future investment projects.

This entry mode, however, has several disadvantages. Though establishing a representative office is comparatively easy, a host of regulatory and start-up costs make them quite expensive to maintain. In addition to high labor costs paid to local employees, representative offices must usually pay high rents, as they tend to be located in major cities where office space is in chronic short supply. Of the total 24,402 representative offices which were operating in China as of 1994, 3,802 were located in Beijing, 3,294 in Shanghai, and 6,918 in Guangzhou. Far fewer have been established in interior locations. Moreover, a representative office cannot issue invoices or receive payment directly for its services to Chinese customers. It has also to pay duties on all imported office equipment. At present, the imposed tariffs on computers, photocopiers, fax machines, video and audio equipment, air conditioners, and other office items, can be as high as 100 percent. Furthermore, a representative office can officially hire local employees only though one of the four approved management service companies, namely Foreign Enterprise Service Co., China International Enterprise Cooperations Corp., China International Intellectech Corp., and China International Talent Development Center. These service companies withhold a maximum of 50 percent of gross pay of local Chinese working in foreign representative offices. Many representative offices have to pay a substantial bonus directly to the employees in order to compensate for the low net pay resulting from the management service company's withholdings.

Many foreign companies continue to use representative offices as their company's China headquarters even after they have established other types of ventures in China. On balance, the merits of this entry mode make it an invaluable way to sample the fruits of China's current economic dynamism and growth.

8.8 Entry Mode 7: Other Options

Branch

One of the newest options for expanding investment is the establishment of branch offices that can undertake business transactions. The 1994 Company Law allows foreign companies to open branches that engage in production and operating activities. A FIE can also open a branch office in another region of the country to expand its operations in China.

Up untill now, only a handful of foreign banks and law firms have been approved to open branch offices. These offices are limited to specified cities and their scope of business is highly regulated. Branch offices may ultimately offer a relatively simple means for establishing or expanding a presence in China, but the fact that they do not have legal-person status means the foreign parent company is liable if civil charges are brought against the branch. To shield the parent company from unlimited damages, foreign companies interested in establishing branch offices in China should designate an offshore subsidiary as the parent.

Build-Operate-Transfer (BOT)

Build-operate-transfer (BOT) is a newly emerging mode of entry into the Chinese market. It is especially useful in the power generation sector and for other large-scale infrastructure projects. For instance, negotiation on one of the first BOT power projects was recently completed. According to officials in Southeastern Guangxi, the final contract for the Laibin B power plant will be signed soon with Electricite de France, Britain's National Power International, and Barclays Bank. Recently, China's State Planning Committee has ratified ten more BOT projects calling for foreign operations: (1) the Summer Palace light rail in Beijing; (2) the Zilanda hydropower plant; (3) the Tuoketro B power station in Inner Mongolia; (4) the State highway 104 in Shandong; (5) the Shenyang elevated expressway in Liaoning; (6) the Wuhan light rail line in Hubei; (7) the Yinglongshan power plant in Zhejiang; (8) the Second Nanjing Yangtse River Bridge in Jiangsu; (9) the Shenyang-Beijing Expressway in Liaoning; and (10) the Shenyang second ring road in Liaoning.

BOT is a guarantee-fee method of cooperation by which an investor identifies a project in a host country, assumes sole responsibility in investing in the construction and operation of the project, and, after recovering investment and obtaining compensation, returns the project to the local organization in the host country. It is a relatively new means of international capital investment, applied usually in projects where building infrastructure facilities calls for a huge investment and great length of time. It is popular in developing countries short on capital and technology. The first BOT project, implemented in China on a trial basis, was the Beijing-Tongxian Expressway, by Beijing civil construction departments and an American company. Construction started in September 1994, with 20 months as the projected time for completion. The approved term of the BOT is 20 years, after which the expressway will be returned to China.

Due in part to difficulties working out financing and equity arrangements, the BOT approach is often used together with other entry modes. Foreign businesses may set up BOT project firms by means of either equity or cooperative joint ventures with Chinese partners or wholly foreign-owned ventures. Because of their ability to provide foreign investors with returns in excess of their proportional contributions to the venture's total registered capital, CJVs have been the vehicles of choice for BOT infrastructure projects.

Franchising and Licensing

Two forms of contractual arrangements most often used in international expansion are franchising and licensing. Both involve a contract between parties in different countries, but franchise contracts cover more aspects of the operation and are typically of a longer duration than licensing. A licensor in one country makes limited rights and/or resources available to the licensee in a foreign country. The rights and/or resources may include patents, trademarks, technology, managerial skills, and so on. These allow the licensee to produce and market a product similar to the one the licensor has already been producing in its home country, without requiring the licensor actually to create a new operation abroad. For instance, licensees in China and other countries have contracts to produce and sell toys and clothing bearing pictures of Mickey Mouse and other Walt Disney characters.

Licensing is a popular method for profiting from a foreign market without committing sizable funds. Since the foreign producer is typically 100 percent locally owned, political risk is minimized. Income from license however, is lower than that from other FDI entry modes, although the return on the marginal investment can be higher. Other potential disadvantages include loss of quality control; establishment of a competitor in a foreign market; improvements of the technology by the local licensee, which then enters the home market; and loss of the opportunity to make a direct investment in the licensee's market.

Most licensing agreements by MNCs have been with their own affiliates or joint ventures in China. Licensing fees have been a way to spread the corporate research and development costs among all SBUs. They are also a means of repatriating profits in a form typically more acceptable to the Chinese government than dividends.

Compared to licensing, a franchise usually includes a broader package of rights and resources. Production equipment, managerial systems, operating procedures, access to advertising and promotional materials, loans and financing may all be part of a franchise. McDonald's and KFC are examples of foreign companies with franchises in China. This arrangement can lead to the creation of a new business in which the franchise is designed to stand in perpetuity.

It is important for foreign licensors or franchisors to familiarize themselves with the legal framework for international licensing and franchising in China. Currently, the Regulations on the Administration of Technology Import Contracts (RATIC), promulgated by the State Council in May 1985, are the most comprehensive. In addition, foreign companies should confirm the identity, legal status, and authority of the potential Chinese recipients. The simplest verification is a review of their business license and, if possible, articles of association. A foreign supplier should also make sure that the relevant planning authorities in China have authorized the proposed project. Moreover, foreign suppliers must be aware that Chinese law tends to encourage the conversion of a licensing contract into an installment sale plan, by forbidding restriction on the licensee's continued use of the knowhow, trademark, or technology received from the foreign firm after expiration of the contract. The RATIC also mandates that license contracts shall generally not exceed 10 years.

8.9 Some Advice to International Executives

Factors Under Consideration

Foreign companies can structure their entry into China in many different ways. Some will be more suitable than others depending upon specific situation and business objectives. A foreign company that is not familiar with the Chinese business environment may want to engage a dependable distributor to sell its goods in China. Those firms that want to minimize investment of capital and resources at the initial stage may find a contract manufacturing arrangement suitable. Some may want to first test the market and establish a relationship with their current and potential customers by setting up a representative office. Those who are knowledgeable about China may want to ask themselves whether they need a partner at all. Under certain circumstances, they can set up a wholly foreign-owned enterprise and put in their own management team, then hire locally to staff their Chinese company.

Various other forms of doing business in China are also available. Foreign firms should make sure they know all possible options before they determine the best one. One factor to consider is that it takes longer to finalize a joint venture in China than in, say, the United States. Even joint ventures with private parties require government approval under China's legal system.

Some options, particularly expanding or buying into an existing FIE or setting up a new one, are attractive because existing legislation and experience make them transparent, feasible, and relatively predictable. Other methods, such as buying into a Chinese enterprise other than an FIE or seeking to establish a branch of the foreign company, may lead investors into uncharted waters. Investors must select among these various options in an environment marked by bureaucratic struggles both within the central government and between the national and local governments.

Inevitably, there are tradeoffs in choosing one entry mode over another. Once a foreign investor decides to pursue a FDI project in China, its choice of entry mode will depend on a wide range of factors such as the project's compatibility with China's national industrial plans, size of the venture, and amount of capital and technology needed. Moreover, businesses must consider factors such as protection of intellectual property rights, competition from Chinese firms, and access to adequate suppliers, target markets, and power sources.

The strategic objective of a project also influences the entry mode selection. If the project is export-oriented, for instance, a WFOE might be a better choice. By manufacturing in the location where factor conditions are optimal and then exporting to the rest of the world, a foreign company may be able to realize substantial location economies and a positive experience curve. This arrangement also gives the company the tight control over marketing that might be required to coordinate a globally dispersed value chain as well as better transfer pricing for avoiding various taxes or tariffs. Thus, foreign companies pursuing global strategies may prefer to establish WFOEs.

When foreign investors expand in China, the optimal entry mode for such companies depends to some degree on the nature of their distinctive competency. In particular, it is imperative to distinguish between technological know-how and managerial know-how. If a company's competitive advantage derives from its control of proprietary technological know-how, licensing and joint venture arrangements are not advisable because of the risk of losing control of that technology. A WFOE might be a better choice in this situation. The licensing or joint venture mode can be used for these companies only if the arrangement is structured in such a way as to reduce the risk of a company's technology being expropriated by licensees or joint venture partners. Companies can arrange to prevent leakage of their most sensitive technologies by only allowing their partners access to production processes that do not expose some kinds of knowledge. Contractual safeguards can also be written into a joint venture contract. Cross-licensing agreements between parties can also protect a foreign investor's technological knowhow, if both parties agree in advance to exchange skills and technologies. Comparatively, the risk of losing control of management skills to franchisees or joint venture partners is not that great. This is one of the reasons that many service companies favor a combination of franchising and subsidiaries to control franchisees in China.

Foreign companies in China tend to start with low risk/low control options and then advance to higher levels of risk and control as they gain experience and build confidence. Initial market entry often starts with import/export or flexible trade. International leasing, countertrade, representative offices, licensing, and franchising may also be considered as trial steps. EJVs or CJVs may be established as investment vehicles with intermediate risks. These modes still dominate in China because they included partnerships with players already experienced in the targeted market. They also reduce risk through cost sharing. Thus, they represent an appropriate entry strategy for early market development tactics.

To secure a stronger presence in China, acquisitions, BOT, WFOEs, or umbrella companies may be required. Indeed, many consider these approaches more risky. They are likely to come at later stages in the development of an international diversification strategy in China. These modes, however, enable foreign investors to better control local operations and, more importantly, become more profitable from the economic boom and market growth. Foreign investors may employ some or all of these alternatives in sequential fashion or use different modes simultaneously with different products or in different regions of China.

In sum, the selection of entry modes in China depends upon the following four groups of factors: (1) firm-specific factors including strategic objectives, degree of global integration, firm size and experience, and its distinctive competencies such as technological and managerial know-how; (2) local market-specific factors including contextual risk, cultural distance, market potential, market knowledge, infrastructure conditions, intellectual property right systems, and government policy and treatment toward FDI; (3) industry-specific factors such as entry barriers, industrial policies of the Chinese government, structural uncertainty, and degree of competition from both local and other foreign firms; and (4) project-specific factors such as contractual risk, project size, amount of investment needed, project orientation (technological, local market, export, or infrastructure-oriented), and availability of appropriate local partners.

Combining Options

Selecting between an EJV and a WFOE is not necessarily an either-or decision. Sometimes a Chinese partner does have a strong distribution network or operates in a restricted sector that is attractive to a foreign investor. In such situations, foreign companies can, for instance, surround their WFOE production operation with EJVs that market and sell their products in China. Motorola in Tianjin does exactly that. Since 1993, Motorola has been laying the groundwork for the biggest U.S. manufacturing venture in China. Its $300-million-plus commitment to China focuses on pagers, simple integrated circuits, cellular phones, and, eventually, automotive electronics. The production site in the Tianjin Economic Development Zone is a WFOE; marketing and sales of products will be done through various EJVs with local partners.

Another approach is to consider an EJV and a WFOE in sequence. A foreign investor can get initial entry as part of an EJV for a fixed period which is normally stipulated in the duration clause of the joint venture contract. At the end of the stipulated term, it can take over the assets from the Chinese partner and continue to run the operation as a WFOE. This is an attractive alternative if the added value of the Chinese partner is significant but limited to the early stages of the venture. Some EJVs have integrated this option in the termination clause of the joint venture contract.

It is also possible to structure a WFOE under the legal umbrella of an EJV. In other words, the project would be an EJV as a legal entity but would be run and operated as a WFOE. Many foreign partners that have increased their equity stakes in existing ventures are going in that direction. In some cases, they turn their Chinese partner into a silent partner with a minority stake.

8.10 Financial Comparison Between EJVs and WFOEs

Comparing financial and operational characteristics of different entry modes, especially EJVs and WFOEs, is essential. For both foreign and local investors, the mode of involvement creates certain unique and long-term resource commitments. Because of the fixed nature of these investments and contractual bindings, some of these commitments are nearly irreversible, at least in the short run. Ownership policy also has implications in terms of control of foreign subsidiaries, integration of production and operation networks, and coordination of functional policies on a regional and worldwide basis. Knowledge of relative financial efficacy and operational characteristics helps investors select their optimum ownership mode, formulate appropriate investment strategies, and work out proper financial strategies such as financing, budgeting, transfer pricing, and dividend policy.

Based on a cross-sectional sample from 1989 to 1991 obtained from the Jiangsu Provincial Commission of Foreign Economic Relations and Trade, I computed financial characteristics for three groups of samples, EJVs, WFOEs, and Chinese domestic firms (CDFs). The data consist of 54 randomly selected EJVs (a control group), 54 WFOEs, and 54 CDFs. In each case, the external financial statements, which each enterprise is required to submit to the Foreign Investment Administration Division of the Commission, were analyzed. The results are revealed in Table 8.1.

Profitability

The profitability measures show some differences between EJVs and the other two groups. Although there is no significant difference in the level of ROA (return on assets) for EJVs and WFOEs, the profit margins show significant disparities. The gross profit margin (sales minus variable costs divided by sales) is lower for WFOEs than for EJVs. However, when all other expenses beyond the direct costs are taken into account, WFOEs are more profitable than EJVs, as shown by their higher operating profit margin (sales minus variable and fixed costs divided by sales). This suggests that the WFOEs, on average, have higher variable costs in relation to total revenue than EJVs, and that they may have lower fixed costs than EJVs due to their lower overhead expenses. The latter may be caused by lower interest and depreciation, and by less allocation of certain social and transportation funds

Table 8.1 Financial Comparison Among EJVs, WFOEs and Chinese Domestic Firms (CDFs)

Variable	EJV	WFOE	*t*	CDF	*t*
Profitability					
ROA before tax	0.21	0.18	-1.33	0.12	-6.03**
ROA after tax	0.14	0.14	-1.46	0.07	-3.88**
Gross profit margin	0.71	0.69	-0.95	0.62	-2.76**
Operating profit margin	0.23	0.25	2.48**	0.17	-4.83**
Efficiency					
Accounts receivable turnover	9.86	10.30	0.42	6.08	-5.65**
Inventory turnover	9.23	9.45	0.12	7.11	-2.30**
Total asset turnover	1.21	1.38	1.83*	1.18	-1.94*
Financial risk					
Current ratio	1.90	2.35	2.67**	1.19	-3.77**
Cash liquidity	0.10	0.09	-0.75	0.07	-1.50
Debt-to-asset ratio	0.37	0.29	-2.68**	0.54	-6.46**
Earnings/interest ratio	13.20	17.50	1.04	7.52	-2.80**
Growth Opportunities					
Domestic sales growth rate	0.18	0.17	-0.78	0.12	-1.84*
Export growth rate	0.08	0.15	2.91**	0.12	1.12
Net profit growth rate	0.14	0.12	-0.56	0.08	-1.90*
Lerner index[#]	0.04	0.05	1.25	0.04	-2.55**
Business Determinants					
Advertising	0.01	0.01	-1.16	<0.01	-8.92**
R&D	0.06	0.08	3.10**	0.01	-4.13**
Sales force marketing	0.06	0.05	-2.78**	0.09	1.21
Credit liberalization	0.07	0.05	-2.00*	0.09	3.22**
Investment size	$145M	$105M	-1.95*	$623M	14.50**

* ** denote 10% and 1% significance level respectively.
[#] Under constant returns, the Lerner index, which is the ratio of marginal profits to marginal revenues, is equal to the ratio of profits to sales.

contributed to the local governments because of no involvement of Chinese partner in the case of WFOEs.

Evidence also indicates that all the profitability ratios are significantly higher for EJVs than for Chinese domestic firms. Moreover, both the mean of, and *t*-value between, the two groups for ROA after taxes differ greatly than for ROA before taxes, indicating that the return difference between EJVs and CDFs is larger when taxes are taken into account because EJVs are subject to preferential tax treatment as compared to CDFs. The remarkable profitability difference between the EJVs and CDFs may be the result of not only discrepancies in tax holidays and exemptions, the retained percentage of foreign exchange earnings, managerial effectiveness and operational efficiency, but also a difference in degree of freedom in formulating and implementing business strategies. Unlike EJVs, CDFs are often restricted by the governments that their objectives, behavior and activities must be in line with the specific requirements of central and local planning bodies. As a consequence, certain CDFs are in the situation of so-called "state policy-led loss or small margin".

Efficiency

Consistent with the common view, the evidence in this study indicates that Chinese domestic state firms are less efficient in managing their assets than EJVs. The accounts receivable, inventory, and total assets turnover ratios are significantly higher for EJVs than for CDFs. Indeed, it was reported that EJVs maintained a better customer network than CDFs and often optimized their inventory levels (Luo and Chen, 1995b).

Like WFOEs, EJVs have a similar level of accounting receivable and inventory turnover, but moderately lower level of total assets turnover, suggesting that fixed assets might be more productive in WFOEs than in EJVs, because WFOEs usually are equipped with new and technology-advanced machinery whereas the Chinese partners of EJVs often invest by used fixed assets.

Liquidity and Financial Risk

As a measure of liquidity, current ratio is significantly lower for EJVs than for WFOEs. A possible reason is that EJVs, which usually have the partnership with Chinese state enterprises, may have better banking relationships, thereby making it possible for them to maintain a low current ratio without impairing their routine business activities. In the mean time, the debt ratio (in respect to total assets) is significantly higher for EJVs than for WFOEs, which may be explained by the fact that many foreign investors in joint ventures,particularly from Hong Kong and Taiwan,often remit only a portion of their undertaken equity, and have to, as a result, rely on bank loans when own capital is insufficient to meet the operational demand.

Other than the liquidity ratio, the other three financial risk and liquidity measures studied apparently differ between EJVs and CDFs. The mean of current ratio for CDFs is as low as 1.19, while the mean of debt ratio is as high as 0.54. One likely reason is that these Chinese domestic firms are actually "wholly state-owned" enterprises from the equity perspective. Therefore, low current and high debt ratios do not necessarily mean that these firms carry higher financial risks.

Growth Opportunities

None of the domestic market growth measures reveal significant differences between EJVs and WFOEs, indicating that both groups of firms have similar growth opportunities. However, export growth rate is significantly higher for WFOEs than for EJVs, suggesting that those foreign investors aiming at pursuing Chinese market entry are more likely to choose the joint venture mode, since utilization of existing market power and distribution networks possessed by the Chinese counterparts is commonly viewed as the best short-term way to enter into the unfamiliar Chinese market. On the other hand, those foreign investors attempting to minimize production cost by manufacturing on a Chinese site with the intent of exporting to international markets are more likely to employ the wholly owned venture mode.

Interestingly, EJVs are significantly different from Chinese domestic firms concerning domestic market growth. The result of this study shows that the Lerner index is significant higher for EJVs than for CDFs, indicating that EJVs have a greater ability to generate excess returns. Furthermore, domestic sales growth and net profit growth are also marginally higher for the EJVs than for the CDFs, suggesting that EJVs are likely to be more concerned with industry selection, or might possess superior competition advantages deriving from proprietary knowledge, advanced technology and intense product and process innovation.

Business Determinants

This study offers evidence that R&D expenditure is less intense for EJVs than for WFOEs, but that EJVs tend to be more advertising intensive, although not at a statistically significant level. The possible reason for higher R&D intensity for WFOEs is that the foreign investors who own certain advanced technology or research and development proprietary knowledge or processes, which could provide their major competitive advantage, might be willing to let their "knowhow" be shared by others, and hence choose the investing mode of wholly-owned ventures. In addition, it is found that sales-force marketing and credit expenses are more intense for EJVs than for WFOEs, suggesting that EJVs are more often to employ sales-force and preferential term-of-payment as marketing tools. The size, as measured by total assets, are not significantly different between these two groups.

The business determinants also show some difference between EJVs and CDFs. On the one hand, advertising and R&D expenditures are more intense for EJVs than for CDFs. Yet, it is expected that advertising intensity for EJVs (WFOEs as well) will be come even greater in that China plans to drop, once it rejoin the General Agreement on Tariffs and Trade, a recently introduced two-tier pricing system for advertising in which foreign firms pay 30 percent more to advertise in China's state-run media than Chinese domestic firms. On the other hand, sales-force marketing and credit granting are significantly lower for EJVs than for CDFs. It appears that Chinese domestic firms have extensively developed personal direct marketing and credit expansion as their primary marketing promotion instruments.

China is now widely recognized as one of most promising investment locations. Its phenomenal growth and increased openness to foreign cooperation, has encouraged more and more foreign companies to take the plunge. The economy has presented foreign investors with both opportunities and challenges. In order to achieve satisfactory financial performance in this market, foreign executives need to understand a variety of tax laws, financing rules, foreign exchange regulations and other policies, and adopt realistic financial strategies. Asset management, financing arrangement, equity distribution, tax avoidance, transfer pricing, exposure hedging, and dividend policy are all crucial elements among them. The findings of this study have offered a basic knowledge about comparative financial characteristics of Sino-foreign joint ventures, that could be beneficial to financial officers for formulation of financial strategies, and to foreign investors for selection of an appropriate entry mode.

8.11 Sharing Arrangement in China

Sharing arrangements are an important aspect of investment since they are closely tied to the firm's core competency contributions, control over subsidiaries, bargaining power with local partners, globally integrated synergy, and parent-subsidiary relations.

Value-generating assets are increasingly taking the form of created assets (e.g., human capital) rather than natural assets. Most of these created assets are intangible and ownership-specific, and often constitute the contribution brought by one party to an EJV. Under these conditions, the equity distribution of the EJV is critical, particularly when the firms are pooling their core competencies into the EJV. Equity distribution can also affect the ability and propensity of an EJV to influence environmental factors.

It has been shown that the degree of interdependence of a multinational network, and the relative strength of an EJV's position within that network, have a negative effect on its vulnerability to host government intervention. That is, the higher the degree of dependence of the EJV on local relationships, the more the venture is prone to political or other contextual risks. This indicates that when an EJV is more dependent on the MNC network, it will be less reliant on the local environment and will hence have a greater capability to reduce or avoid local risks and uncertainties. In general, if a venture's interaction with the local environment is high, the parent should decentralize more power and disperse more resources to the venture. Conversely, since the foreign partner's control over local operations is positively related to its equity status, higher ownership will lead to a lower degree of dependence on local relationships. As a result, it is likely that the greater the portion of equity owned by foreign investors, the lower the risks and uncertainties assumed by EJVs. Although large MNCs are likely to be capable of bearing more risks, empirical evidence indicates that the willingness of American firms to commit equity in a foreign market is inversely related to the perception of uncertainty of doing business in the host country.

In China and other developing countries, foreign investors are typically able to exercise somewhat greater control than even their equity levels would suggest. This is due to the nature of their contribution (e.g., advanced technology), and more sophisticated knowledge of available control mechanisms. This greater control, a result of competency and managerial efficiency, may lead to greater effectiveness than would be the case elsewhere.

Contingency theory suggests that sharing arrangement must consider the particular industry, firm, and country factors faced by entering firms. Harrigan (1985) provides evidence that industry-specific and strategic factors contingently influence the success of joint ventures; the former are mainly structural factors in the host market, the latter are primarily firm-specific competitive or competency advantages. Since the ownership advantage explains a firm's resource commitment, sharing arrangement is thus an elaborate allocation of resources according to the local industrial structure so as to maximize the integrated synergy generated from the interaction between firm resources and host country markets and industries. Since, as stated earlier, type of project selection involves a consideration of both resource commitment and indigenous industry conditions, this selection is likely to strongly interact with sharing arrangement, and the interaction may impact the EJV performance. To be more specific, EJVs are likely to contribute more equity in technologically-advanced projects after controlling risk and other relevant factors. This action can make an investor enjoy more competitive advantages over either foreign or domestic rivals.

Recently, Luo (1995, 1996) has examined the relationship between sharing arrangement and EJV performance. The key findings can be summarized as follows:

First, the majority and split status of sharing arrangement have a significant influence on EJV's overall performance. However, these two different sharing arrangements have different univariate effects on the multi-dimensional EJV performance. While the split-arrangement has a significantly positive impact on accounting return and asset efficiency, the majority-arrangement has a non-significant effect on these efficiency measures.

Second, the majority status of sharing arrangement is not significantly related to operational risks. This is contrary to the predictions by other scholars. Indeed, although the majority status of sharing arrangement enables the foreign parent firm (majority equity holder) to have greater power to control the EJV, operational uncertainties resulting from the contextual settings may outweigh those arising from contractual factors. Additionally, the univariate analysis suggests that there is no systematic and positive relationship between majority status and EJV's efficiency. Alternatively, the split status of sharing arrangement is significantly and positively related to ROI, asset turnover, and domestic sales growth. Thus, split control is a principal means by which success may be achieved because the local economy, politics and culture in China are so far removed from the experience of most Western firms and managers as to make dominant foreign control extremely risky; for Chinese investors, the shortage of advanced technology and managerial skills makes dominant control by them equally risky. The above evidence also suggests that the measurement of sharing arrangement by using the 'percentage' approach is not appropriate.

Third, the relationship between sharing arrangement and EJV performance is significantly moderated by project-type selection. The majority status positively interacts with technologically-advanced projects, and this interaction has a significant effect on EJV performance. This finding implies that advanced-technology represents an essential competency which can increase the competitive power and hence result in larger market share or high market growth.

China is by far the biggest and most impressive economy of the developing countries. When one considers that it also has a population of 1.3 billion people, approximately a quarter of the population of the earth, the potential of its future market is clear. A number of factors exist which make the selection of entry mode difficult and risky. Economically, there are a myriad of neo-mercantilism rules and regulations which both restrict and control the flow of FDI within the territory. Realistically, putting aside the actual content of Chinese law, it is important to note that there are few legal guarantees for foreign companies, a fact which by itself increases the risks of investing in China. These environmental factors surely have a critical influence on the choice of entry mode for foreign companies.

These fears, however, are likely to diminish following China's admission into the World Trade Organization, an eventuality which is currently being delayed by the United States. The Chinese economy will continue to lurch forward as the authorities maintain their pragmatic and ad-hoc attitude toward market reform and foreign investment. The uncertainties inherent in transforming economies are a source of challenges as well as opportunities. In China, as elsewhere, those investors best prepared to circumvent the former and exploit the latter are apt to survive and prosper. In fact, the growing complexity of operations of many MNCs in China, and the need to better explore market opportunities and more closely coordinate numerous strategic business units in China, has led many firms to set up an inter-SBUs network in China whereby different entry modes are flexibly adopted and strategically integrated.

Bibliography and Further Readings

Beamish, P.W. (1993). 'The Characteristics of Joint Ventures in the People's Republic of China'. *Journal of International Marketing*, vol.1, pp. 29-48.

Beamish, P.W. and Banks, J.C. (1987). 'Equity Joint Ventures and the Theory of the Multinational Enterprise'. *Journal of International Business Studies*, vol.18, pp. 1-16.

Harrigan, K.R. (1985). *Strategies for Joint Ventures*. Lexington, MA: D.C. Heath.

Killing, P.J. (1983). 'How to Make a Global Joint Venture Work'. *Harvard Business Review*, May-June, pp. 120-127.

Luo, Y. (1995). 'Linking Strategic and Moderating Factors to Performance of International Joint Ventures in China'. *Mid-Atlantic Journal of Business*, vol.31, pp. 5-23.

Luo, Y. (1996). *Foreign Parent Investment Strategies and International Joint Venture Performance: Chinese Evidence*. Unpublished Ph.D dissertation, Temple University, Philadelphia, PA.

Luo, Y. and Chen, M. (1995a). 'Financial Performance Comparison Between International Joint Ventures and Wholly Foreign-Owned Enterprises in China'. *The International Executive*, vol.37, pp. 599-613.

Luo, Y. and Chen, M. (1995b). 'A Financial Primer for Investors in China'. *Business Horizons*, vol.38, issue 4, pp. 32-36.

Osland, G.E. and Cavusgil, S.T. (1996). 'Performance Issues in U.S.-China Joint Ventures'. *California Management Review*, vol.38, pp. 106-130.

Pan, Y. (1996). 'Influences on Foreign Equity Ownership Level in Joint Ventures in China'. *Journal of International Business Studies*, vol.27, pp. 1-26.

Randall, D. and Telesio, P. (1995). 'Planning Ahead'. *The China Business Review*, January-February, pp. 14-18.

Shan, W. (1991). 'Environmental Risks and Joint Venture Sharing Arrangements', *Journal of International Business Studies*, vol.22, pp. 555-578.

Shenkar, O. (1990). 'International Joint Ventures' Problems in China: Risks and Remedies'. *Long Range Planning*, vol.23, pp. 82-90.

Tateisi, N. (1996). 'How to Invest in China'. *The Columbia Journal of World Business*, Summer, pp. 66-75.

Teagarden, M.B. (1990). *Sino-U.S. Joint Venture Effectiveness*. Unpublished Ph.D dissertation, University of Southern California, Los Angeles, CA.

Vanhonacker, W. (1997). 'Entering China: An Unconventional Approach'. *Harvard Business Review*, March-April, pp. 130-140.

Yan, A. and Gray, B. (1994). 'Bargaining Power, Management Control, and Performance in United States-China Joint Ventures: A Comparative Case Study', *Academy of Management Journal*, vol.37, pp. 1478-1517.

Appendix 1

Sample Contract For International Joint Venture Formation

CHAPTER 1. GENERAL PROVISIONS

In accordance with the Law of the People's Republic of China and other relevant Chinese laws and regulations concerning International Joint Venture Formation (involving Chinese and Foreign Investment), _____ Company and _____ Company, adhering to the principles of equality, mutual benefit, and friendly consultation, agree to establish a joint venture enterprise in _____, the People's Republic of China, in accordance with the following contract.

CHAPTER 2. PARTIES TO THE JOINT VENTURE

Article 1

The Parties to this contract are as follows:
_____ Company (hereafter referred to as Party A), registered with _____ in China, with its legal address at _____ (street), _____ (district), _____ (city), _____ (province), China.

Legal representative:
    Name:
    Position:
    Nationality:

_____ Company (hereafter referred to as Party B), registered with _____, with its legal address at _____.

Legal representative:
    Name:
    Position:
    Nationality:

(Note: In case there are more than two investors, they will be called Party C, D..... in proper order).

CHAPTER 3. ESTABLISHMENT OF THE JOINT VENTURE COMPANY

Article 2

In accordance with the Law of the People's Republic of China and other relevant Chinese laws and regulations concerning International Joint Venture Formation, both parties to the joint venture agree to set up the _____ limited liability joint venture company (hereafter referred to as the joint venture company.)

Article 3

The name of the joint venture company is _____ Limited Liability Company.
The foreign language name is _____.
The legal address of the joint venture company is at _____(street), _____ (city), _____ (province).

Article 4

All activities of the joint venture company shall be governed by the laws, decrees, and pertinent rules and regulations of the People's Republic of China.

Article 5

The organizational form of the joint venture company is a limited liability company. Each party to the joint venture company is liable to the joint venture company within the limit of the capital subscribed by said party. The profits, risks, and losses of the joint venture company shall be shared by the parties in proportion to their contributions of registered capital.

CHAPTER 4. PURPOSE, SCOPE, AND SCALE OF PRODUCTION AND BUSINESS

Article 6

The purpose of the parties to the joint venture is to enhance economic cooperation and technical exchange, improve product quality, develop new products, and gain competitive positions in the world market in terms of quality and price by adopting advanced and appropriate technology and scientific management methods, so as to increase economic results and ensure satisfactory economic benefits for each investor.
(Note: This article shall be written according to the specific situation in the contract).

Article 7

The productive business scope of the joint venture company is to produce _____ products, provide maintenance services after the sale of the products, and research and develop new products.
(Note: To be written in the contract according to specific conditions).

Article 8

The production scale of the joint venture company is as follows:

1. The production capacity after the joint venture begins operations is _____.

2. The production scale may be increased up to _____ with the development of production and operations. The product varieties may be developed into _____.
(Note: To be written according to the specific situation).

CHAPTER 5. TOTAL AMOUNT OF INVESTMENT AND REGISTERED CAPITAL

Article 9

The total amount of investment of the joint venture company is _____RMB (or foreign currency agreed upon by both parties).

Article 10

Investment contributed by the parties is _____RMB, which will be the registered capital of the joint venture company, of which:
Party A shall pay _____RMB, accounting for _____% of total investment; Party B shall pay _____RMB, accounting for _____%.

Article 11

Both Party A and Party B will contribute the following as their investment:

Party A:
cash	_____RMB
machines and equipment	_____RMB
premises	_____RMB
rights to use of the site	_____RMB
industrial property	_____RMB
other	_____RMB

Total Investment in RMB   _____RMB

Party B:
cash	_____RMB
machines and equipment	_____RMB
premises	_____RMB
rights to use of the site	_____RMB
industrial property	_____RMB
other	_____RMB

Total Investment in RMB   _____RMB
(*Note: When contributing capital goods or industrial property as investments, Party A and Party B shall include a separate contract regarding these investments as part of this main contract*).

Article 12

The registered capital of the joint venture company shall be paid in _____ installments by Party A and Party B according to the respective proportions of their investment.

Each installment shall be as follows:

(Note: To be written according to the specific conditions).

Article 13

In case any party to the joint venture intends to assign all or part of its investment subscribed to a third party, consent shall be obtained from the other party to the joint venture, and approval from an examination and approval authority is required. When one party to the joint ventures assigns all or part of its investment, the other party has preemptive rights.

CHAPTER 6. RESPONSIBILITIES OF EACH PARTY TO THE JOINT VENTURE

Article 14

Party A and Party B shall be responsible respectively for the following matters:

Responsibilities of Party A:

Handling of applications for approval, registration, business licenses, and other matters concerning the establishment of the joint venture company with the relevant Chinese departments;

Processing applications for rights to use of a site with the authority in charge of land;

Organizing design and construction of the premises and other engineering facilities for the joint venture company;

Providing cash, machinery and equipment, and facilities - in accordance with the stipulations in Article 11;

Assisting Party B in processing import customs declarations for the machinery and equipment contributed by Party B as investment, and arranging transportation of such within Chinese territory;

Assisting the joint venture company in purchasing or leasing equipment, materials, raw materials, office supplies and equipment, means of transportation, communication facilities and so on;

Assisting the joint venture company in contacting and arranging for basic utilities, such as water, electricity, transportation, and so on;

Assisting in recruiting Chinese management personnel, technical personnel, workers, and other needed personnel for the joint venture;

Assisting foreign workers and staff in applying for entry visas, work licenses, and in processing their travel documents; and

Responsibly handling other matters entrusted by the joint venture company.

Responsibilities of Party B:

Providing cash, machinery, equipment, and industrial property - in accordance with the stipulations in Article 11 - and shipping capital goods that have been contributed as investment, such as machinery and equipment, to the Chinese port:

Handling matters entrusted by the joint venture company, such as selecting and purchasing machinery and equipment outside of China, and so on;

Providing necessary technical personnel for the installation, testing, and trial runs of the equipment, as well as for future production and inspection;

Training technical personnel and workers for the joint venture company;

In the case where Party B is a licenser, Party B shall be responsible for the stable production of qualifying products by the joint venture company based on the design capacity within the stipulated period; and

Being responsible for handling other matters entrusted by the joint venture company.

(Note: To be written according to the specific situation).

CHAPTER 7. TRANSFER OF TECHNOLOGY

Article 15

Both Party A and Party B agree that a technology transfer agreement shall be signed between the joint venture company and Party B (or a third party) so as to obtain the advanced production technology needed for realizing the production scale stipulated in Chapter 4 of the contract, including technology necessary for product design, manufacturing, testing, material prescription, maintenance of standard of quality, and training of personnel.

(Note: To be written according to the specific conditions).

Article 16

Party B offers the following guarantees on the transfer of technology:
(Note: This article applies only when Party B is responsible for transferring technology to the joint venture company).

1. Party B guarantees that the overall technology, such as the design, technological processes, tests, and inspection of products, will be integrated, precise, and reliable. The technology should be sufficient to satisfy the requirements of the purposes of the joint venture's operation and be able to meet the quality standards and production capacity stipulated in the contract;

2. Party B guarantees that the technology stipulated in this contract and the technology transfer agreement shall be fully transferred to the joint venture company and pledges that the technology provided shall be truly advanced.

3. Party B shall compile a detailed list of the technology and technological services provided at various stages, as stipulated in the technology transfer agreement, comprising an appendix to the contract and a guarantee of performance;

4. The drawings, technological conditions, and other detailed information are part of the transferred technology and shall be offered on time;

5. Within the valid period of the technology transfer agreement, Party B shall provide the joint venture company with improvements of the technology and improved information and technological materials in a timely manner, without charging separate fees; and

6. Party B shall guarantee that the technological personnel and the workers in the joint venture company will master all of the technology transferred within the period stipulated in the technology transfer agreement.

Article 17

In case Party B fails to provide equipment and technology in accordance with the stipulations in this contract and in the technology transfer agreement or in case any deceptions or concealments on the part of Party B are discovered, Party B shall be responsible for compensating for the resulting direct losses to the joint venture company.

Article 18

The technology transfer fee shall be paid in royalties. The royalty rate shall be _____ % of the net sales value of the products produced.

The term for royalty payments is the same as the term of the technology transfer agreement stipulated in Article 19 of this contract.

Article 19

The term for the technology transfer agreement signed by the joint venture company and Party B is _____ years. After the expiration of the technology transfer agreement, the joint venture company shall have the right to continue using, researching, and developing the imported technology.

(Note: The term for a technology transfer agreement is generally no longer than ten years, and it shall be approved by the Ministry of Foreign Economic Relations and Trade or by other examination and approval authorities entrusted by the Ministry of Foreign Economic Relations and Trade).

CHAPTER 8. SELLING PRODUCTS

Article 20

The products of the joint venture company will be sold both on the Chinese market and on the overseas market, with the exports accounting for _____ %, and the domestic market for _____ %.

(Note: An annual percentage and amounts for outside and inside selling will be written out according to the practical situation. In normal conditions, the amount for export shall at least meet the foreign exchange expenses of the joint venture company).

Article 21

Products may be sold on the overseas markets through the following channels:

The joint venture company may sell its products directly in international markets, which will account for _____ % of production;

The joint venture company may sign sales contracts with Chinese foreign trade companies, entrusting them as sales agents or exclusive sales agencies, which may account for _____ %; and

The joint venture company may entrust Party B to sell its products, which may account for _____ %.

Article 22

The joint venture's products to be sold in China may be handled by Chinese materials and commercial departments by means of agency or exclusive sales, or they may be sold by the joint venture company directly.

Article 23

In order to provide maintenance service for the products sold both in China or abroad, the joint venture company may set up sales branches for maintenance service both in China or abroad subject to the approval of the relevant Chinese department.

Article 24

The trademark of the joint venture's product is _____.

CHAPTER 9: THE BOARD OF DIRECTORS

Article 25

The date of registration of the joint venture company shall be the date of the establishment of the board of directors of the joint venture company.

Article 26

The board of directors is composed of _____ directors, of which _____ shall be appointed by Party A, _____ by Party B. The chairman of the board shall be appointed by Party A, and its vice-chairman by party B. The term of office for the directors, chairman, and vice-chairman is four years. Their term of office may be renewed if they are re-appointed by the relevant party.

Article 27

The highest authority of the joint venture shall be its board of directors, which shall decide all major issues concerning the joint venture company. Unanimous approval shall be required before any decisions are made concerning major issues. As for other matters, approval by majority or a simple majority shall be required.
(Note: The main contents shall be listed according to article 36 of the Regulations for the Implementation of the Joint Venture Law).

Article 28

The chairman of the board is the legal representative of the joint venture company. Should the chairman be unable to exercise his responsibilities for some reason, he shall authorize the vice-chairman or any other director to represent the joint venture company temporarily.

Article 29

The board of directors shall hold a meeting at least once every year. The meeting shall be called and presided over by the chairman of the board. The chairman may convene an interim meeting based on a proposal made by more than one third of the total number of directors. Minutes of the meeting shall be placed on file.

CHAPTER 10. BUSINESS MANAGEMENT OFFICE

Article 30

The joint venture company shall establish a management office that shall be responsible for management of daily business affairs. The management office shall have a general manager, appointed by party _____; _____ deputy general managers, _____ by party _____; _____ by party _____. The general manager and deputy general managers shall be appointed by the board of directors for terms of _____ years.

Article 31

The responsibility of the general manager is to carry out the decisions of the board and to organize and conduct the daily management of the joint venture company. The deputy general managers shall assist the general manager in his or her work.

Several department managers may be appointed by the management office. They shall be responsible for the work of their respective departments, follow directives of the general manager and deputy general managers, and report directly to them.

Article 32

In case of graft or serious dereliction of duty on the part of the general manager and/or deputy general managers, the board of directors shall have power to dismiss them at will.

CHAPTER 11. PURCHASE OF EQUIPMENT

Article 33

The joint venture company shall give first priority to finding sources in China for the purchase of required raw materials, fuel, parts, means of transportation, articles for office use, and so on, where their quality would be equivalent to that obtained from the country of Party B.

Article 34

In case the joint venture company entrusts Party B to purchase equipment from overseas markets, the persons appointed by Party A shall be invited to take part in the purchasing.

CHAPTER 12. PREPARATION AND CONSTRUCTION

Article 35

During the period of preparation and construction, an office shall be set up by the board of directors. This office shall consist of _____ persons, among whom _____ persons will be from Party A, _____ from Party B. This office shall have one manager recommended by Party _____, and one deputy manager by Party _____. The manager and deputy manager shall be appointed by the board of directors.

Article 36

The preparation and construction office is responsible for the following: examining the project designs; signing project construction contracts; organizing the purchasing and inspection of relevant equipment and materials; developing the project construction schedule; preparing the budget; controlling project expenditures and accounting procedures; and maintaining records of documents, drawings, files, and materials during the construction phase of the project.

Article 37

A technical group shall be organized with several technical personnel appointed by Party A and Party B. This group, under the leadership of the preparation and construction office, is in charge of all aspects of the project, including project design, quality control, as well as equipment, materials, and use of technology.

Article 38

Remuneration for services and expenses of the preparation and construction office staff shall be covered in the project budget as agreed upon by both parties.

Article 39

After having completed the project, the preparation and construction office shall be dissolved by the board of directors.

CHAPTER 13. LABOR MANAGEMENT

Article 40

The labor contract covering recruitment, employment, dismissal and resignation, wages, labor insurance, welfare, rewards, penalties, and other matters concerning the staff and the workers for the joint venture company shall be drawn up between the joint venture company and the trade union of the joint venture company as a whole or with individual employees in accordance with the Regulations of the People's Republic of China on Labor Management in Joint Ventures Using Chinese and Foreign Investment and Its Implementation Rules.

After being signed, the labor contracts shall be filed with the local labor management department.

Article 41

The appointment of high-ranking administrative personnel recommended by both parties, their salaries, social insurance, welfare, and standards for traveling expenses shall be decided upon by the board of directors.

CHAPTER 14. TAXES, FINANCE, AND AUDITS

Article 42

The joint venture company shall pay taxes in accordance with Chinese laws and other relevant regulations.

Article 43

Staff members and workers for the joint venture company shall pay individual income taxes according to the Individual Income Tax Law of the People's Republic of China.

Article 44

Allocations for reserve and expansion funds for the joint venture company, as well as welfare funds and bonuses for staff and workers, shall be set aside in accordance with the stipulations of the Law of the People's Republic of China on Joint Ventures Using Chinese and Foreign Investment. The annual proportion of allocations shall be decided by the board of directors according to the business situation of the joint venture company.

Article 45

The fiscal year of the joint venture company shall be from January 1 to December 31. All vouchers, receipts, statistical statements, reports, and account books shall be written in Chinese.
(Note: A foreign language may be used concurrently with mutual consent).

Article 46

The examination of the joint venture's finances shall be conducted by an auditor registered in China, and the reports shall be submitted to the board of directors and general manager.

In case Party B considers it necessary to employ a foreign auditor registered outside of China to undertake the annual financial audit, Party A shall give its consent. However, all associated expenses shall be borne by Party B.

Article 47

In the first three months of each fiscal year, the manager shall prepare the previous year's balance sheet, profit and loss statement, and a proposal regarding the disposal of profits, and he will submit them to the board of directors for examination and approval.

CHAPTER 15. DURATION OF THE JOINT VENTURE

Article 48

The duration of the joint venture company is _____ years. The establishment of the joint venture company shall start from the date of issuance of the business license of the joint venture.

An application for extension of duration, proposed by one party and unanimously approved by the board of directors, shall be submitted to the Ministry of Foreign Economic Relations and Trade (or the examination and approval authority entrusted by it) six months prior to the expiration date of the joint venture.

CHAPTER 16. THE DISPOSAL OF ASSETS AFTER EXPIRATION OF THE DURATION

Article 49

Upon the expiration of the joint venture agreement (or termination before the date of expiration), liquidation shall be carried out according to relevant laws. The liquidated assets shall be distributed in accordance with the proportions of investment contributed by Party A and Party B respectively.

CHAPTER 17. INSURANCE

Article 50

Insurance policies carried by the joint venture company for various kinds of risks shall be underwritten by the People's Insurance Company of China. The type, value, and duration of the insurance shall be determined by the board of directors in accordance with the stipulations of the People's Insurance Company of China.

CHAPTER 18. AMENDMENTS, ALTERATIONS, AND DISCHARGE OF THE CONTRACT

Article 51

Amendments of the contract shall come into force only after a written agreement is signed by Party A and Party B and approved by the original examination and approval authority.

Article 52

In case of an inability to fulfill the contract, or to continue operations due to heavy losses for successive years as a result of a force majeure, the duration of the joint venture and the contract may be terminated prior to the time of expiration after unanimous agreement by the board of directors and approval by the original examination and approval authority.

Article 53

Should the joint venture company be unable to continue its operations or achieve the business purpose stipulated in its contract, due to the fact that one of the contracting parties fails to fulfill the obligations prescribed by the contract and articles of association or seriously violates the stipulations of the contract and articles of association, that party shall be deemed in breach of contract. The other party shall have the right to terminate the contract and to claim damages in accordance with the provisions of the contract after approval by the original examination and approval authority. In case Party A and Party B of the joint venture company both agree to continue operations, the party that fails to fulfill obligations shall be liable for the economic losses thus suffered by the joint venture company.

CHAPTER 19. LIABILITIES FOR BREACH OF CONTRACT

Article 54

Should either Party A or Party B fail to pay contributions on schedule as defined in Chapter 5 of this contract, the party in breach of contract shall pay the other party _____ % of the contribution starting from the first month after the expiration of the time limit. Should the party in breach fail to pay after three months, _____ % of the contribution shall be paid to the other party, which shall have the right to terminate the contract and to claim damages from the party in breach in accordance with the stipulations in article 53 of the contract.

Article 55

Should all or part of the contract and its appendices go unfulfilled, owing to the fault of one party, the party in breach shall bear the responsibility. Should it be the fault of both parties, they shall bear their respective responsibilities accordingly.

Article 56

In order to guarantee the performance of the contract and its appendices, both Party A and Party B shall provide each other with bank guarantees for their respective contributions according to the contract.

CHAPTER 20. FORCE MAJEURE

Article 57

Should either of the parties to the contract be prevented from executing the contract by force majeure, such as an earthquake, typhoon, flood, fire, war, or other unforeseen events, this party shall notify the other party by cable without delay within fifteen days, thereafter provide detailed information of the events and a notarized document explaining the reason for the party's delay or inability to execute all or part of the contract. Both parties shall decide through negotiations whether to terminate the contract, to exempt part of the obligations necessitated for implementation of the contract, or to delay the execution of the contract, according to the effect of the force majeure events on the performance of the parties in carrying out the stipulations of the contract.

CHAPTER 21. APPLICABLE LAW

Article 58

The formation of this contract, its validity, interpretation, execution, and settlement of disputes shall be governed by the related laws of the People's Republic of China.

CHAPTER 22. SETTLEMENT OF DISPUTES

Article 59

Any disputes arising from the execution of (or in connection with) the contract shall be settled through friendly consultation between both parties. In case no settlement can be reached through consultation, the dispute shall be submitted for arbitration to the Foreign Economic and Trade Arbitration Commission of the China Council for the Promotion of International Trade in accordance with established rules of procedure. The arbitral award is final and binding upon both parties.

Any disputes arising from the execution of (or in connection with) the contract shall be settled through friendly negotiation between both parties. In case no settlement can be reached, the dispute shall be submitted to the _____ Arbitration Organization in _____ for arbitration in accordance with its rules of procedure. The arbitral award is final and binding upon both parties.

Any disputes arising from the execution of (or in connection with) the contract shall be settled through friendly negotiation between both parties. In case no settlement can be reached through negotiation, the dispute shall be submitted for arbitration.

Arbitration shall take place in the defendant's country. If in China, arbitration shall be conducted by the Foreign Economic and Trade Arbitration Commission of the China Council for the Promotion of International Trade in accordance with its rules of procedure.

If in _____, arbitration shall be conducted by _____ in accordance with its rules of procedure.

The arbitral award is final and binding on both parties.

(Note: When formulating contracts, only one of the above-mentioned provisions can be used).

Article 60

During arbitration, the contract shall be executed continuously by both parties except for matters in dispute.

CHAPTER 23. LANGUAGE

Article 61

The contract shall be written in Chinese and in _____. Both languages are equally legally binding. In the event that any discrepancy arises between the two aforementioned versions, the Chinese version shall prevail.

CHAPTER 24. EFFECTIVENESS OF THE CONTRACT AND MISCELLANEOUS CONCERNS

Article 62

The appendices drawn up in accordance with the principles of this contract are an integral part of this contract, including: the project agreement, technology transfer agreement, and sales agreement.

Article 63

The contract and its appendices shall come into force beginning on the date of approval by the Ministry of Foreign Economics Relations and Trade of the People's Republic of China (or its entrusted examination and approval authority).

Article 64

Should notices in connection with any party's rights and obligations be sent by either Party A or Party B by telegram, telex, or facsimile, a written letter shall be required immediately afterward. The legal address of Party A and Party B listed in this contract shall be the posting address.

Article 65

This contract is signed in _____, China, by the authorized representatives of both parties on _____, 19_____.

For Party A   For Party B
(Signature)   (Signature)

Appendix 2

List of China's Foreign Investment Laws and Regulations

1 Law on Civil Procedure of the People's Republic of China (Promulgated on 9 April 1991);

2 The Company Law of the People's Republic of China (Promulgated on 29 December 1993);

3 Law of the People's Republic of China on Bankruptcy of Enterprises (Trial Implementation) (Promulgated in December 1986);

4 Provisional Regulations of the People's Republic of China on Private Enterprises (Promulgated by the State Administration for Industry and Commerce in 1988);

5 Measures for the Implementation of the Provisional Regulations of the People's Republic of China on Private Enterprises (Promulgated by the State Administration for Industry and Commerce on 16 January 1989);

6 Customs Law of the People's Republic of China (Adopted and promulgated at the 19th Session of the Standing committee of the Sixth National People's Republic of China on 22 January 1987);

7 Law of the People's Republic of China on Import and Export Commodity Inspection (Promulgated on 21 February 1989);

8 Implementing Rules to the Law on the Inspection of Import and Export Commodities of the People's Republic of China (Promulgated by the Standing Administration for the Inspection of Import and Export Commodities on 23 October 1992);

9 Rules of the People's Republic of China on the Origin of Export Goods (Adopted at the Standing Conference of the State Council on 28 February 1992);

10 Measures for the Implementation of the Rules of the People's Republic of China on Origin of Export Goods (Promulgated by the Ministry of Foreign Economic Relations and Trade on 1 April 1992);

11 Checklist of the People's Republic of China on Main Procedures for Manufacture and Processing of Original Goods with Imported Elements (Promulgated by the Ministry of Foreign Economic Relations and Trade on 1 April 1992);

12 Regulations on the Administration of Technological Import Contracts in the People's Republic of China (Promulgated by the State Council on 24 May 1985);

13 Detailed Rules for the Implementation of the Regulations of the Administration of Technological Import Contracts in the People's Republic of China (Approved by the State Council on 30 December 1987 and promulgated by the Ministry of Foreign Economic Relations and Trade on 20 January 1988);

14 Taxation Management Law for the People's Republic of China (Adopted at the 27th Session of the Standing Committee of the Seventh National People's Congress on 4 September 1992);

15 Provisional Regulations on Value-Added Taxes for the People's Republic of China (13 December 1993);

16 Detailed Implementation Rules for the Provisional Regulations of Value-Added Taxes for the People's Republic of China (Promulgated by the Ministry of Finance on 25 December 1993);

17 Provisional Regulations on Consumption Taxes for the People's Republic of China (Promulgated by the Ministry of Finance on 13 December 1993);

18 Detailed Implementation Rules for the Provisional Regulations on Consumption Taxes for the People's Republic of China (Promulgated by the Ministry of Finance on 25 December 1993);

19 Provisional Regulations of Business Taxes in the People's Republic of China (Promulgated by the Ministry of Finance on 13 December 1993);

20 Detailed Implementation Rules for the Provisional Regulations of Business Taxes in the People's Republic of China (Promulgated by the Ministry of Finance on 25 December 1993);

21 Patent Law of the People's Republic of China (Adopted at the Fourth Session of the Standing Committee of the Sixth National People's Congress on 12 March 1984);

22 Implementation Regulations for the Patent Law of the People's Republic of China (Approved by the State Council and Promulgated by the Patent Office of the People's Republic of China on 21 December 1992);

23 Trademark Law of the People's Republic of China (Adopted at the 24th Session of the Standing Committee of the Fifth National People's Congress on 23 August 1982);

24 Law on Economic Contracts Involving Foreign Investment in the People's Republic of China (Adopted at the 10th Session of the

Standing Committee of the Sixth National People's Congress on 21 March 1985);

25 Rules for the Procedure of Arbitration at the Chinese International Economic and Trade Arbitration Commission (Amended and adopted at the First Session of the Standing Committee of the Second Chinese Council for the Promotion of International Trade and the Chinese International Chamber of Commerce on 17 March 1994);

26 Regulations of the People's Republic of China for Controlling the Registration of Enterprises as Legal Persons (Promulgated by the State Administration for Industry and Commerce on 13 June 1988);

27 Detailed Rules for the Implementation of the Regulations of the People's Republic of China for Controlling the Registration of Enterprises as Legal Persons (Enforced from 1 December 1988);

28 Regulations on Granting and Transfer of Land Use Rights for Valuable Consideration in Cities and Towns in the People's Republic of China (Promulgated on 19 May 1990);

29 Individual Income Tax Law of the People's Republic of China (Promulgated on 10 September 1980);

30 Implementing Regulations of the Individual Income Tax Law of the People's Republic of China (Promulgated by the State Council on 28 January 1994);

31 Accounting Regulations for Foreign Funded Enterprises in the People's Republic of China (Promulgated on 24 June 1992);

32 Provisions of the People's Republic of China on Financial Management of Foreign-Funded Enterprises (Promulgated on 24 June 1992);

33 Provisional Regulations on Management of Export Goods by the Ministry of Foreign Economic Regulations and Trade (Issued by the Ministry of Foreign Economic Relations and Trade in December 1992);

34 Provisions of the Ministry of Foreign Economic Relations and Trade and the State Administration for Industry and Commerce on Contracts for and Management of Sino-Foreign Joint Ventures (Issued by the Ministry of Foreign Economic Relations and Trade on 13 September 1990);

35 Interpretation by the Ministry of Foreign Economics Relations and Trade on Certain Articles of Detailed Implementation Rules on the Law on Foreign-Funded Enterprises in the People's Republic of China (Issued by the Ministry of Foreign Economic Relations and Trade on 5 December 1991);

36 Implementation Rules of the Ministry of Foreign Economic Relations and Trade Concerning the Verification and Determination of Export-Oriented Enterprises and Technologically Advanced Enterprises with Foreign Investment (Promulgated by the Ministry of Foreign Economic Relations and Trade on 27 January 1987);

37 Supplementary Provisions for the Implementation Rules of the Ministry of Foreign Economic Relations and Trade Concerning the Verification and Determination of Export-Oriented Enterprises and Technologically Advanced Enterprises with Foreign Investment (Promulgated by the Ministry of Foreign Economic Relations and Trade on 2 February 1992);

38 Implementation Rules for the Ministry of Foreign Economic Relations and Trade Concerning Applications for Import and Export Licenses by Foreign Investment Enterprises (Promulgated by the Ministry of Foreign Economic Relations and Trade on 5 December 1991);

39 Interim Provisions on the Term of Joint Ventures of Chinese Foreign Equity Joint Ventures (Approved be the State Council on September 1990 and Promulgated by the Ministry of Foreign Economic Relations and Trade on 22 October 1990);

40 Rules of the Customs Administration of the People's Republic of China concerning the Control of Imported Materials and Parts Required by Foreign Investment Enterprises for the Fulfillment of Export Contracts (Promulgated by the General Customs Administration on 24 November 1986);

41 Provisional Rules of the People's Bank of China Concerning Renminbi Loans Against Mortgage on Foreign Exchange by Enterprises with Foreign Investment (Published by the Xinhua News Agency on 12 December 1986);

42 Provisional Rules of the People's Bank of China Concerning Provisions for Foreign Exchange Guarantees by Organizations within Chinese Territory (Promulgated by the People's Bank of China on 20 February 1987);

43 Provisional Regulations Concerning the Ratio Between Registered and Total Investments in Chinese Foreign Equity Joint Ventures (Promulgated by the State Administration for Industry and Commerce on 1 March 1987);

44 Rules by the Bank of China concerning Loans for Foreign Investment Enterprises (Approved by the State Council on 7 April 1987 and promulgated by the Bank of China on 26 April 1987);

45 Provisions on the Contributions Made by Parties to Joint Ventures Using Chinese and Foreign Investments (Approved by the State Council on 23 December 1987 and promulgated by the Ministry of Foreign Economic Relations and Trade and the State Administration for Industry and Commerce on 1 January 1988);

46 Provisions of the Ministry of Labor and Personnel of the People's Republic of China on the Autonomous Rights of Enterprises with Foreign Investment in the Hiring of Personnel and on Salaries and Wages, Insurance, and Welfare Expenses (Promulgated by the Ministry of Labor and Personnel on 26 November 1986);

47 Labor Law of the People's Republic of China (Adopted at the Eighth Session of the Standing Committee of the Eighth National People's Congress on 5 July 1994);

48 Foreign Trade Law of the People's Republic of China (Adopted at the Seventh Session of the Standing Committee of the Eighth National People's Congress on 12 May 1994);

49 Provisional Regulations on the Guidance of Foreign Investment Orientations (Published by the Xinhua News Agency on 27 June 1995);

50 Directory of Industries for the Guidance of Foreign Investment Orientations (Published by the Xinhua News Agency on 27 June 1995).

Appendix 3

The Law of the People's Republic of China on Sino-Foreign Equity Joint Ventures

(Adopted on 1 July 1979 at the Second Session of the Fifth National People's Congress, and amended pursuant to the Decision to Amend the Law on Chinese-Foreign Equity Joint Ventures in the People's Republic of China, passed on 4 April 1990 at the Third Session of the Seventh National People's Congress).

Article 1

The People's Republic of China, in order to expand international economic cooperation and technological exchange, permits foreign companies, enterprises, and other economic organizations or individuals (hereinafter referred to as the foreign party) to jointly establish and operate equity joint ventures within the territory of the People's Republic of China with Chinese companies, enterprises, or other economic organizations (hereinafter referred to as the Chinese party) based on the principles of equality and mutual benefit, and upon the approval of the Chinese government.

Article 2

The Chinese Government shall protect in accordance with law the investments of the foreign party in an equity joint venture, the profits due to it, and its other lawful rights and interests under the Agreement, Contract, and Articles of Association approved by the Chinese Government.

All the activities of an equity joint venture shall comply with the provisions of the laws, decrees, and relevant rules and regulations of the People's Republic of China.

The state will not nationalize or expropriate equity joint ventures except under special circumstances, based on the requirements of social and public interests, where equity joint ventures may be expropriated in accordance with legal procedures, and corresponding compensation shall be provided.

Article 3

The Agreement, Contract, and Articles of Association of an equity joint venture signed by the parties to the venture shall be submitted to the state department in charge of foreign economic relations and trade for examination and approval (hereinafter referred to as the Examination and Approval Authority). The Examination and Approval Authority shall decide within three months to approve or disapprove. After an equity joint ventures has been approved, it shall register with the state department in charge of Administration of Industry and Commerce, obtain its Business License, and commence business operations.

Article 4

The form of an equity joint venture shall be a limited liability company. The proportion of the foreign party's contribution to the registered capital of an equity joint venture shall in general not be less than 25%.

The parties to the venture shall share profits and bear risks and losses in proportion to their respective contributions to the registered capital.

The transfer of a party's contribution to the registered capital must be agreed upon by each party to the venture.

Article 5

The parties to an equity joint venture may make their investments in cash, in kind, in industrial property rights, etc.

The technology and equipment contributed by a foreign party as its investment must be advanced technology and equipment which is truly suited to the needs of China. Compensation shall be paid for losses caused by deception through intentional provision of outdated technology and equipment.

The investment of a Chinese party may include providing the right to use a site during the term of operation of the equity joint venture. If the right to use a site is not a part of the investment by a Chinese party, the venture shall pay the Chinese Government a fee for its use.

The various investments mentioned above shall be specified in the Contract and Articles of Association of the equity joint venture, and the value of each contribution (except for the site) shall be appraised and determined through discussions between parties to the venture.

Article 6

An equity joint venture shall establish a board of directors with a size and composition stipulated in the Contract and the Articles of Association after consultation between the parties to the venture; and each party to the venture shall appoint and replace its own director(s). The chairman and the vice-chairman of the board shall be determined through consultation between the parties to the venture or elected by the board. Where a director appointed by the Chinese party of the foreign party serves as chairman, a director appointed by the other party shall serve as vice-chairman. The board of directors shall decide important issues concerning the equity joint venture based on the principles of equality and mutual benefit.

The functions and powers of the board of directors shall be to discuss and decide, pursuant to the provisions of the Articles of Association of the equity joint venture, all important issues concerning the venture, namely: the development plan of the enterprise, production and business programs, the budget, distribution of profits, plans concerning labor and wages, termination of business, and the appointment or hiring of the general manager, the deputy general manager(s), the chief engineer, the chief accountant, and the auditor, as well as their functions and powers and their remuneration, etc.

The positions of general manager and deputy general manager(s) (or the factory manager and deputy factory manager(s)) shall be assumed by nominees made by the respective parties to the venture.

The employment and dismissal of the staff and workers of an equity joint venture shall be stipulated according to law in the Agreement or Contract between the parties to the venture.

Article 7

From the gross profit earned by an equity joint venture, after payment of the venture's income tax in accordance with the provisions of the tax laws of the People's Republic of China, deductions shall be made for the reserve fund, the bonus and welfare fund for staff and workers, and the enterprise development fund as stipulated in the Articles of Association of the venture; the net profit shall be distributed to the parties to the venture in proportion to their respective contributions to the registered capital.

Any equity joint venture may enjoy preferential treatment in the form of tax reductions and exemptions in accordance with provisions of state laws and administrative regulations relating to taxation.

When a foreign party uses its share of the net profit as reinvestment within the territory of China, it may apply for a refund of part of the income tax already paid.

Article 8

An equity joint venture shall, on the basis of its Business License, open a foreign-exchange account with a bank or another financial institution which is permitted by the state foreign-exchange control authority to engage in foreign-exchange business.

Matters concerning the foreign exchange of an equity joint venture shall be handled in conformity with the foreign-exchange control regulations of the People's Republic of China.

An equity joint venture may, in the course of its business activities, raise funds directly from foreign banks.

The various items of insurance of an equity joint venture shall be obtained from China's insurance companies.

Article 9

An equity joint venture's plans for production and business operations shall be filed for the record with the department in charge, and implemented through economic contracts.

For the raw and processed materials, fuel, auxiliary equipment, etc. needed by an equity joint venture, priority shall be given to purchasing in China, but such purchases may also be made directly on the international market with foreign exchange raised by the equity joint venture itself.

An equity joint venture shall be encouraged to sell its products outside the territory of China. Export products may be sold on foreign markets by an equity joint venture directly or by related entrusted institutions; they may also be sold through China's foreign-trade institutions. The products of an equity joint venture may also be sold on the Chinese market.

When necessary, an equity joint venture may set up branch institutions outside China.

Article 10

The net profit received by a foreign party after fulfillment of its obligations under the law and provisions of agreements and contracts, the funds received by a foreign party upon the expiration or termination of an equity joint venture, as well as other funds, may be remitted abroad, in the currency stipulated in the joint venture contract, in accordance with foreign-exchange control regulations.

The foreign party shall be encouraged to make deposits in the Bank of China that foreign exchange which may be remitted abroad.

Article 11

After payment of individual income taxes under the tax laws of the People's Republic of China, wage income and other legitimate income of foreign staff and workers within an equity joint venture may be remitted abroad in accordance with foreign-exchange control regulations.

Article 12

The term of operation of equity joint ventures may be agreed upon differently according to different lines of business and different circumstances. The term of operation of equity joint ventures engaged in some lines of business shall be fixed, while the term of operation of equity joint ventures engaged in other lines of business may or may not be fixed. Where the parties to an equity joint venture with a fixed term of operation agree to extend the term, they shall submit an application to the Examination and Approval Authority not later than six months prior to the expiration of the operation term. The Examination and Approval Authority shall decide, within one month of receipt of the application, to approve or disapprove.

Article 13

If serious losses are incurred by an equity joint venture, or one party fails to fulfill its obligations under the Contract and the Articles of Association, or a *force majeure* event occurs, etc., the contract may be terminated after consultation and agreement between the parties to the venture, subject to approval by the Examination and Approval Authority and to registration with the state department in charge of Administration of Industry and

Commerce. In case of losses caused by breach of contract, economic responsibility shall be borne by the breaching party.

Article 14

When a dispute arises between the parties to a venture which the board of directors is unable to resolve through consultation, the dispute shall be settled by conciliation or arbitration by an arbitration institution of China, or through arbitration by another arbitration institution agreed upon by the parties to the venture.

Article 15

This law shall come into force on the date of its promulgation. The power to amend this law is vested in the National People's Congress.

Appendix 4

The Law of the People's Republic of China on Sino-Foreign Cooperative Joint Ventures

(Adopted at the First Session of the Seventh National People's Congress on 13 April, 1988).

Article 1

The Law is formulated in order to expand economic cooperation and technological exchange with foreign countries and to encourage, according to the principles of equality and mutual benefit, foreign enterprises, economic organizations or individuals (hereafter referred to as the foreign cooperator) to establish with Chinese enterprises or other economic organizations (hereafter referred to as the Chinese cooperator) Chinese-foreign cooperative joint ventures (hereafter referred to as cooperative joint ventures) within the territory of the People's Republic of China.

Article 2

In establishing a cooperative joint venture, the Chinese and foreign cooperators shall, in accordance with the provision of this Law, and the provisions of investment or conditions of cooperation, determine the distribution of earnings or profits, the sharing of risks and losses, the manner of operation and management, and the disposal of property. The Chinese and foreign cooperators shall determine such distribution in advance with regard to the termination of the cooperative joint venture.

A cooperative joint venture which meets the conditions for being a legal person under Chinese law shall acquire the status of a Chinese legal person in accordance with the law.

Article 3

The state shall protect, according to law, the legitimate rights and interests of the cooperative joint venture and the Chinese and foreign cooperators.

The cooperative joint venture must abide by Chinese laws and regulations and must not injure the social and public interests of China.

The relevant state authorities shall exercise supervision over the cooperative joint venture according to law.

Article 4

The state shall encourage the establishment of productive export-oriented or technologically advanced cooperative joint ventures.

Article 5

In applying for the establishment of a cooperative joint venture, such documents as the Agreement, the Contract, and the Articles of Association, signed by both the Chinese and foreign cooperators, shall be submitted for examination and approval to the department in charge of foreign economic relations and trade under the State Council (hereafter referred to the Examination and Approval Authority). The Examination and Approval Authority shall, within 45 days of receipt of the application, decide whether to grant approval.

Article 6

When the application for the establishment of a cooperative joint venture is approved, the cooperators shall, within 30 days of receipt of the Certificate of Approval, apply to the Administrative Authority for Industry and Commerce for registration and then obtain a Business License. The date of issuance of the Business License of a cooperative joint venture shall be the date of its establishment.

A cooperative joint venture shall, within 30 days of its establishment, register with the Tax Authority.

Article 7

If, during the period of cooperation, the Chinese and foreign cooperators agree, after consultation, to make major modifications to the cooperative joint venture Contract, they shall report to the Examination and Approval Authority for approval; if the modifications are related to matters of statutory industrial and commercial registration or tax registration, they shall register with the Administrative Authority for Industry and Commerce or the Tax Authority, respectively.

Article 8

The investment or requirements for cooperation contributed by the Chinese and foreign cooperators may be provided in cash, in kind, in the right to use land, industrial property rights, non-patent technology, and other property rights.

Article 9

The Chinese and foreign cooperators shall, in accordance with the law and regulations and the provisions of the cooperative joint venture Contract, duly fulfill their obligations in contributing the full investment and providing the required cooperation. In case of failure to do so within the prescribed time, the Administrative Authority for Industry and Commerce shall set a time limit for fulfillment of these obligations; if such obligations remain unfulfilled within the time limit, the matter shall be handled by the Examination and Approval Authority and the Administrative Authority for Industry and commerce according to relevant state rules.

The investment or requirements for cooperation provided by the Chinese and Foreign cooperators shall be verified by an accountant registered in China, or another relevant authority, who shall provide a Verification Certificate.

Article 10

If the Chinese or foreign cooperator wishes to assign the whole or a part of its rights and obligations as prescribed in the cooperative joint venture Contract, it must have the consent of the other cooperator or cooperators, and report to the Examination and Approval Authority for approval.

Article 11

The cooperative joint venture shall conduct its operations and managerial activities in accordance with the approved Contract and the Articles of Association without interference in its autonomous rights of operation and management.

Article 12

A cooperative joint venture shall establish a board of directors or directors of a joint managerial committee which shall, according to the Contract or the Articles of Association of the cooperative joint venture, decide on major issues concerning the cooperative joint venture. If a Chinese or foreign cooperator assumes the chairmanship of the board of directors or the directorship of the joint managerial committee, the other cooperator shall assume the vice-chairmanship of the board or the deputy directorship of the joint managerial committee. The board of directors or the joint managerial committee may decide the appointment or employment of a general manager, who shall then take charge of the routine operations and management of the cooperative joint venture. The general manager shall be responsible to the board of directors or the joint managerial committee.

If a cooperative joint venture, after its establishment, chooses to entrust a third party with its operation and management, it must obtain the unanimous agreement of the board of directors or the joint managerial committee, report to the Examination and Approval Authority for Approval, and register the charge with the Administrative Authority for Industry and Commerce.

Article 13

The employment, dismissal, remuneration, welfare, labor protection, and labor insurance, etc. of the workers and staff of a cooperative joint venture shall be specified and provided for in contracts concluded in accordance with the law.

Article 14

The workers and staff of a cooperative joint venture shall, in accordance with the law, establish their trade unions to carry out trade union activities and protect their legal rights and interests.

A cooperative joint venture shall provide the necessary conditions for the venture's trade unions to carry out their activities.

Article 15

A cooperative joint venture must establish its account books within the territory of China, file its accounting statements according to accounting rules, and accept supervision by financial and tax authorities.

If a cooperative joint venture violates the provisions of the preceding paragraph and fails to establish its account books within the territory of China, the financial and tax authorities may impose a fine, and the Administrative Authority of Industry and Commerce may order the cooperative joint venture to suspend its business operations or may revoke its Business License.

Article 16

A cooperative joint venture shall, on presentation of its Business License, open a foreign exchange account with a bank or any other financial institution which is permitted by the state exchange control authority to deal in foreign exchange.

Any matters concerning foreign exchange by cooperative joint ventures shall be handled in accordance with the regulations of the state on foreign exchange control.

Article 17

A cooperative joint venture may obtain loans from financial institutions both within and outside the territory of China.

Any loans to be used by the Chinese cooperator or the foreign cooperator as investment or as a requirement for cooperation, and any guarantees in relation to the loan, shall be provided by the cooperator concerned on his own account.

Article 18

Each kind of insurance coverage of a cooperative joint venture shall be furnished by an insurance institution within the territory of China.

Article 19

A cooperative joint venture may, within its approved scope of operations, import the materials it needs and export its products. A cooperative joint venture may purchase, on both the domestic market and the world market, those raw materials, fuels, etc. which are needed and fall within its approved scope of operations.

Article 20

A cooperative joint venture shall balance its own foreign exchange receipts and expenditures. If a cooperative joint venture is unable to balance expenditures, it may, in accordance with the state regulations, apply to relevant authorities for assistance.

Article 21

A cooperative joint venture shall, in accordance with the state tax regulations, pay taxes, and may enjoy preferential treatment through tax reductions or exemptions.

Article 22

The Chinese and foreign cooperators shall distribute earnings or profits, and undertake risks and losses, in accordance with the provisions in the cooperative joint venture Contract.

If the Chinese and foreign cooperators agree in the cooperative joint venture Contract that the whole of the fixed assets of the cooperative joint venture shall be allocated to the ownership of the Chinese cooperative at the expiration of the cooperative joint venture, it may be agreed in the cooperative joint venture Contract that the foreign cooperator shall have its investment returned prior to the end of the period of cooperation. If the return of the foreign cooperator's investment will occur prior to the payment of income tax, applications must be made to the financial and tax authorities, which shall examine and approve the application in accordance with state regulations concerning taxation.

If, according to the provisions of the preceding paragraph, the foreign cooperator will have its investment returned prior to the end of the period of cooperation, the Chinese and foreign cooperators shall, in accordance with relevant laws and provisions in the cooperative joint venture Contract, both be liable for any debts incurred by the cooperative joint venture.

Article 23

The profits received by the foreign cooperator after fulfillment of its obligations as required by the law and the cooperative joint venture Contract and any other legitimate income and funds the foreign cooperator may receive after termination of the cooperative joint venture may be remitted abroad according to law.

The wages, salaries, and other legitimate income earned by the foreign personnel of cooperative joint ventures may, after individual income tax has been paid, be remitted abroad according to law.

Article 24

Upon expiration or early termination of the term of a cooperative joint venture, its assets, claims, and liabilities shall be liquidated according to legal procedures. The Chinese and foreign cooperators shall, in accordance with the provisions in the cooperative joint venture Contract, determine the ownership of the venture's properties.

A cooperative joint venture shall, upon expiration or termination, cancel its registration with the Administrative Authority for Industry and Commerce and the tax authorities.

Article 25

The period of a cooperative joint venture shall be determined through consultation by the Chinese and foreign cooperators and shall be clearly specified in the cooperative joint venture Contract. If the Chinese and foreign cooperators agree to extend the period of cooperation, they shall apply to the Examination and Approval Authority 180 days prior to the expiration of the cooperation term. The Examination and Approval Authority shall, within 30 days of receipt of the application, decide whether to grant approval.

Article 26

Any dispute between the Chinese and foreign cooperators arising from performance of the Contract or the Articles of Association of a cooperative joint venture shall be settled through consultation or mediation. If the Chinese and foreign cooperators are unable or do not wish to settle a dispute through consultation or mediation, the Chinese and foreign cooperators may submit the case to a Chinese arbitration institution or any other arbitration institution in accordance with the arbitration clause in the cooperative joint venture Contract or a written agreement on arbitration concluded after occurrence of the dispute.

The Chinese or foreign cooperator may bring a suit in a Chinese court if no arbitration clause is provided by the cooperative joint venture Contract or if no written agreement on arbitration is concluded after occurrence of the dispute.

Article 27

The detailed rules for implementation of this Law shall be formulated by the department in charge of foreign economic relations and trade under the State Council and be reported to the State Council for approval, and shall be effective after approval.

Article 28

This Law shall come into force on the day of promulgation.

Appendix 5

Law of the People's Republic of China on Enterprises Operated Exclusively with Foreign Capital

(Adopted at the Fourth Session of the Sixth National People's Congress on 12 April, 1986).

Article 1

With a view to expanding economic cooperation and technological exchange with other countries, and promoting the development of its national economy, the People's Republic of China permits foreign firms, other economic entities, or individuals (hereafter referred to as foreign investors) to set up enterprises exclusively with foreign capital in China (hereafter referred to as wholly foreign-owned enterprises) and protects the lawful rights and interests of the enterprises so established.

Article 2

As referred to in the present Law, wholly foreign-owned enterprises are those established in China by foreign investors exclusively with their own capital in accordance with the relevant Chinese laws. The term does not include branches set up in China by foreign investors.

Article 3

Wholly foreign-owned enterprises shall be conducive to the development of China's national economy. Such enterprises shall use advanced technology and equipment or market all or most of their products outside China.

Provisions will be made by the State Council regarding the lines of business that the state forbids wholly foreign-owned enterprises to engage in or on which it places certain restrictions.

Article 4

The investments made by a foreign investor in China, the profits he earns, and his other lawful rights and interests shall be protected by Chinese laws.

The wholly foreign-owned enterprise must abide by Chinese laws and statutes and must do nothing detrimental to China's public interest.

Article 5

Except under special circumstances, the state shall not nationalize or expropriate wholly foreign-owned enterprises. Should it prove necessary to do so in the public interest, legal procedures will be followed, and reasonable compensation will be made.

Article 6

The application to establish a wholly foreign-owned enterprise shall be submitted for examination and approval by the department under the State Council which is in charge of foreign economic relations and trade or by other authorities entrusted with such powers by the State Council. The department or said authorities shall, within 90 days from the date when such application is received, make a decision on whether to grant approval.

Article 7

Within 30 days after receiving a Certificate of Approval, the foreign investor should apply to the authorities in charge of the Administration of Industry and Commerce for Registration and a Business License. The date of issue of the Business License shall be deemed to be the date of establishment of the enterprise.

Article 8

The wholly foreign-owned enterprise, which meets the conditions for being a legal person under Chinese law, shall acquire the status of a Chinese legal person in accordance with the Law.

Article 9

The wholly foreign-owned enterprise must make investments in China within the period approved by the department in charge of examination and approval. If it fails to do so, the authorities in charge of the Administration of Industry and Commerce may revoke the Business License.

The authorities in charge of the Administration of Industry and Commerce shall inspect and monitor the investment situation of a wholly foreign-owned enterprise.

Article 10

In the event of a separation, merger, transfer, or other major change, the wholly foreign-owned enterprise must report to and obtain approval from the authorities in charge of examination and approval and register the change with the authorities in charge of the Administration of Industry and Commerce.

Article 11

The production and business programs of the wholly foreign-owned enterprise shall be reported to the appropriate authorities for the record.

The enterprise shall be free from interference in its operations and management so long as these are conducted in accord with the approved Articles of Association.

Article 12

The wholly foreign-owned enterprise shall employ Chinese workers and administrative staff under contracts concluded according to law. These contracts shall include provisions related to employment, dismissal, remuneration, welfare, occupational safety, and workers' insurance.

Article 13

Workers and administrative staff in the employment of the wholly foreign-owned enterprise may set up trade unions in accordance with the law, and such unions may conduct activities to protect the lawful rights and interests of the employees.

The enterprise shall provide necessary facilities for the activities of these trade unions.

Article 14

The wholly foreign-owned enterprise shall set up account books in China, conduct independent auditing, and, in conformity with the regulations, submit its fiscal reports and statements to the financial and tax authorities for supervision.

If the enterprise refuses to maintain account books in China, the financial and tax authorities may impose a penalty on it, and the authorities in charge of the Administration of Industry and Commerce may order it to suspend operations or revoke its Business License.

Article 15

Within the scope of operations approved, the wholly foreign-owned enterprise may purchase, either in China or on the world market, raw and semi-finished materials, fuels, and other materials it needs. When these are available from both sources, preference should be given to Chinese sources.

Article 16

The wholly foreign-owned enterprise shall apply to insurance companies in China for such insurance coverage as is needed.

Article 17

The wholly foreign-owned enterprise shall pay taxes in accordance with relevant state regulations. It may enjoy preferential treatment including reduction of taxes or exemption from taxes.

If the enterprise reinvests a portion of its after-tax profits in China, it may, in accordance with relevant state regulations, apply for a refund of the income tax paid on the reinvested amount.

Article 18

The wholly foreign-owned enterprise shall handle its foreign exchange matters in accordance with relevant state regulations.

The enterprise shall open an account with the Bank of China or with a bank designated by the Chinese authorities in charge of foreign exchange control.

The enterprise should take care to balance its foreign exchange receipts and payments. If, with the approval of the appropriate authorities, the enterprise markets its products in China and subsequently experiences an imbalance in foreign exchange, the said authorities shall be responsible for helping it to eliminate the imbalance.

Article 19

The foreign investor may remit abroad profits legitimately earned from the enterprise, as well as other lawful earnings and any funds left over after the enterprise is liquidated.

Wages, salaries, and other legitimate income earned by foreign employees in the enterprise may be remitted abroad after the payment of personal income tax in accordance with Chinese Law.

Article 20

The foreign investor should apply for and secure approval for the duration of operations for its enterprise from the authorities in charge of examination and approval. When an extension of the duration of operations is desired, application must be made to the said authorities 180 days before the duration of operations expires. The authorities in charge of examination and approval shall, within 30 days of the date of receipt of the extension application, make a decision on whether to grant approval.

Article 21

When terminating operations, the wholly foreign-owned enterprise shall give timely notification and proceed with liquidation in accordance with relevant legal requirements.

A foreign investor may not dispose of the assets of the enterprise except for the purpose of liquidation.

Article 22

At the termination of operations the wholly foreign-owned enterprise should nullify its registration with the authorities in charge of the Administration of Industry and Commerce and return its Business License.

Article 23

In accordance with the present Law, the detailed rules and regulations for the implementation of this Law shall be formulated by the department under the State Council which is in charge of foreign economic relations and trade and shall go into effect after approval by the State Council.

Article 24

The present Law comes into force on the date of its promulgation.

Appendix 6

Provisions of the State Council of the People's Republic of China for the Encouragement of Foreign Investment

(Promulgated on 11 October 1986)

Article 1

These provisions are hereby formulated in order to improve the investment environment, facilitate the absorption of foreign investment, introduce advanced technology, improve product quality, and expand exports in order to generate foreign exchange and develop the national economy.

Article 2

The state encourages foreign companies, enterprises, and other economic entities or individuals (hereafter referred to as foreign investors) to established Chinese-foreign equity joint ventures, Chinese-foreign cooperative ventures, and wholly foreign-owned enterprises (hereafter referred to as enterprises with foreign investment) within the territory of China. The state grants special preferences to the enterprises with foreign investment listed below:

1. Production enterprises whose products are mainly for export, which have a foreign exchange surplus after deducting from their total annual foreign exchange revenues the annual foreign exchange expenditures incurred in production and operation and the foreign exchange needed for the remittance abroad of the profits earned by foreign investors (hereafter referred to as export enterprises).

2. Production enterprises possessing advanced technology supplied by foreign investors which are engaged in developing new products, and upgrading and replacing products in order to increase foreign exchange

generated by exports or for import substitution (hereafter referred to as technologically advanced enterprises).

Article 3

Export enterprises and technologically advanced enterprises shall be exempt from payment to the state of all subsidies to staff and workers, except for the payment or allocation of funds for labor insurance, welfare costs, and housing subsidies for Chinese staff and workers in accordance with the provisions of the state.

Article 4

The site use fees for export enterprises and technologically advanced enterprises, except for those located in busy urban sectors of large cities, shall be computed and charged according to the following standards:

1. RMB 5-20 per square meter per year in areas where the development fee and the site use fee are computed and charged together;

2. Not more than RMB 3 per square meter per year in site areas where the development fee is computed and charged on a one-time basis or in areas developed by the above-mentioned enterprises themselves. Exemptions for specified periods of time from these aforementioned fees may be granted at the discretion of local people's governments.

Article 5

Export enterprises and technologically advanced enterprises shall be given priority in obtaining water, electricity, transportation services, and communications facilities needed for their production and operation. Fees shall be computed and charged in accordance with the standards of local state enterprises.

Article 6

Export enterprises and technologically advanced enterprises, after examination by the Bank of China, shall be given priority in receiving loans for short-term revolving funds necessary for production and distribution, as well as for other necessary credit.

Article 7

When foreign investors in export and technologically advanced enterprises remit abroad profits distributed to them by such enterprises, the amount remitted shall be exempt from income tax.

Article 8

After the expiration of the period for the reduction or exemption of enterprise income tax in accordance with the provisions of the state, export enterprises whose value of export products amounts to 70% or more of the value of their products in that same year may pay enterprise income tax at one-half the rate of the present tax.

Export enterprises in special economic zones or in economic and technological development zones, and other export enterprises that already pay enterprise income tax at a rate of 15% and that comply with the foregoing conditions, shall pay enterprise income tax at a rate of 10%.

Article 9

After the expiration of the period of reduction or exemption of enterprise income tax in accordance with the provisions of the state, technologically advanced enterprises may extend for three years the payment of enterprise income tax, at a rate reduced by one-half.

Article 10

Foreign investors who reinvest the profits distributed to them by their enterprises in order to establish or expand export enterprises or technologically advanced enterprises for a period of operation of not less than five years, after application to and approval by the tax authorities, shall be refunded the total amount of enterprise income tax already paid on the reinvested portion. If the investment is withdrawn before the period of operation reaches five years, the amount of enterprise income tax refunded shall be repaid.

Article 11

Export products of enterprises with foreign investment, except crude oil, finished oil, and other products subject to special state provisions, shall be exempt from the consolidated industrial and commercial tax.

Article 12

Enterprises with foreign investment may arrange the export of their products directly or may also export by consignment to agents in accordance with state provisions. For products that require an export license, in accordance with the annual export plan of the enterprise, an application for an export license may be made every six months.

Article 13

Machinery and equipment, vehicles used in production, raw materials, fuel, bulk parts, spare parts, machine component parts, and fittings (including imports restricted by the state), which enterprises with foreign investment need to import in order to carry out their export contracts, do not require further applications for examination and approval and are exempt from the requirement for import licenses. The customs department shall exercise supervisions and control, and shall inspect and release such imports on the basis of the enterprise Contract or the export contract.

The imported materials and items mentioned above are restricted to use by the enterprises and may not be sold on the domestic market. If they are used in products to be sold domestically, import procedures shall be handled in accordance with provisions, and taxes shall be computed according to the governing sections.

Article 14

Under the supervision of the foreign exchange control departments, enterprises with foreign investment may mutually adjust their foreign exchange surpluses and deficiencies among each other.

The Bank of China and other banks designated by the People's Bank of China may provide cash security services and may grant loans in Renminbi to enterprises with foreign investment.

Article 15

The people's government at all levels and relevant departments in charge shall guarantee the right of autonomy of enterprises with foreign investment and shall support enterprises with foreign investment in managing themselves in accordance with international advanced scientific methods.

With the scope of their approved contracts, enterprises with foreign investment have the right to determine production and operation plans, raise funds, use funds, purchase production materials, and sell products and determine wage levels and forms of wages and bonuses, and set up an allowance system.

Enterprises with foreign investment may, in accordance with their production and operation requirements, determine their own organizational structure and choose personnel, and increase or dismiss staff and workers. They may recruit and employ technical personnel, managerial personnel, and workers in the locality. The unit to which such employed personnel belong shall provide its support and shall permit their transfer. Staff and workers who violate the rules and regulations, and thereby cause negative consequences, may, in accordance with the seriousness of the case, be given differing sanctions, up to that of discharge. Enterprises with foreign investment that recruit, employ, dismiss, or discharge staff and workers shall file a report with the local labor and personnel department.

Article 16

All districts and departments must implement the Circular of the State Council concerning Firmly Curbing the Indiscriminate Levy of Charges on Enterprises. The people's governments at the provincial level shall formulate specific methods to strengthen supervision and administration.

Enterprises with foreign investment that encounter unreasonable charges may refuse to pay and may also appeal to the local economic committees up to level of the State Economic Commission.

Article 17

The people's government at all levels and relevant departments in charge shall strengthen the coordination of their work, improve efficiency in handling matters, and promptly examine and approve matters reported by enterprises with foreign investment that require response and resolution. The Agreement, Contract, and Articles of Association of an enterprise with foreign investment shall be examined and approved by the departments in charge under the State Council. The Examination and Approval Authority must within three months from the date of receipt of all documents decide to approve or disapprove them.

Article 18

Export enterprises and technologically advanced enterprises mentioned in these provisions shall be confirmed jointly as such by the foreign economic relations and trade departments where such enterprises are located and the relevant departments in accordance with the enterprise Contract, and certification shall be issued.

If the actual results of the annual export enterprise are unable to realize the goal of a surplus in the foreign exchange balance, as stipulated in the enterprise Contract, the taxes and fees which have already been reduced or exempted in the previous year shall be made up in the following year.

Article 19

These provisions are applicable to all enterprises with foreign investment, except those articles stating that they are to be applied to export enterprises or technologically advanced enterprises.

These provisions apply from the date of implementation to those enterprises with foreign investment that have obtained approval for establishment before the date of implementation of these provisions and that qualify for the preferential terms of these provisions.

Article 20

For enterprises invested in and established by companies, enterprises, and other economic organizations or individuals from Hong Kong, Macao, or Taiwan, matters shall be handled by reference to these provisions.

Article 21

The Ministry of Foreign Economic Relation and Trade shall be responsible for interpreting these provisions.

Article 22

These provisions shall go into effect on the date of issue.

Appendix 7

Income Tax Law of the People's Republic of China for Foreign-Invested Enterprises

Promulgated on 9 April 1991

Article 1

Income tax shall be paid in accordance with the provisions of this Law by enterprises with foreign investment within the territory of the People's Republic of China on their income derived from production, business operations, and other sources.

Income tax shall be paid in accordance with the provisions of this Law by foreign enterprises on their income derived from production, business operations, and other sources within the territory of the People's Republic of China.

Article 2

Enterprises with foreign investment referred to in this Law mean Chinese-foreign equity joint ventures, Chinese-foreign contractual joint ventures, and foreign-capital enterprises that are established in China.

Foreign enterprises referred to in this Law mean foreign companies, enterprises, and other economic organizations which have establishments or places in China and engage in production or business operations or those without establishments or places in China, but which have income from sources within China.

Article 3

Any enterprise with foreign investment which establishes its head office in China shall pay its income tax on income derived from sources inside and outside China. Any foreign enterprise shall pay its income tax on income derived from sources within China.

Article 4

The taxable income of an enterprise with foreign investment and an establishment or a place set up in China to engage in production or business operations by a foreign enterprise shall be the amount remaining from its gross income in the tax year after the cost, expenses, and losses have been deducted.

Article 5

The income tax on enterprises with foreign investment and the income tax which shall be paid by foreign enterprises on the income from production or business operations at their establishments in China shall be computed at the rate of 30%, and a local income tax shall be computed at the rate of 3%.

Article 6

The state shall, in accordance with industrial policies, guide the orientation of foreign investment and encourage the establishment of enterprises with foreign investment which adopt advanced technology and equipment and export all or a greater part of their product.

Article 7

The income tax of enterprises with foreign investment established in special economic zones, foreign enterprises which have establishments in special economic zones engaged in production or business operations, and enterprises with foreign investment of a production nature in economic and technological development zones shall be levied at the reduced rate of 15%.

The income tax of enterprises with foreign investment of a production nature established in coastal economic open zones or in the old urban districts of cities where the special economic zones or the economic and technological development zones are located shall be levied at the reduced rate of 24%.

The income tax of enterprises with foreign investment in coastal economic open zones, in the old urban districts of cities where the special economic zones or the economic and technological development zones are located, or in other regions defined by the State council, which are within the scope of energy, communications, harbor, wharf, or other projects encouraged by the state, may be levied at the reduced rate of 15%. The specific rules shall be regulated by the State Council.

Article 8

Any enterprise with foreign investment of a production nature scheduled to operate for a period of not less than ten years shall, from the year it begins to make a profit, be exempted from income tax in the first and second years and allowed a 50% reduction from the third to fifth years. However, the income tax exemption or reduction for enterprises with foreign investment engaged in the exploitation of resources such as petroleum, natural gas, rare metals, and precious metals shall be regulated separately by the State Council. Enterprises with foreign investment which actually operate for a period of less than ten years shall repay the amount of income tax exempted or reduced.

Regulations promulgated by the State Council before the establishment of this Law, which provide preferential treatment including exemption from or reduction of income tax on enterprises engaged in energy, communications, harbor, wharf, and other major production projects for a period longer than that specified in the preceding paragraph, or which provide preferential treatment of exemption from or reduction of income tax on enterprises engaged in major projects of a non-production nature, shall remain applicable after this Law comes into force.

Any enterprise with foreign investment which is engaged in agriculture, forestry, or animal husbandry and any other enterprise with foreign investment which is established in remote, underdeveloped areas may, upon approval by the competent department for tax affairs under the State Council of an application filed by the enterprise, be allowed a 15% to 30% reduction of the amount of income tax payable for a period of another ten years following the expiration of the period of tax exemption as provided for in the preceding two paragraphs.

After this Law comes into force, any modification to the provisions of the preceding three paragraphs of this Article shall be submitted by the State Council to the Standing committee of the National People's Congress for decision.

Article 9

The exemption or reduction of local income tax on any enterprise with foreign investment which operates in an industry or undertakes a project encouraged by the state shall, in accordance with the actual situation, be at the discretion of the people's government of the province, autonomous region, or municipality directly under the Central Government.

Article 10

Any foreign investor of an enterprise with foreign investment which reinvests its share of profit obtained from the enterprise directly into that enterprise by increasing its capital, or uses the profit as capital investment to establish other enterprises with foreign investment to operate for a period of not less than five years shall, upon approval by the tax authorities of an application filed by the investor, be refunded 40% of the income tax already paid on the reinvested amount. Where other preferential provisions are provided by the State Council, such provisions shall apply. If the investor withdraws its reinvestment before the expiration of a period of five years, it shall repay the refunded tax.

Article 11

Losses incurred in a tax year by any enterprise with foreign investment and by an establishment set up in China by a foreign enterprise to engage in production or business operations may be made up with the income of the following tax year. Should the income of the following tax year be insufficient to make up for said losses, the balance may be made up by income in subsequent years, over a period not exceeding five years.

Article 12

Any enterprise with foreign investment shall be allowed, when filing a consolidated income tax return, to deduct from the amount of tax payable the foreign income tax already paid abroad on income derived from sources outside China. The deductible amount shall, however, not exceed the amount of income tax otherwise payable under this Law in respect to income derived from sources outside China.

Article 13

The payment of receipt of charges or fees in business transactions between an enterprise with foreign investment, or an establishment in China set up by a foreign enterprise to engage in production or business operations, and its associated enterprises, shall be made in the same manner as the payment or receipt of charges or fees in business transactions between independent enterprises. Where the payment or receipt of charges or fees is not made in the same manner as in business transactions between independent enterprises and results in a reduction of the taxable income, the tax authorities shall have the right to make a reasonable adjustment.

Article 14

When an enterprise with foreign investment or a foreign enterprise engaged in production or business operations in China is established, moves to a new site, merges with another enterprise, breaks up, winds up, or makes a change in any of the main entries on its registration, it shall present the relevant documents to and go through tax registration with, the local tax authorities after the relevant event, change or cancellation is registered by the Administrative Agency for Industry and Commerce.

Article 15

Income tax on enterprises and local income tax shall be computed on an annual basis and paid in advance in quarterly installments. Such payments shall be made within 15 days from the end of each quarter, and the final settlement shall be made within five months from the end of each tax year. Any excess payment shall be refunded, and any deficiency shall be repaid.

Article 16

Any enterprise with foreign investment or a foreign enterprise engaged in production or business operations in China shall file its quarterly provisional income tax return with the local tax authorities within the period of advance tax payments, and it shall file an annual income tax return together with the final accounting statements within four months from the end of the tax year.

Article 17

Any enterprise with foreign investment or an establishment or place set up in China by a foreign enterprise to engage in production or business operations shall submit its financial and accounting systems to the local tax authorities for reference. All accounting records must be complete and accurate, with legitimate vouchers as the basis for entries.

If the financial and accounting bases adopted by enterprises with foreign investment or foreign enterprises with establishments in China engaged in production or business operations contradict the tax provisions of the State Council, tax payment shall be computed in accordance with the provisions of the State Council.

Article 18

When any enterprise with foreign investment goes into liquidation, and if the balance of its net assets or the balance of its remaining property after deduction of the enterprise's undistributed profits, various funds, and liquidation expenses exceeds the enterprise's paid-in capital, the excess portion shall be liquidation income on which income tax shall be paid in accordance with the provisions of this Law.

Article 19

Any foreign enterprise which has no establishment or place in China but derives profit, interest, rental, royalty, and other income from sources in China, or has an establishment or place in China but the said income is not effectively connected with such an establishment, shall pay an income tax of 20% on such income.

For the payment of income tax in accordance with the provisions of the preceding paragraph, the income beneficiary shall be the taxpayer, and the payer shall be the withholding agent. Taxes shall be withheld from each payment by the payer. The withholding agent shall, within five days, turn the amount of taxes withheld from each payment over to the State Treasury and submit a withholding income tax return to the local authorities.

Income tax shall be reduced or exempted on the following income:

1. The profit derived by a foreign investor from an enterprise with foreign investment shall be exempted from income tax.

2. Income from interest on loans made to the Chinese government or Chinese state banks by international financial organizations shall be exempted from income tax.

3. Income from interest on loans made at a preferential interest rate to Chinese state banks by foreign banks shall be exempted from income tax.

4. Income tax on royalties or the supply of technical know-how in scientific research, exploitation of energy resources, development of the communications industries, agriculture, forestry and animal husbandry production, and the development of important technologies may, upon approval by the appropriate department for tax affairs under the State Council, be levied at the reduced rate of 10%. Where the technology supplied is advanced or the terms are preferential, exemption from income tax may be allowed.

Where the preferential treatment of reduction and exemption of income tax on profit, interest, rental, royalties, and other income other than those provided for in this Article is required, it shall be regulated by the State Council.

Article 20

The tax authorities shall have the right to inspect the financial, accounting, and tax affairs of enterprises with foreign investment and establishments or places set up in China by foreign enterprises to engage in production or business operations, and have the right to inspect tax withholding made by the withholding agent and its payment of the withheld tax into the State Treasury. The entities inspected must report the facts and provide relevant information. They may not conceal or refuse to report any facts.

When making an inspection, the tax officials shall produce identification and be responsible for confidentiality.

Article 21

Income tax payable according to this Law shall be computed in Renminbi (RMB). Income in foreign currency shall be converted into Renminbi according to the exchange rate quoted by the state exchange control authorities for purposes of tax payment.

Article 22

If any taxpayer fails to pay taxes within the prescribed time limit, or if the withholding agent fails to turn over the tax withheld within the prescribed time limit, the tax authorities shall, in addition to setting a new time limit for tax payment, impose a surcharge for overdue payment, equal to 0.2% of the overdue tax for each day in arrears, starting from the first day the payment becomes overdue.

Article 23

The tax authorities shall set a new time limit for registration or submission of documents and may impose a fine of RMB 5,000 or less on any taxpayer or withholding agent which fails to go through tax registration or makes a change or cancellation in registration with the tax authorities within the prescribed time limit, fails to submit an income tax return, final accounting statements, or withholding income tax return to the tax authorities within the prescribed time limit, or fails to submit its financial and accounting systems to the tax authorities for reference.

Where the tax authorities have set a new time limit for registration or submission of documents, they shall impose a fine of RMB 10,000 or less on the taxpayer or withholding agent which has again failed to meet the time limit for going through registration or making a change in registration, or for submitting an income tax return, final accounting statements, or withholding income tax returns from the tax authorities. Where the circumstances are serious, the legal representative and the person directly responsible shall be prosecuted for their criminal liability, by applying *mutatis mutandis* the provisions of Article 121 of the Criminal Law.

Article 24

Where the withholding agent fails to fulfill its obligation to withhold tax as provided in this Law, and does not withhold or withholds an amount less than should have been withheld, the tax authorities shall set a time limit for the payment of remaining amount of tax due, and may impose a fine up to but not exceeding 100% of the amount of tax that should have been withheld.

Where the withholding agent fails to turn the tax withheld over to the State Treasury within the prescribed time limit, the tax authorities shall set a new time limit and may impose a fine of RMB 5,000 or less on the withholding agent; if the new time limit is again unmet, the tax authorities shall pursue the taxes according to law and may impose a fine of RMB 10,000 or less on the withholding agent. If the circumstances are serious, the legal representative and the person directly responsible shall be prosecuted for their criminal liability by applying *mutatis mutandis* the provisions of Article 121 of the Criminal Law.

Article 25

Where any person evades tax by deception or concealment or fails to pay taxes within the time limit prescribed by this Law and, after the tax authorities pursued the payment of tax, fails again to pay it within the new prescribed time limit, the tax authorities shall, in addition to recovering the taxes due, impose a fine up to but not exceeding 500% of the amount of tax due. Where the circumstances are serious, the legal representative and the person directly responsible shall be prosecuted for their criminal liability by applying the provisions of Article 121 of the Criminal Law.

Article 26

Any enterprise with foreign investment, foreign enterprise, or withholding agent, in case of a dispute with the tax authorities on payment of tax, must pay tax according to the relevant regulations first. Thereafter, the taxpayer or withholding agent may, within 60 days from the date of receipt of the tax payment certificate issued by the tax authorities, apply to the tax authorities at the next higher level for reconsideration. The higher tax authorities shall make a decision within 60 days after receipt of the application for reconsideration. If the taxpayer or withholding agent is not satisfied with the decision, it may institute legal proceedings in the people's court within 15 days from the date of notification of the decision regarding reconsideration.

If the party concerned is not satisfied with the punishment meted out by the tax authorities, it may, within 15 days from the date of receipt of the notification of punishment, apply for reconsideration to the tax authorities at the next higher level than that which made the punishment decision. Where the party is not satisfied with the decision made after reconsideration, it may institute legal proceedings in the people's court within 15 days from the date of receipt of the new decision. The party concerned may, however, directly institute legal proceedings in the people's court within 15 days from the date of receipt of the notification to punish. If the party concerned does not apply reconsideration to the higher tax authorities or institute legal proceedings in the people's court within the lime limit, and if the punishment is not fulfilled, the tax authorities which made the decision to punish may apply to the people's court for compulsory execution.

Article 27

Where any enterprise with foreign investment which was established before the promulgation of this Law would be subject to higher tax rates or enjoy less preferential treatment of tax exemption or reduction than before the entry of this Law, the law and relevant regulations of the State Council in effect before the entry of this Law shall apply. If any such enterprise has no approved period of operation, the laws and relevant regulations of the State Council in effect before the entry of this Law shall apply within the period prescribed by the State Council. Specific rules shall be regulated by the State Council.

Article 28

Where the provisions of the tax agreements concluded between the government of the People's Republic of China and foreign governments are different from the provisions of this Law, the provisions of the respective agreements shall apply.

Article 29

Rules for implementation shall be formulated by the State Council in accordance with this Law.

Article 30

This Law shall enter into force on 1 July 1991. The Income Tax Law of the People's Republic of China for Chinese-Foreign Equity Joint Ventures and the Income Tax Law of the People's Republic of China for Foreign Enterprises shall be annulled on the same date.

Appendix 8

Notice of the State Council on Regulations of Value-Added, Excise, Business, and other Taxes Applicable to Foreign-Invested Enterprises

According to the Decision of the Standing Committee of the National People's Congress or the Provisional Regulations on Value-Added Tax, Excise Tax, Business Tax, and Other Taxes Applicable to Foreign-Invested Enterprises and Foreign Enterprises (hereafter referred to as the Decision) discussed and approved by the Fifth Session of the Standing Committee of the Eighth National People's Congress, some relevant issues concerning sorts of taxation applicable to foreign invested enterprises and foreign enterprises are to be noted as follows:

1. Issues Concerning Sorts of Taxation Applicable to Foreign Invested Enterprises and Foreign Enterprises

Besides the Provisional Regulations on Value-Added Tax of the People's Republic of China, the Provisional Regulations on Excise Tax of the People's Republic of China, the Provisional Regulations on Business Tax of the People's Republic of China, and the Law on Income Tax for Foreign-Invested Enterprises and Foreign Enterprises of the People's Republic of China, the following provisional regulations shall also be applied to foreign invested enterprises and foreign enterprises, in accordance with the Decision:

    1. Provisional Regulations for Value-Added Tax on Land of the People's Republic of China, promulgated by the State Council on 31 December 1993;

    2. Provisional Regulations on Resource Tax of the People's Republic of China, promulgated by the State Council on 25 December 1993;

    3. Provisional Regulations on Stamp Duty of the People's Republic of China, promulgated by the State Council on 6 August 1988;

4. Provisional Regulations Butchery Duty, promulgated by the Government Administration Council of the Central People's Government on 19 December 1950;

5. Provisional Regulations on Urban Real Estate, promulgated by the Government Administration Council of the Central People's Government on 8 August 1951;

6. Provisional Regulations on Vehicle and Boat License Duty, promulgated by the Government Administration Council of the Central People's Government on 13 September 1951;

7. Provisional Regulations on Deed Tax, promulgated by the Government Administration Council of the Central People's Government on 3 April 1950;

During the process of tax reforms, the State Council will successively modify and formulate several new provisional regulations on taxation, which foreign invested and foreign enterprises shall implement accordingly.

2. Issues Concerning Resolution of the Added Tax Burden on Foreign Invested Enterprises and Foreign Enterprises After Alteration of the Levied Value-Added Tax, Excise Tax, and Business Tax

1. Foreign invested enterprises approved and established by 31 December 1993, which have had an added tax burden due to alterations of levied value-added taxes, excise taxes, and business taxes, may submit an application to the tax authority to have the added taxes repaid. The tax authority may, within the approved business period, ratify to repay the added taxes to foreign invested enterprises. The term of expiration shall not exceed five years. If the business period is not provided for, the added tax mentioned above shall be refunded to foreign invested enterprises if the application is submitted and approved by the tax authority within a period of five years.

2. If both a value-added tax and excise tax are levied upon foreign invested enterprises, the part which exceeds the original paid tax burden shall be returned according to the ratio of the value-added tax and excise tax paid.

3. Foreign invested enterprises whose products are produced directly for export or sold to export enterprises for export may, according to the Provisional Regulations on Value-Added Tax of the People's Republic of China, handle the taxation once and for all on the Customs Declaration of Exports and Tax Paid Certificate.

4. Foreign invested enterprises may, in principle, handle the taxation due from the added tax burden at the end of a year. However, if the added tax burden is a relatively large amount, they may apply to pay it quarterly, and clear off the balance at the end of the year.

5. Issues concerning refunds of value-added and excise taxes shall be exclusively conducted by the National Taxation Bureau. The national treasuries at all levels shall conscientiously verify all items. The tax calculations, application procedures, and approval of tax refunds are to be separately formulated by the National Taxation Bureau.

6. Issues concerning refunds of business taxes shall be provided by the people's government of each province, autonomous region, and municipality directly under the Central Government.

3. Issues Concerning Taxation of Sino-Foreign Cooperatively Exploited Oil Resources

A value-added tax at the rate of 5% shall be levied upon the crude oil and natural gas exploited through Sino-foreign cooperation, together with a charge for the utilization of minerals in accordance with the present regulations. Resource taxes, however, shall not be levied for the time being. The value-added tax, when being levied, shall not be credited against taxation of purchased items. The taxation shall not be repaid when the crude oil and natural gas is exported.

The regulations above shall be applicable, *mutatis mutandis*, to offshore oil fields independently operated by the China National Offshore Oil Corporation.

The present notice shall be implemented from the date of 1 January 1994.

Appendix 9

Supplementary Provisions of the Ministry of Foreign Trade and Economic Cooperations Concerning the Implementing Rules on Confirmation and Examination of Export-Oriented and Technologically-Advanced Foreign-Invested Enterprises

(Promulgated on March 2, 1992)

With a View To Further Improving The Confirmation And Examination System For Two Types Of Enterprises, The Following Provisions Are Hereby Formulated To Supplement the 'Implementing Rules on Confirmation and Examination of Export Enterprises and Technologically Advanced Enterprises with Foreign Investment' issued on January 27, 1987.

Article 1

All foreign invested enterprises which apply for confirmation as export enterprises or technologically advanced enterprises (hereinafter referred to as 'the two types of enterprises') should, except in cases defined by Section 2, Article 5 of these Supplementary Provisions, be enterprises which produce tangible products.

Article 2

The examination and confirmation authorities for the two types of enterprises are the Ministry of Foreign Economic Relations and Trade (hereinafter referred to as MOFERT) and the foreign economic relations and trade departments of provinces, autonomous regions, municipalities under the central government, cities with enlarged planning power, and special economic zones (hereinafter referred to as the provincial-level examination and confirmation authorities). MOFERT may entrust, in written form, the provincial-level examination and confirmation authorities with the tasks of examining the two types of enterprises approved and confirmed by MOFERT. While MOFERT is in charge of confirmation and examination of enterprises established by units affiliated to ministries, commissions, and bureaus under the State Council, MOFERT may also entrust, in written form, their confirmation or examination to the ministries, commissions, and bureaus under the State Council.

The provincial-level examination and confirmation authorities which need to entrust the work of confirming and examining export enterprises to foreign economic relations and trade departments at a lower level because of the great number of export enterprises located in their regions must submit proposals accordingly to the Ministry of Foreign Economic Relations and Trade for approval.

Article 3

After registering and obtaining business licenses from the administrative departments for industry and commerce, foreign invested enterprises may apply to the examination and confirmation authorities for confirmation as one of the two types of enterprises; The examination and confirmation authorities may either base examination and confirmation on such documents as contracts for Chinese-foreign joint ventures, application forms for wholly foreign-owned enterprises, and project feasibility study reports, or on the actual export performance of operating enterprises, application of advanced technologies, and results of contract implementation.

Article 4

Examination of export enterprises:

1. Certified export enterprises with foreign investment should apply to the examination and confirmation authorities for assessment within 90 days after the end of the first complete calendar year since the start of production. They should submit statements of export performance for the previous year and the balance sheets on their annual foreign exchange income and expenditures to the examination and confirmation authorities before the end of March.

2. A positive balance of operating forex income and expenditures in a given year, as realized by an enterprise, is defined as the amount of operating foreign exchange income in that year which exceeds the amount of operating

foreign exchange expenditures, excluding any carryover balance from the previous year.

3. The value of domestic sales and exports of the same kind of products of an enterprise shall be computed on the basis of actual factory prices during the same period. In the absence of comparable domestic sale prices, the value of export products may be computed by converting into Renminbi the foreign exchange earned through exporting products. This conversion should be based on the closing buying prices of foreign currencies on the date of receipt of the foreign exchange at the forex transaction center in the region where the enterprise is located.

For certain enterprises, the export value shall be computed according to the following methods. Enterprises which process overseas buyers' materials shall have their processing fees counted as export value. Foreign trade companies that purchase products from other enterprises for export or entrust other enterprises with the task of processing and exporting products, shall compute export value against the certificates of actual export quantities issued by foreign trade companies, according to the factory prices of the products and processing fees respectively. The value of domestic products settled in foreign exchange payment shall not be counted in the enterprises' export value.

The above provisions shall apply to calculating export value during the examination of export enterprises. Under the current system, the scope and definition of export statistics of foreign invested enterprises remains unchanged.

4. The assessment of export enterprises by the examination and confirmation authorities should be conducted once a year through consultation with the departments of finance, taxation, foreign exchange control, and customs under the people's governments at the same level.

Article 5

Confirmation and examination of technologically advanced enterprises:

1. Technologically advanced enterprises should meet the following criteria:
(1) They should generally belong to the sectors and projects in which the State encourages foreign investment;

(2) They should make use of internationally advanced and appropriate technologies and equipment, and their products should constitute new developments within China or advancements in terms of quality and technical performance, compared to similar domestic products;

(3) Generally, there should be signed technological transfer agreements or special clauses on technological transfer included in the joint venture contracts: Stipulations should be made concerning the detailed contents of technology to be transferred, time frames required to reach technological and product standards, and programs for localizing the production of parts and components, etc.

Projects of a general processing nature with imported machinery and equipment that perform better and more efficiently than domestically made equipment or projects which mainly assemble imported parts cannot be certified as technologically advanced enterprises.

2. High-tech and new technology development projects that really develop advanced technologies may apply for confirmation and examination as technologically advanced enterprises, even though they produce no tangible products.

3. In confirming and examining technologically advanced enterprises, the examination and confirmation authorities shall make arrangements with those industrial, scientific and technical departments in charge of the applications. These have the responsibility for organizing the assessment and involving experts who shall make assessment reports.

4. Certified technologically advanced enterprises with foreign investment should apply to the examination and confirmation authorities for examination within 90 days after the end of the first complete calendar year since the start of production. Foreign invested enterprises which apply for examination as technologically advanced enterprises should provide the examination and confirmation authorities with detailed reports on their production, sales operations, implementation of technology transfer, product quality, and progress made in localizing production.

5. Unless re-examination is deemed necessary by the examination and confirmation authorities, technologically advanced enterprises which have successfully passed the examination normally do not have to go through such examinations again on an annual basis.

Article 6

Apart from the required items for examination of the two types of enterprises, the examination should also cover the results of contract implementation by all invested parties. Investors or enterprises that seriously violate or fail to implement their contracts, stick to their commitments, or apply their investments as stipulated shall be regarded as disqualified through examination.

Article 7

Enterprises which begin to apply for confirmation as one of the two types of enterprises after they have already gone into production may have their examination and confirmation procedures carried out simultaneously.

Article 8

If any of the two types of enterprises fail to pass the examination for three consecutive years, they shall be deprived of their title as one of the two types of enterprises.

Article 9

The examination and confirmation authorities should present lists of the two types of enterprises which have been qualified or disqualified to the departments of finance, taxation, customs, banking, and land administration, under the people's governments at the same level, by May 31 of every year.

Article 10

The provincial-level examination and confirmation authorities should submit for MOFERT's records lists of the two types of enterprises confirmed in the previous year by January 31 every year. They should also submit to MOFERT the results of examinations of the two types of enterprises during the previous year by May 31 every year, and submit lists of enterprises which have failed to pass the examination for three consecutive years.

Article 11

Wherever the "Implementing Rules for Confirmation and Examination of Export Enterprises and Technologically Advanced Enterprises with Foreign Investment" runs counter to these Supplementary Provisions, these Supplementary Provisions shall prevail.

Appendix 10

Patent Law of the People's Republic of China

(Adopted by the fourth Session of the Standing Committee of the Sixth National People's Congress on March 12, 1984; amended according to the decision by the 27th Session of the Standing Committee of the Seventh National People's Congress on September 4, 1992)

CHAPTER 1: GENERAL PROVISIONS

Article 1

This Law is enacted to protect patent rights for inventions-creations, to encourage inventions-creations, to foster the spread and applications of inventions-creations, and to promote the development of science and technology to meet the needs of socialist modernization.

Article 2

In this Law, 'inventions-creations' means inventions, utility models, and designs.

Article 3

The Patent Office of the People's Republic of China receives and examines patent applications and grants patent rights for inventions-creations that conform with the provisions of this Law.

Article 4

Where the invention-creation for which a patent is applied for relates to security or other vital interests of the State, and is required to be kept secret, the application shall be treated in accordance with the relevant prescriptions of the State.

Article 5

No patent rights shall be granted for any invention-creation that is contrary to the laws of the State or social morality or that is detrimental to public interest.

Article 6

If a service invention-creation has been made by a person in execution of tasks directed by an organization (entity) to which he or she belongs, or made mainly by using the material means of an entity, the right to apply for the patent belongs to the entity. For any non-service invention-creation, the right to apply for the patent belongs to the inventor or creator. If the patent application was filed by an entity owned by the public, after it has been approved the patent rights shall be held by the entity. If it was filed by an entity under collective ownership or by an individual, the patent rights shall then be owned by the entity or individual.

For a service invention-creation made by any staff member or worker of a foreign enterprise, or of a Chinese-foreign joint venture enterprise located in China, the right to apply for a patent belongs to the enterprise. For any non-service invention-creation, the right to apply for a patent belongs to the inventor or creator. After the application is approved, the patent rights shall be owned by the enterprise or the individual that applied for it.

The owner or holder of patent rights is referred to as the 'patentee'

Article 7

No entity or individual shall prevent an inventor or creator from filing an application for a patent for a non-service invention-creation.

Article 8

For an invention-creation made with the cooperation of two or more entities, or made by an entity commissioned for research or design by another entity, the right to apply for a patent belongs, unless otherwise agreed upon, to the entity or entities which made or jointly made the invention-creation. After the application is approved, the patent rights shall be owned or held by the entity or entities that applied for it.

Article 9

Where two or more applicants file applications for a patent for an identical invention-creation, the patent rights shall be granted to the applicant whose application is filed first.

Article 10

The right to apply for a patent and the patent rights may be assigned to another party.

Any assignment by an entity under ownership by the whole public, of the rights to apply for a patent, or of the patent rights, must be approved by a competent authority at a higher level.

Any assignment, by a Chinese entity or individual, of the right to apply for a patent, or of the patent right, to a foreigner must be approved by the relevant State Council department.

Where the right to apply for a patent or the patent rights are assigned to another party, the parties involved must conclude a written contract which will come into force after it is registered and announced by the Patent Office.

Article 11

After the grant of the patent right for an invention or utility model, except as otherwise provided for in the law, no entity or individual may make, use, or sell the patented product, or use the patented process, or use or sell products directly obtained by using the patented process for production or business purposes, without the authorization of the patentee.

After the grant of the patent rights for a design, no entity or individual may, without the authorization of the patentee, make or sell the product or incorporate the patented design for production or business purposes.

After the grant of the patent right, except as otherwise provided for in the law, the patentee has the right to prevent any other person from importing, without the patentees authorization, the patented product, or the product directly obtained by using the patented process, for the uses mentioned in the preceding two paragraphs.

Article 12

Any entity or individual exploiting the patent of another must, except as provided for in Article 14 of this Law, conclude with the patentee a written license contract for exploitation and pay the patentee a fee for use of that patent. The licensee has no right to authorize any other entity or individual, other than that referred to in the contract, to exploit the patent.

Article 13

After the publication of the application for a patent for invention, the applicant may require the entity or individual exploiting the invention to pay an appropriate fee.

Article 14

The relevant departments of the State Council and the People's Governments of provinces, autonomous regions or municipalities directly under the Central Government have the power to decide, in accordance with the State plan, that any entity under ownership by the public that is within their system or directly under their administration, and that holds the patent rights to an important invention-creation, may be allowed to designate entities to exploit that invention-creation. The exploiting entity shall, according to the prescriptions of the State, pay a fee for exploitation to the entity holding the patent right.

Any patent held by a Chinese individual or entity under collective ownership, which is of great significance to the interests of the State or to the public interest, and is in need of being spread and applied, may, after approval by the State Council, be treated according to the preceding paragraph.

Article 15

The patentee has the right to affix a patent marking and to indicate the number of the patent on the patented product or on the packaging of that product.

Article 16

The entity owning or holding the patent right shall make an award to the inventor or creator of a service invention-creation. Upon exploitation of the patented invention-creation, the entity shall make an award to the inventor or creator based on the extent of the dispersion, application, and economic benefits resulting from use of that patent.

Article 17

The inventor or creator has the right to be named as such in the patent document.

Article 18

Where any foreigner, foreign enterprise, or other foreign organization having no habitual residence or business office in China files an application for a patent in China, the application shall be treated under this Law in accordance with agreements concluded between the country to which the applicant belongs, or in accordance with any international treaty to which both countries are party, or on the basis of the principle of reciprocity.

Article 19

Where any foreigner, foreign enterprise, or other foreign organization having no habitual residence or business office in China applies for a patent, or has other patent matters to attend to in China, they shall appoint a patent agency designated by the State Council of the People's Republic of China to act as their agent.

Where any Chinese entity or individual applies for a patent or has other patent matters to attend to in the country, they may appoint a patent agency to act as their agent.

Article 20

Where any Chinese entity or individual intends to file an application in a foreign country for a patent for an invention-creation made in China, first an application must be made for a patent within China at the Patent Office. With the sanction of the relevant department of the State Council, a patent agency shall be designated by the State Council to act as an agent for the patentee outside China.

Article 21

Until the publication or announcement of the application for a patent, staff members of the Patent Office and persons involved have the duty to keep its contents secret.

CHAPTER 2: REQUIREMENTS FOR GRANTING PATENT RIGHTS

Article 22

Any invention or utility model for which patent rights may be granted must possess novelty, inventiveness, and practical applicability.

Novelty means that, before the date of filing, no identical invention or utility model has been disclosed in publications in China or abroad, or has been publicly used or made known by any other means, nor has any other person previously filed an application which described the identical invention or utility model with the Patent Office and which was published after the said filing date.

Inventiveness means that, as compared with the technology existing before the date of filing, the invention or utility model has prominent substantive features and represents notable progress.

Practical applicability means that the invention or utility model can be made or used to produce effective results.

Article 23

Any design for which patent rights may be granted must not be identical with or similar to any design which, before the date of filing, has been publicly used or disclosed in publications in China.

Article 24

An invention-creation for which a patent is applied does not lose its novelty if, within six months before the date of filing, one of the following events occurs:

(1) it is first exhibited at an international exhibition sponsored or recognized by the Chinese Government;

(2) it is first made public at an authorized academic or technological meeting;

(3) it is disclosed by any person without consent of the applicant.

Article 25

For any of the following, no patent rights shall be granted:

(1) scientific discoveries;

(2) rules and methods for mental activities;

(3) methods for the diagnosis or treatment of disease;

(4) animal and plant varieties;

(5) substances obtained by means of nuclear transformation.

For processes used in producing products referred to in item (4) of the preceding paragraph, patent rights may be granted in accordance with the provisions of this Law.

CHAPTER 3: APPLYING FOR PATENTS

Article 26

When an application for a patent for an invention or utility model is filed, a request, description, abstract, and claims shall also be submitted.

The request shall state the title of the invention or utility model, the name of the inventor or creator, the name and address of the applicant, and other related matters.

The description shall set forth the invention or utility model in a manner sufficiently clear and complete as to enable a person skilled in the relevant field of technology to carry it out. Where necessary, drawings should be included.

The abstract shall state briefly the main technical points of the invention or utility model.

The claims shall state the extent of requested patent protection. They shall be supported by the description.

Article 27

Where an application for a patent for design is filed, a request along with drawings or photographs of the design shall be submitted. A product incorporating the design and the class to which that product belongs should be indicated.

Article 28

The date on which the Patent Office receives the application shall be the filing date. If the application is sent by mail, the date of mailing indicated by the postmark shall be the filing date.

Article 29

Where any applicant files in China an application for a patent within twelve months from the date in which the patent for an invention or utility model was first filed in a foreign country, or within six months from the date on which they first filed for a patent for design, the applicant has the right of priority, in accordance with any agreement concluded between the said foreign country and China, or with any international treaty to which both countries are party, or on the basis of the principle of mutual recognition.

Where, within twelve months from the date on which any applicant filed first in China an application for a patent for invention or utility model, they file with the Patent Office an application for a patent for the same subject matter, they have the right of priority.

Article 30

Any applicant who claims the right of priority shall make a written declaration when the application is filed, and submit, within three months, a copy of the patent application document which was first filed. If the applicant fails to make the written declaration or to meet the time limit, the claim to the right of priority shall be deemed not to have been made.

Article 31

Generally, an application for a patent for invention or utility model shall be limited to one invention or utility model. Two or more inventions or utility models belonging to a single general inventive concept may be filed as one application.

Generally, an application for a patent for design shall be limited to one design incorporated in one product. Two or more designs which are incorporated in products belonging to the same class and are sold or used in sets may be filed as one application.

Article 32

An applicant may withdraw his or its application of a patent at any time before the patent right is granted.

Article 33

An applicant may amend his or its application for a patent, but the amendment to the application for patent or invention or utility model may not go beyond the scope of the disclosure contained in the initial description and claims, and the amendment to the application for a patent for design may not go beyond the scope of the disclosure as shown in the initial drawings or photographs.

CHAPTER 4: EXAMINATION AND APPROVAL OF THE PATENT APPLICATION

Article 34

Where, after receiving an application for a patent for invention, the Patent Office, upon preliminary examination, finds the application to be in conformity with the requirements of this Law, it shall publish the application promptly eighteen months from the date of filing. Upon the request of the applicant, the Patent Office may publish the application earlier.

Article 35

Upon the request of the applicant, made at any time within three years from the date of filing a patent for invention, the Patent Office will proceed to examine the application as to its substance. If, without justified reason, the applicant fails to meet the time limit for requesting examination as to substance, the application shall be deemed to have been withdrawn.

The Patent Office may, on its own initiative, proceed to examine the substance of any application for a patent for invention when it deems it necessary.

Article 36

When the applicant for a patent for invention requests examination as to substance, they shall furnish reference materials concerning the invention that were developed before the filing date.

The applicant for a patent for invention who has filed an application for a patent for the same invention in a foreign country shall, at the time of requesting examination as to substance, furnish documents and results concerning any search made for the purpose of examining that application in that country. If, without any justified reason, the said documents are not furnished, the application shall be deemed to have been withdrawn.

Article 37

Where the Patent Office, after it has made the examination as to the substance of the application for a patent for an invention, finds that the application is not in conformity with the provisions of this Law, it shall notify the applicant and request a submission, within a specified time limit, of the applicants observations or amendments to the application. If, without any justified reason, the time limit is not met, the application shall be deemed to have been withdrawn.

Article 38

Where, after the applicant has made the observations or amendments, the Patent Office finds that the application for a patent for invention is still not in conformity with the provisions of this Law, the application shall be rejected.

Article 39

Where it is found after examination as to substance that there is no cause for rejection of the application for a patent for invention, the Patent Office shall make a decision to grant the patent rights for the invention, issue the certificate of patent for invention, and register and announce it.

Article 40

Where it is found after preliminary examination that there is no cause for rejection of the application for a patent for a utility model or design, the Patent Office shall make a decision to grant the patent rights for the utility model or design, issue the relevant patent certificate, and register and announce it.

Article 41

Where, within six months from the date of the announcement of the grant of the patent right by the Patent Office, any entity or individual considers that the grant of the said patent right is not in conformity with the relevant provisions of this Law, they may request the Patent Office to revoke the patent rights.

Article 42

The Patent Office shall examine the request for revocation of the patent rights, make a decision revoking or upholding the patent rights, and notify the person who made the request and the patentee. The decision revoking the patent rights shall be registered and announced by the Patent Office.

Article 43

The Patent Office shall set up a Patent Reexamination Board. Where any party is not satisfied with the decision of the Patent Office concerning rejection of the application, or revocation or upholding of patent rights, such party may, within three months from the date of receipt of notification, request the Patent Reexamination Board to reexamine the case. The Patent Reexamination board shall, after reexamination, make a decision and notify the applicant, the patentee, or the person who made the request for revocation of patent rights. Where the applicant for a patent for invention, the patentee of an invention, or the person who made the request for revocation of the invention patent rights is not satisfied with the decision of the Patent Reexamination board, they may, within three months from the date of receipt of notification, institute legal proceedings in the people's court.

The decision of the Patent Reexamination Board concerning reexamination of a utility model or design is final.

Article 44

Any patent right which has been revoked shall be deemed to have been non-existent from the beginning.

CHAPTER 5: DURATION, CESSATION, AND INVALIDATION OF PATENT RIGHTS

Article 45

The duration of patent rights for inventions shall be twenty years. The duration of patent rights for utility models or patent rights for designs shall be ten years, counting from the filing date.

Article 46

The patentee shall pay an annual fee beginning with the year in which the patent right was granted.

Article 47

In any of the following cases, the patent rights shall cease before the expiration of its duration:

(1) where an annual fee is not paid as required;

(2) where the patentee abandons the patent rights in a written declaration

Any cessation of the patent rights shall be registered and announced by the Patent Office.

Article 48

Six months after the date of announcement of patent rights being granted by the Patent Office, any entity or individual who considers that said granting of patent rights is not in conformity with this Law, may request the Patent Reexamination Board to declare the patent rights invalid.

Article 49

The Patent Reexamination Board shall examine the request for invalidation of the patent rights, make a decision, and notify the person who made the request and the patentee. The decision declaring the patent rights invalid shall be registered and announced by the Patent Office.

Where any party is not satisfied with the decision of the Patent Reexamination Board in declaring the patent rights for an invention invalid or upholding the patent rights for an invention, such party may, within three months from receipt of the notification of the decision, institute legal proceedings in the people's court.

The decision of the Patent Reexamination Board with respect to declaring patent rights for utility models or designs invalid is final.

Article 50

Any patent right which has been declared invalid shall be deemed to have been non-existent from the beginning.

The decision of invalidation shall have no retroactive effect on any judgment or order on patent infringement which has been pronounced and enforced by the people's court, on any decision concerning the handling of patent infringement which has been made and enforced by the administrative authority for patent affairs, on any contract for patent licensing, and on any assignment of patent rights which have been performed prior to the invalidation decision. However, the damages caused to another person in bad faith on the part of the patentee shall be compensated.

If, pursuant to the provisions of the preceding paragraph, no repayment (by the patentee or the assignor of the patent rights to a licensee, or the assignee of the patent rights, for the fee for the exploitation of the patent or of the price for the assignment of the patent rights) is obviously contrary to the principle of equity, the patentee or the assignor shall repay all or part of the fee for the exploitation of the patent, or the price for the assignment of the patent right, to the licensee or the assignee of the patent rights.

The provisions of the second and third paragraph of this Article shall apply to patent rights which have been revoked.

CHAPTER 6: COMPULSORY LICENSE FOR EXPLOITATION OF THE PATENT

Article 51

Where any entity which is qualified to exploit the invention or utility model has made requests for authorization from the patentee of an invention or utility model to exploit the patent in reasonable terms and such efforts have not been successful within a reasonable period of time, the Patent Office may, upon the application of that entity, grant a compulsory license to exploit the patent of an invention or utility model.

Article 52

Where a national emergency or any extraordinary state of affairs occurs, or where the public interest so requires, the Patent Office may grant a compulsory license to exploit the patent of an invention or utility model.

Article 53

Where the invention or utility model for which the patent right was granted is technically more advanced than another invention or utility model for which a patent right has been granted earlier, and the later invention or utility model depends on the exploitation of the earlier invention or utility model, the Patent Office may, upon the request of the later patentee, grant a compulsory license to exploit the earlier invention or utility model.

Where, according to the preceding paragraph, a compulsory license is granted, the Patent Office may, upon the request of the earlier patentee, also grant a compulsory license to exploit the later invention or utility model.

Article 54

The entity or individual requesting, in accordance with the provisions of this Law, a compulsory license for exploitation shall furnish proof that they have not been able to conclude a reasonable license contract for exploitation with the patentee.

Article 55

The decision of the Patent Office to grant a compulsory license for exploitation of a patent shall be registered and announced.

Article 56

Any entity or individual that is granted a compulsory license for exploitation shall not have exclusive rights to exploit and shall not have the right to authorize exploitation by others.

Article 57

The entity or individual that is granted a compulsory license for exploitation shall pay to the patentee a reasonable exploitation fee, the amount of which shall be fixed by both parties in consultation. Where the parties fail to reach an agreement, the Patent Office shall adjudicate.

Article 58

Where the patentee is not satisfied with the decision of the Patent Office to grant a compulsory license for exploitation, or with the adjudication regarding the exploitation fee, they may, within three months from the receipt of the notification, institute legal proceedings in the people's court.

CHAPTER 7: PROTECTION OF PATENT RIGHTS

Article 59

The extent of protection of the patent rights for inventions or utility models shall be determined by the terms of the claims. The descriptions and appended drawings may be used to interpret the claims.

The extent of protection of the patent rights for designs shall be determined by the products incorporating the patented design as shown in drawings or photographs.

Article 60

If any exploitation of the patent occurs without the authorization of the patentee, it constitutes an infringement of patent rights. The patentee or any interested party may request the administrative authority for patent affairs to handle the matter or may directly institute legal proceedings in the people's court. The administrative authority for patent affairs shall have the power to order the infringement to stop and to order compensation for damages. Any party dissatisfied may, within three months form the receipt of notification, institute legal proceedings in the people's court. If such proceedings are not instituted within this time limit, and if the order is not complied with, the administrative authority for patent affairs may approach the people's court for compulsory execution of the judgement.

When any infringement dispute arises, if the patent for an invention is a process for the manufacture of a new product, any entity or individual manufacturing identical products shall furnish proof of the processes used in the manufacture of their products.

Article 61

Prescription for instituting legal proceedings concerning the infringement of patent rights is two years counted from the date on which the patentee or any interested party obtains or should have obtained knowledge of the infringement.

Article 62

None of the following shall be deemed an infringement of patent rights:

(1) Where, after the sale of the patented product that was made by the patentee or with the authorization of the patentee, any other person uses or sells that product;

(2) Where any person uses or sells a patented product not knowing that it was made and sold without the authorization of the patentee;

(3) Where, before the date of filing of the application for patent, any person who has already made the identical product, used the identical process, or made necessary preparations for its making or using, continues to make or use it within the original scope only;

(4) Where any foreign means of transport which temporarily passes through the territory, territorial waters, or territorial air space of China uses the patent concerned for its own needs in its devices and installations in

accordance with an agreement concluded between the country to which the foreign means of transport belongs and China, or in accordance with any international treaty to which both countries are parties, or on the basis of the principle of reciprocity;

(5) Where any person uses the patent concerned solely for the purposes of scientific research and experimentation.

Article 63

Where any person passes off the patent of another person as though it were their own, such passing off shall be treated in accordance with Article 60 of this Law. If the circumstances are serious, the person directly responsible shall be prosecuted for criminal liability, by applying *mutatis mutandis* Article 127 of the Criminal Law.

Where any person passes any unpatented product or process off as a patented product or process, such person shall be ordered by the administrative authority of patent affairs to stop the passing off, make a public correction, and pay a fine.

Article 64

Where any person, in violation of the provisions of Article 20 of this Law, unauthorizedly files in a foreign country an application for a patent that divulges an important secret of the State, that person shall be subject to disciplinary sanction by the entity to which he or she belongs or the competent authority concerned at the higher level. If the circumstances are serious, he or she shall be prosecuted for criminal liability according to the Law.

Article 65

Where any person usurps the right of an inventor or creator to apply for a patent for a non-service invention-creation, or usurps any other rights or interests of the inventor or creator, as prescribed by this Law, he or she shall be subject to disciplinary sanction by the entity to which he or she belongs or by a competent authority at a higher level.

Article 66

Where any staff member of the Patent Office, or any staff member concerned of the State, acts wrongfully out of personal considerations or commits fraudulent acts, they shall be prosecuted for criminal liability by applying *mutatis mutandis* Article 188 of the Criminal Law.

CHAPTER 8: SUPPLEMENTARY PROVISIONS

Article 67

Any application for a patent filed with the Patent Office, and any other proceedings, shall be subject to the payment of a prescribed fee.

Article 68

The Implementation Regulations of this Law shall be drawn up by the Patent Office and shall enter into force after approval by the State.

Article 69

This Law shall enter into force on April 1, 1985.

Appendix 11

Implementation Rules for International Copyright Treaties

(Promulgated by Decree No. 105 of the State council on September 25, 1992)

Article 1

These Rules are formulated to implement international copyright treaties and to protect the legitimate rights and interests of owners of copyrighted foreign works.

Article 2

Protection of foreign works shall be carried out through application of the copyright Law of the People's Republic of China (hereinafter referred to as 'the Copyright Law'), the Implementation Regulations of the Copyright Law of the People's Republic of China, the Regulations on Protection of Computer Software, and these Rules.

Article 3

The international treaties mentioned in these Rules shall refer to the Berne Convention for the Protection of Literary and Artistic Works, to which China is a party, and bilateral agreements relating to copyrights that China has concluded with foreign countries.

Article 4

Foreign works mentioned in these Rules shall include:
(1) works of which the author, or one of the co-authors, or other copyright owners or co-owners is a national or permanent resident of a country party to international copyright treaties;

(2) works not authored by a national or a permanent resident of a country party to international copyright treaties that have been first published or published simultaneously in a country party to international copyright treaties;

(3) works created by others on commission in which a joint venture enterprise, a cooperative enterprise, or an enterprise with sole foreign investment is supposed to be the owner or one of the co-owners of the copyright, according to contract.

Article 5

In the case of unpublished foreign works, the term of protection shall be governed by Article 20 and Article 21 of the Copyright Law.

Article 6

The term of protection of foreign works of applied art shall be 25 years commencing from the making of the work.

The preceding paragraph shall not apply to the use of works of fine arts, including drawings of cartoon characters, on industrial goods.

Article 7

Foreign computer programs shall be protected as literary works. They are therefore not subject to registration, and enjoy a term of protection of 50 years commencing from the end of the first year of publication.

Article 8

Foreign works created by compiling unprotectable materials shall be protected in accordance with Article 14 of the Copyright Law, provided that originality is shown in the selection and arrangement of such materials. Such protection, however, shall not prevent another person from using the same materials to create other compilations.

Article 9

Foreign video recordings shall be protected as cinematographic works if treated as such works under international copyright treaties.

Article 10

Prior permission of the copyright owner shall be required to translate a published foreign work, if created in Chinese, into the language of a minority nationality.

Article 11

Copyright owners of foreign works shall have the right to authorize any form of public performances of their works and any communication to the public of performances of their works.

Article 12

Copyright owners of foreign cinematographic works, including video recordings made for television, shall have the right to authorize the public performance of their works.

Article 13

Prior permission from the copyright owner shall be required of newspapers and periodicals which want to reprint foreign works, except in reprinting articles on current political, economic, and other social topics.

Article 14

Copyright owners of foreign works shall retain the right to authorize or prohibit rental of copies of their works after the authorized sale of such copies.

Article 15

Copyright owners of foreign works shall have the right to prohibit the import of the below types of copies of their works:
    (1) infringing copies;
    (2) copies coming from a country where their works are not protected.

Article 16

In the case of public performances, recordings, and broadcasting of foreign works, provisions of the Berne Convention shall apply. Where collective administration organizations exist, prior permission of such organizations shall be required.

Article 17

Foreign works which, at the date on which international copyright treaties enter into force in China, have not fallen into the public domain in their countries of origin shall be protected until expiration of their valid terms as prescribed in the Copyright Law and these Rules.

The preceding paragraph shall not apply to use of foreign works that have taken place before international treaties enter into force in China.

A Chinese person or legal person who owned and used a particular copy of a foreign work for a particular purpose before international copyright treaties enter into force in China may continue to make use of that copy of the work without liability, provided that the copy is neither reproduced nor used in any manner that unreasonably prejudices the legitimate rights and interests of the copyright owner.

The application of the above three paragraphs of this Article shall be subject to provisions of bilateral agreements relating to copyright that China has concluded with the countries concerned.

Article 18

Articles 5, 12, 14, 15, and 17 of these Rules shall also apply to sound recordings.

Article 19

Where pre-existing administrative regulations relating to copyright may conflict with these Rules, these Rules shall apply. Where these Rules may conflict with international copyright treaties, international copyright treaties shall apply.

Article 20

The implementation in China of international copyright treaties shall be the responsibility of the National Copyright Administration in China.

Article 21

The interpretation of these Rules shall be the responsibility of National Copyright Administration of China.

Article 22

These Rules shall enter into force on September 30, 1992.

About the Author

Dr. Luo (Ph.D, Temple University 1995) is an assistant professor of international management at the College of Business Administration, University of Hawaii. As a CBA Teaching Excellence Award recipient, he teaches strategic management, multinational management, global business, global management of technology, external environment of international business, and Chinese management   at undergraduate and MBA levels. His research interests are in the area of international management, with focus on global strategy, international cooperative ventures, foreign direct investment, and Chinese management and business. Dr. Luo has published over fifty research articles in professional journals since he started his academic career in 1986 when he published his first article on international business in a leading journal in China. Since 1995, his research has appeared or is in press in such referred journals as *Journal of International Business Studies, Organization Science, Journal of International Management (2 papers), Management International Review (3 papers), International Business Review (2 papers), The International Executive (2 papers), Long Range Planning (2 papers), Journal of Small Business Management, Business Horizons, Bulletin of Economic Research, Asia-Pacific Journal of Management (3 papers), International Journal of Management, Human Systems Management, Group and Organization Management, Journal of Applied Management Studies, Journal of Business and Management, Mid-Atlantic Journal of Business, Journal of Transnational Management Development*, among others. His book *"China 2000: Emerging Business Issues"* was published by Sage. Recently, Dr. Luo has over thirty other publications such as book chapters and referred proceedings. He is a frequent reviewer for numerous journals and publishers including *Academy of Management Journal* and University of Chicago Press. Before he came to the United States in July 1992, Dr. Luo had also taught a variety of courses in business and management at leading universities in China, published twenty-five articles on international business in major national journals, and served as a provincial official in charge of international business for six years.

For Product Safety Concerns and Information please contact our EU
representative GPSR@taylorandfrancis.com Taylor & Francis Verlag GmbH,
Kaufingerstraße 24, 80331 München, Germany

Printed and bound by CPI Group (UK) Ltd, Croydon, CR0 4YY
08/05/2025
01864373-0002